From BUST TO BOOM

Finding God in the Middle of the Oil Boom

CHRISTIAN DELL

WESTBOW PRESS®
A DIVISION OF THOMAS NELSON & ZONDERVAN

Some names and/or relationships have been changed due to the sensitivity of events recorded.

WestBow Press books may be ordered through booksellers or by contacting:

WestBow Press
A Division of Thomas Nelson & Zondervan
1663 Liberty Drive
Bloomington, IN 47403
www.westbowpress.com
1 (866) 928-1240

ISBN: 978-1-4908-7988-8 (sc)
ISBN: 978-1-4908-7989-5 (hc)
ISBN: 978-1-4908-7987-1 (e)

Library of Congress Control Number: 2015907478

Print information available on the last page.

WestBow Press rev. date: 07/30/2015

Special thanks to Bobbi—Your dedication, patience, honesty and integrity made this project possible.

PREFACE

This isn't about me. I'm a secondary character in this play we call life. My life is not my own, and frankly: I'm glad. I did a terrible job when it sat in my hands. We may not always make bad choices, but what remains is that without Christ, we cannot affect our post death outcome.

But this is here and now. So what do we do with it? What is the goal of it all? To make money or find love? To become famous? To procreate? These things can give some level of satisfaction, but what do we do when these are lost to the cruel realities of this world? After all, we have no eternal claim on such items.

This book looks to explore these questions, and shows what happens when the God of all creation is given the reins.

It's scary to give control to someone you don't know or trust. When we think of Christianity, we think rules, traditions and a loss of mind. In actuality, He is not found in these. He is found in grace, love, mercy, peace and forgiveness. He is found in relationship with Him. He is in our deepest struggles, highest moments, biggest blessings and worst days. He is not a stern God with crossed arms, but one who runs to those who come to Him. Our days are short, and we must answer the question: who is God, and will we have faith that He should be in control of our eternity?

Despite all the sin we've committed, Christ gave the option to be forgiven. This part is most important. It's the only way to

God, and while many believe they are good people, all of them have told a lie, gossiped, hated, or looked lustfully at another. And that was just yesterday.

We may have sinned, but the gift is still available.

And a part of us denies that could be a possibility.

Some people think they have no chance and they're too horrible for God to accept them.

I want to remind you: Moses killed a man. David stole a man's wife. Paul persecuted, condemned and sent Christians to their death. But out of God's forgiveness, they were all redeemed by accepting the gift of Christ. His life for ours. However, God won't force you to take it, since that would deny a person's free will.

By now, perhaps you're thinking, "I don't need to be preached to." I say that if I believe this is The Truth, I'd be remiss not to give it. Even avowed atheist Penn Jillette from Penn and Teller says that a Christian must really hate a person to not warn of Hell if they believe it's true, and he's absolutely right. He sees that if we believe such a statement is Truth, then it must be our passion above all else to share the beautiful news that a gift is open to all!

A truth is considered to be narrow. It is either correct or false. I can give all sorts of evidence that point to the truth of Christ, but those clues will not save a person. It takes a willing faith that Christ not only died for our sins, but that His way is the narrow path.

C.S. Lewis pointed out that Christ was one of 3 things. He was either a liar, leading people with false statements and claiming to be God when He knew he wasn't, a lunatic who made extreme claims and thought He was God; or He was telling the truth and is the Lord. Christ left no other options. We must take His claim and decide: was He telling the truth when He states, "I am the way, the truth and the life No one may come to the Father except through me."

Our afterlife depends on taking a step out and putting faith in the only way to be saved.

I state all this to get to the point of this book: My story is not to brag about my path. Instead, this is the bumbling, erratic journey of a person trying to find their way in the world. I am a man ever trying to give up control to a God who says, "Seek ye first the kingdom of God, and all else will be added unto you."

This book is for both the believer and non-believer. We all wonder where God is in each day, and I'm here to tell you that when you have eyes to see, you can look back and see his hand guiding the smallest details of your life, despite the mistakes you'll make till the end.

CHAPTER 1

The baggy sat on the table. We stared.

A warm summer day glistened outside the slider, dancing on the faded wood of the deck. I turned my head back to the baggy, set against a backdrop of *Family Guy* keeping the television busy. My apartment was adorned with scarlet carpet and white-washed walls, interrupted by posters of Guitars and 60's icons.

"How much should we take?" I asked.

"I don't know, an 8th each?" Tanya said.

A flutter of nerves played in my stomach. My first attempt at mushrooms had resulted in a light head and some happy feelings, but nothing more.

"Well, screw it. Let's go for it. No time like the present," I responded, a small charge of confidence pushing through the nerves.

We grabbed grape juice to wash them down and packed apples for our walk. For so long, we had discussed how fun it would be to take 'shrooms and enjoy nature.

We thought about campus with the waning summer displays of color and surrounding trees in the Arboretum set at the back edge of the University. To be on a beautiful college campus in the midst of a psychedelic trip sounded fantastic.

Friends had boasted of how vibrant the colors looked and what fun psychedelic trips were. Added into our appreciation of nature, and a campus trip seemed vital.

We assured ourselves it'd be fun, and started to chomp on the dried, crusty mushrooms. We did everything we could to get the bitter cardboard down, gulping grape juice to wash away the gravel on our tongues.

With psychedelic cardboard in our stomachs, we began the 2 mile float to campus. We turned off the well-traveled backwoods highway for a dirt road. The sky and far-off bushels of colors sharpened as we walked between a dead, washed-out cornfield and forlorn-looking trees.

"It's kickin' in. Things are getting vivid and look really defined," I said.

"I'm starting to feel something too. I can't wait to get there," she responded.

We sauntered past a series of long turkey barns emanating gobbles with a quaint two-story house staring back. The world was coming in waves. The colors would start to rise off the canvas, like the world had become HD. Soon, the edges and outlines slowly blurred back to a sober state. The drugs were grasping for control over our strings as they prepared to play us like marionettes.

We reached an intersection of dirt and pavement and a bigger wave started to wash over. We perceived the need for a safe-zone where our pulsing bodies could weather such a sensual assault. So we sat down on a grass lot next to the intersection.

I thought about the oddity of the scene: two college students lying on a random plot of splotchy, matted grass; seemingly oblivious to the world. Then again, in a college town, perhaps that was our best hiding spot.

The grass soothed our bare skin while our minds started to sink into deeper levels of abstract thought. Clouds spun patterns of a spiritual trance as we fought to separate fact from fiction. Billowy, white puffs danced in acid swirls that grew and spun, uniform and even. Tanya commented that she saw boxes and shifting diamonds in her cloud soup. The marionette strings were being tugged harder as the drugs continued their crawling occupation over our own mental and physical controls. Reality was slipping away—a train that had left the station as we peered down the tracks, watching it turn the curve out of sight.

My mind was always my strongest ally and worst enemy with drugs. While lying in the grass, staring at the sky, my gray brain-blob vomited overwhelming thought processes. Abstract questioning of morals and eternal dilemmas were taking over the last vestiges of logical thought. The sense of an individual self sputtered to a halt.

We realized a trip to campus was impossible as the waves of the drugs rose higher.

The decision was made: head back.

I threw up purple on the grass. The mixture of grape juice and apple chunks spewed out with a surprising ease onto the grass outline of where my body had been. The strings were pulling harder, tugging without my consent, so I tried to calm down by focusing on reality.

This was a trip. It would be over in a couple of hours. I was fine. I was okay.

But much like when things are out of your hands, I couldn't get myself to believe my own words. Feelings of panic were storming in.

I called the girl I was dating, wondering if she could give us a ride.

"Where are you?" I asked.

"Hanging out with some friends, why's that?" she said.

"Oh, because Tanya and I are tripping on some 'shrooms right now and could use a ride."

She laughed. "Really? You're doing mushrooms?"

"Yeah. I like learning from drugs. I feel like I discover a lot about myself," I said. A dread crept in with the realization that this lesson might be out of my league.

"Ah. Well, no, I'm not around. Sorry."

We hung up. I didn't think she would have anyway.

We headed back down the dirt road. As we passed the turkey farm, the owner was out, methodically raking his lawn. I watched his hands pull the rake as a few leaves moved with each stroke. His eyes focused on us, following the two star-trippers as we shuffled down the dusty, summer caked road. Our feet fought to keep moving, and nerves pricked at the stares of Old Man Farmer while the mushrooms played like a kid with a demented soundboard. The rake scraped. The farm dog barked. And a wave of gobbles rippled down the turkey barn.

Scrape.

Bark.

Gobble.

Scrape. Bark. Gobble.

Pupils dilated and legs staggered as we stumbled along. The farmer continued to watch, only adding to the uneasiness. A showdown between old-fashioned and hippie-produce had the keen-eyed farmer winning without trying.

It was sensory-overload mixed with feelings of helplessness.

We stopped between the cornfield and dead trees, unable to continue walking. I was dry-heaving, trying to keep sanity amidst the deep panic of being trapped in an invisible cage.

"I have 4 more hours of this?"

I choked each time words attempted to break past my lips, so we sat down, unable to walk. We were a million miles from safety and a mile and a half from home.

"I need to call for a ride," I said, as my fingers searched through my phone for anyone who might be a life line.

Tanya nodded and looked off into the rotting swamp and prickly trees.

I ran through my phone list, calling any name that might be of use. Some didn't pick up. One was in Chicago. Another on the other side of the state.

It was getting difficult to talk for long periods. Anxiety and a reeling mind were the drug's toys as they choked me out and forced sputtering fragments over the phone.

"You can't help. You're useless to me," I told one friend as I hung up.

We left some voicemails and decided staring at a small swamp infested with dead trees was making things worse. We crossed to the other side of the road and plopped down to scan the vast field of decaying, old plant matter. A lone, barely green tree stood at the center. I longed for that island oasis floating out of reach among the broken stalks.

Time crawled and we sat. I had the urge to hold Tanya's hand while my mind fought illogical and sporadic thoughts, but I kept to myself, mustering what courage I could.

Fear pushed upwards. Without peace, the future's outcome proved overwhelming.

The minutes crawled by like centuries. We didn't talk much, but when we did – it was to try to calm the other.

We felt on the edge of the world and at the end of time. We were trapped in Wonderland, with a theme of death and decay stitching itself to our sensibilities. The hope of the sunshine was drowned out by a possibility of slipping out of reality forever, minds wanting to sizzle in a psychosis of talking toasters and forked-tongue dragons.

My phone rang.

"You guys okay?" Todd asked.

"Yeah. I'm really sorry. We're having a bad trip and really need a ride," I said.

"I'm on my way. I left as soon as I got your message. I'm sorry, I was with Erin and didn't have my phone, but I'll be there in 15 minutes."

Fifteen minutes were 15 years. Each time I looked at my phone, I felt lucky if a minute had passed. The flooding emotions of despair made salvation seem as though it were a mirage, left to tease us with a gift we could never receive. We were the controlled toys of our drugs, left with no ability to make our own choices on outlook or hope. With battered souls, we tried desperately to hold onto the faith that he was coming. The wait felt like hours, but as soon as we were in his pick-up, a wave of calm and freedom washed over.

This wouldn't be the last time I was saved at wit's end.

CHAPTER 2

Some mornings I awoke to a freshly packed pipe placed gently before my face. The day was spent continually packing it again, recharging as soon as we felt the high fading away. We'd sit on the deck and talk, play guitar and watch seasons of favorite TV shows to pass the useless time of our day.

Even though the days were relaxing, I was weighed down by the need for a substance in order to feel a normal level of happy. The amount always increased to reach the same place, but nothing brought contentment. A small piece was forever missing.

I knew something was wrong, but I was too busy treating life with an attitude of "if I could just..." If I could just get that job. If I could have that woman. Just one more fix. It was a never ending search for fulfillment. The smack of an imperfect life hurt, and I didn't know how to cope.

Drugs were the stereotypical escape from that slap, but they also served a couple of other purposes. I was convinced they were to expand a seeking mind. I held a glorifying admiration of a hippie culture marinated in music, art and rebellion. This, coupled with misplaced fantasies of enlightenment behind each hit drove me to plumb the depths of various drugs. I felt like an explorer of the untapped reaches of my mind, when the reality was I was escaping worthlessness.

Some of my drug-induced writings during college are now rather appalling to me. If one were to read them, he might ask, "Is this the same guy? Enlightened, philosophical hippie to fundamentalist, evangelical Christian? What drug did he do that warped him so much as to become a Jesus Freak?"

I professed arguments for relative truth as my peers and education fortified such commentary. I can't blame them, considering the thoughts, in a way, made sense. We'd all bought the lie that an intelligent person's ideas were solely his own creation and that the inner-self was the guide to truth.

There was no recognition that our inner-self could be just as imperfect as our feelings, emotions and thoughts. We were sure to supplement the notion of self-truth with the elitist ego of the drug culture; when, in fact, it all was a sham of pride in ourselves, striking down the possibility that we weren't seeing the consequences of life clearly.

Philosophies such as, "Drugs can expand your mind. As long as sex is between two consenting adults, then it's okay. Drinking relieves stress. What I do with my body is of no concern to you." became a mantra for me to repeat over and over, until I didn't question its source or legitimacy.

I learned these things inside and out.

Among the plethora of arguments my 'expanding' mind took on was one titled, "The effects of marijuana, along with its benefits and personal gratification."

It was a favorite topic.

Go figure.

Even though I was cloaking problems in drugs and transcendence, there wasn't the deep despair that one might expect. It was more a daily routine of chasing away the small bouts of depression that bit and scratched inside. I went to class, worked, had various girlfriends, worked out, and partied. But for a drug user, all of that "normal" life is an alibi. Living that normal life is to show yourself that everything is okay.

"No problem here. Move along and let me enjoy my trip," I say.

"He seems normal," they say.

"I am. I'm like every other college student," I say. Then I'd pull out my guitar and Hendrix poster.

However, the deep truth I ignored was the hole inside that everyone talked about. It was the knowledge that even if I crawled into a bed with a beautiful girl, I was alone. The awareness that as soon as the high ended, I needed more to get back. I don't know how many parties I went to where I felt miserably alone.

While I explored the lifestyle of a typical college student, I maintained decent grades and an out-going social life. I held several jobs at one time, usually had a girlfriend and figured saying I believed in Christ was good enough to keep me out of Hell.

Things could have been a lot worse…but comfortable was far more dangerous.

The path from casual drug use made its way downwards.

Suddenly, it made no sense to be paying for my own drugs.

I started selling some weed here and there. After a few months of slinging sporadically, I began buying bigger. Quarter pounds of weed turned into half pounds, halves into wholes. One night while purchasing, I sat staring at several pounds sitting on my table. Something came over me, and I felt nervous and convicted. Getting caught with this could ruin my life. So I vowed, "never again."

I understood. You're not alone in the drug game and you're never safe from someone trying to cover his own butt. I'd get phone calls, texts and people bringing others to my place. And while I had rules against all of those actions, it didn't matter. People would outright ask for something over the phone. Stoners didn't always have the best of memories. I'd chew them out, but the damage was already done.

Friends got robbed at gun point and people were beaten up. Revenge was plotted. The sheriff's department shot one guy while raiding his on-campus townhouse. The chaotic events swirled about, and I chose to get out before my ticket got pulled.

Drug-dealing was also an ego game. You had to be friendly and honorable to bring in people, but cut-throat in standing up for yourself. I learned how to take care of "me", bringing more self-centered attitudes into the mix. And unfortunately, these life lessons weren't being learned in just the game of drugs. Everywhere I looked, it was the self-absorbed, confident and "get mine first" attitudes that were flourishing. Friends and successful people appeared to have a formula, and I wanted it.

For most my life, I had tried to be kind, giving and humble. I was raised on "Be kind to others and be generous. Give to others, and turn the other cheek," but I soon figured out, "If you turn the other cheek, people will walk all over you."

So while I tried my best to be a good person, I simply ended up feeling like a door-mat with low self-esteem. Too often, I felt slighted and taken advantage of. My pain settled in the idea that being nice was getting me nowhere.

Having a friend who embodied what I wanted made it worse. He was funny, seemed confident, and always had girls lining up. I studied his every move. When we'd go to the bar, I watched how he interacted with others. The confidence and a bit of swagger dressed in humble-pie was noted. His "don't care" attitude with girls, and disdain for being walked on matched up with what I thought was the secret. I carefully observed, and the biggest takeaway was that I needed to serve myself. "I could be nice, but I should get mine first."

Flailing about with low self-esteem and drugs forced a change to my approach on life. My attitude became focused on making sure I wasn't the one who got trampled. I tried to retain the Christian principles of being a good person, without letting other people get the best of me. All of my goals were morphing.

Instead of being a sensitive friend to girls, I tried not to care. There were several girls I used for my own enjoyment in an effort to separate my feelings from my desires. One girl I was seeing injured me, so out of spite I went to her best friend. Others I just stopped talking to. The pattern was showing itself as I cared less about what people thought, and cared more about being the guy who wasn't afraid to offend. It was about confidence at all costs.

But while I was trying harder to become what I thought would win, I was losing in spades. I put together quite a string of girls who dumped me, or chased after my friends. The dots weren't connecting, and as the problems accumulated and depression grew worse, I just pressed harder into my theory.

CHAPTER 3

Let's go back to my beginning.

When you drive through West Michigan, you can choose to ride major thoroughfares cutting into the heartland, or you can take to the lakeside. If you follow the curving road along the Lakeshore, you'll drive right through my home town. It's a typical small tourist town located on the beautiful sandy shores of Lake Michigan.

My childhood was surrounded by beaches and churches. Not such a bad life to live. Our town was quiet and conservative, always looking to provide an enjoyable experience for the summer beach goers, and then to kick them out as quickly as possible at fall's beginning.

When you cruise along the beach and gaze towards the lake with the lighthouse in the distance, you're transported to a scene reminiscent of a California getaway. Growing up in such an atmosphere led to complacency. While wars raged and starvation took its toll on the rest of the world, I was enjoying rollerblades and burritos.

Even though our family was living in a 1950's sitcom for most days, the complacency was a facade for several years. During that short span of time, we were broke, and it placed an obstacle between my family and the American Dream. My mom and I discussed the situation years later.

"We didn't know how we were going to make it," she said. Her face was relaxed, honesty evident in the matter-of-fact tone she used. Sunlight poured in through the large windows, lighting the scenic beach escape outside their house in the Upper Peninsula.

I stared at the marblesque countertop in the kitchen of the new house.

"It was really that bad?" I asked, trying to remember any signs of such despair.

She nodded and took another sip of coffee.

"Yup. Right after your father split from the company, we weren't sure what we were going to do or what was going to happen."

I caught her eyes with mine as realizations settled in.

"I had no clue. I never noticed anything out of the ordinary. You guys never seemed to be worried," I said.

"We were, but we trusted the Lord," she paused. "But that's why you couldn't play hockey when you wanted to."

Memories flooded in of when I was 9 or 10, lying in the top bunk, anxiously awaiting the post-parental conference summary. I begged my parents to play hockey, so they gently told me they would talk about it.

I rolled over to see Mom at eye height. My eyes peeked over the stained bunk-bed railing, looking for some sign of approval on her face.

"Your father and I talked about it, and I'm sorry honey, but we won't be able to do hockey this year," she said.

"But why not?"

"There's a lot of reasons, but one of them is that the drive is too far," she answered.

I was sad, but didn't argue. I couldn't understand why other children could play hockey, but I wasn't allowed.

"Ok," I responded.

She kissed me good night and I rolled over to chase after sleep with disappointment shrouding me.

I looked back at my mom in the modern kitchen, with it's dark woods and expensive tiles. I studied her face. They had pulled the ultimate con-job, never letting us in to the struggles that were raging behind the familial scene. I couldn't hold it against her though. They provided an amazing childhood and stuck to their faith.

My shoes never had holes. I was able to at least play a sport. If I needed a musical instrument, I got it. To me, there was nothing wrong. We had struggled through hard financial woes, yet the faith my parents embraced was apparent without my ever noticing. Their words had always been supportive and trusting. They held fast to the truth that God would provide in every situation.

And their perseverance was rewarded with Dad's company settling in and doing well. There were issues that rattled my parents, but they never gave up belief in God, or in the family structure. We always knew we would make it.

The turbulence didn't stop in my kid days. Once I was in college, our family experienced various scenarios that completely changed the dynamic of our family forever. There was unfortunate suffering of my grandparents, which put stress on my mother, there were sicknesses, and a cancer diagnosis.

During these crises, I had a perfect environment to do whatever I wanted without being caught. My parents were so focused on other issues that I slipped under the radar. There were weekends of drinking and smoking with my best friends, all night fireworks runs through the middle of town, jumping conversion vans, shooting Airsoft at random people, spray-painting cars, and causing havoc for which I somehow never received any punishment. All of it was my way of doing what I thought everyone else was doing. The pressure to top someone else's antics was always there. The only consequences that chased me were the levels of reputation I had the opportunity to build. My friends and I were supposedly the good kids, but on our own time we found anyway possible to have fun, legal or illegal.

Through this time of chaos, God placed a man in my life that set a foundation for the future. While things were spinning for this typical high school student, Aaron patiently listened. Odd philosophies crept in and life issues beat on the door of sensibility, but he gently guided and encouraged. We would sit in coffee shops or at his house for hours on end, talking over any and every issue of life.

Aaron was the new youth pastor at a church Mom and I attended during my high school years. After a falling out with our last church, God had led us to Aaron's step. The head pastor was a long-time friend of Mom's, which gave us a welcoming place to go. Immediately, Aaron became involved in my life. Soon I was playing in the worship band, meeting with him once or twice a week and going regularly on Sundays. I was living what most considered a good Christian life. I knew the right answers, and could hold interesting discussions on God and life.

Despite the positive influences, I continued to relax in my faith, considering myself "saved and done". My wayward path had nothing to do with what Aaron did or did not do, but was a progression of my own desires.

With a withering adherence to God, I sailed into the sea of college and left behind the buoy that Aaron represented.

College was the place where my life view became philosophical and liberal. We were all trying to carve out our own niche, and many times it came at the cost of absolute truth. We explored, attempting to be on the cutting edge of some new ideology. I felt prompted to leave behind faith for a more critical, skeptical mindset that focused on affirmation and feel-good.

This thought-process had a profound effect, pushing me to forsake my conservative Christian roots for something that supposedly would jive more with love and peace. My music and reading tastes sought new boundaries. The decorations in my room went from band posters of psuedo-rebellious youth to outliers like Hendrix and Bob Dylan. Acceptance and tolerance were the new words that replaced truth and righteousness.

Along with the new words came "fresh" ideas about our country and who we were as a people. Instead of pride in America's founding, I was being instructed in our terrible colonialist past. I believed we were on the cusp of a new movement in America, one which forced us to leave behind the old, antiqued ideas of a former culture. In subtle ways, Christianity was being chipped away from my life. Whether it was the scientific instruction that posited natural origin of existence at the expense of a creator, or the events on campus that promoted diversity; it seemed Christians were the one group who could not be affirmed or encouraged by the administration.

Being involved in this atmosphere day in and day out, I constructed a new world view. Things needed to be changed. We needed to make a difference. All the ills of society were our fault, and they required a complete overhaul to be useful. I was told such crimes committed by western culture were perpetrated by those who peered out from behind the Bible. So often I'd heard people smarter than I lambast it for being factually incorrect, naïve and vicious. It was attributed to bigots, hate-mongers and close-minded fools. I didn't want to be any of those.

But at the same time, the teachings of Jesus always resonated. People never seemed to speak a bad word about Jesus himself. The lessons to love your enemy, give to the poor, take care of orphans and widows all held some figurative spot in each person's heart.

These teachings seemed to be the base for the progressive credo, which drove me to accept the parts with which I enthusiastically agreed. It was obvious that a spiritual side in this world existed, and I couldn't deny it. There was too much going on which could not be explained by a simple scientific conclusion. Knowing there had to be something more, I looked for other ways to get Christ's instruction without the demands of the Bible. Such an option would grant me the opportunity to dump everything on its pages that required a person to look hate-filled and intolerant.

I went exploring and grabbed whatever felt right. This spiritual search jump-started my dive into Eastern philosophy, Buddhism, meditation, and even a dabbling into astrology. With absolutely no foundation left standing, I gave myself permission to follow all natural desires while ignoring the consequences. I considered myself free to make the choices I wanted, and followed the rules when I wanted.

Christianity put the burden of Christ's pain and death squarely on my shoulders. I ran from such knowledge. The choices did have consequences, and there was no penance I could pay to solve it. Instead, I had to come before Him and accept that I was not the master of my own life, and that only He could save me.

So I rejected that truth and instead grasped for immediate satisfaction in life, wondering how I could balance getting what I wanted while still getting to Heaven. I was the poster boy for such an approach, and I slipped deeper into a depressed and hopeless state. No matter how hard I paddled, the shore seemed to creep farther into the horizon.

Chapter 4

By the end of of college, I felt I was finally learning how to apply myself in tasks at hand. For so long, life had been a lazy grasp for what I needed, figuring all things would come to me one way or another. Social activities consumed most of my attention, though my last several semesters saw dramatic improvement in grades and study habits. I felt I was on course for the rest of my life.

And then the time came for my college audit to assure the school I had what was needed to move into its College of Education. The sidewalk lazily curved its way under the highway and between rising brick structures. I noticed the clean lines separating the concrete sections that directed my feet. All of creation around me represented a standardization, a fleeing from the spastic chaos of nature. The air was a thick, hanging coolness that toyed with my comfort. I approached a tall building that sat between the river and me, mundane from the years I had spent entering and exiting its doors.

I strolled into the dark brick structure and onto the elevator, pressing the button for the top floor. I had set-up an audit with my counselor whom I'd never met. The elevator dumped me out to a big view of the city skyline through tinted bay windows. Spires of human achievement tore holes in the sky, shimmering with reflections of other buildings in their blue-tinted panes of glass. The winding river flowed with a lackadaisical meander towards the big lake. Turning to my left, I saw a man dressed in casual clothes with a greyish-white beard. His eyes were kind behind thin rimmed glasses, and he smiled immediately.

"Christian?" he asked.

"Yup, that's me," I responded.

I dropped into a seat across the table, and pulled out various papers and folders.

"Kind of a cool day out today," he commented.

"Yeah, but it's nice. You can tell summer is coming around. A few more weeks and I won't need this sweatshirt," I said.

He smiled.

"So are you ready to graduate?" he asked, beginning to organize the papers I spread before him.

"Oh yeah. Definitely ready. I'm looking forward to doing College of Ed and getting into the workforce."

His gaze was warm.

"I can understand that," he said. "Well, let's just double check to make sure you have everything you need, and that way we can start your College of Ed app. Once you get that finished, then you should be on your way to starting in the fall."

I looked down at the papers he was scouring. They held my GPA's, classes, credits and various personal information. The pile sat thick, with stats and info of all kinds.

"So far so good. You've got the classes you need to start the English College of Ed. Your overall GPA looks good, and your extras seem to fit."

The words felt refreshing as they washed away the anxiety. The corners of my lips were turning upward as giddiness rose from within. Finally, I would be done with what felt like too long of a precursor. My life would start rolling forward, and I'd be well on my way to having control over my own classroom. Images of being Mr. D popped into my head.

"Hmm," his lips tightened and pulled downwards. "We may have a problem. I didn't notice this at first."

I leaned over to watch his pen circle a group of classes.

"See these classes?" he asked.

"Yeah…" my brow knit together as my heartbeat increased.

"Well, the problem is that your GPA for these classes is too low. These four classes are required to get into the English Department, and they require a GPA of 3.0," he said, looking at me with sympathy.

I examined the classes separated by the red circle, and followed the dotted line to the section GPA. It was 2.5. I searched my brain, wondering what had gone wrong.

And then it struck me. These were classes I took after transferring, being in a band and suffering an attack of mono. The slump reflected school being the last priority.

I slumped back in my chair.

"There's nothing I can do about it?" I asked. "Even though my cumulative GPA is just fine?" The joy deserted me in an forlorn sigh. My feet suddenly felt like they had been swallowed up by cement.

He shook his head and pulled off his glasses. A hand went towards his forehead, working out knots and smoothing the white long hair on top of his head. I could tell he battled having to bring bad news to another undergrad.

"I'm sorry. You can re-take the classes, take a few other classes, and then you could re-apply."

I did the math. That would be 2+ years of school in order to become an English teacher, on top of the 5 I had already completed. I weighed 7 years of tuition against the beginning salary of a teacher, and it wasn't encouraging.

"Man. I had no clue," I said.

"I'm sorry, but if you want to re-take those classes to up your GPA, you can."

I feigned a smile. "Well, thank you for your help. I'll have to figure out what I'm going to do."

My papers found their way into my backpack. We shook hands, and he wished me the best of luck. I walked towards the elevator and gazed out the windows. The city moved without me. Everyone's world traveled forward and each car followed its planned direction. I stepped onto the elevator through the open, accepting doors. As they closed me into the steel box, I leaned against the wall and gave a light sigh.

"Well, I guess I'm not going to be a teacher," I said to myself.

The walk back to the bus stop was a shade shy of reality. People were blurred and autonomous. I slumped onto the bus and gazed out the window, my eyes becoming lazy while my mind worked overtime. "How could I have screwed that up so bad? What am I going to do now? What will I do for work? Where now?"

Those around me were following their daily routine, seemingly carrying out unchanged plans for future houses and little families. The bridge I had planned on crossing to the rest of my life was burning before my eyes. The timbers smoldered and snapped as smoke curled skyward. The river below was deep and rushing, mocking that I would never be able to go the way I had planned for the past several years. The river carried away the formula to settle into a quiet life of teaching and writing. I'd begun college with no clue as to where I was going, and I ended on the same cliff. I stared at a bridge burned by my own failures, with no blame to pass.

I got home, called Tanya and ran headfirst into becoming numb to the situation. As the high passed and clarity began to return, an excitement came over me. This wasn't the end. Instead, I was free to to do what I saw fit. The change gave an excuse to pick up from responsibilities and the chance to start fresh. But little did I know God was lining things up despite my own failures. He was pursuing me while I pursued great thoughts of men and drugs.

I had built a house of cards out of my ideologies about life, and He decided it was time to let it fall. So, while the destruction of my career plans was reaching its full cascade, my false sense of security in my romantic relationships was about to blow up in a massive fireworks display.

CHAPTER 5

Women filled an empty spot, and my supposed "failed" approach of being nice, kind, open, honest and caring disintegrated with an epiphany. Most college women were not looking for the quality guy, even if they complained and cried about how there were no "good guys". In actuality, most were looking for the guy they could have fun with, and it just so happened the seemingly confident, arrogant boys tended to be the most fun. It seemed they came with a lot of baggage and self-interest, which brought plenty of melancholy women to confide in me over long talks about this one or that one. Why couldn't they just find a quality man? They would ask, look at me and say, "Kind of like you. You're such a 'good guy', any girl would be lucky to have you."

"Except you. You obviously would not consider yourself lucky to have me," I thought. Not to say I didn't come with my own baggage. I had no clue that my dependency on how a woman made me feel, and my perceived success in all my previous relationships hid the real truth. I had switched approaches, becoming the arrogant, self-absorbed guy, even though the cards were falling no matter what I tried.

What was going wrong? I was no longer the one dumping love-stricken girls, but was the one being kicked to the curb.

My previous long-term relationship had lasted for over two years, and after that I'd sought an oasis of solace. Seven plus years of roller-coaster relationships had taken its toll. But trying the "less complicated" connections of sex only or first time dates was not satisfying. It just caused havoc and complication in my life. Friends around me were finding their special someones, and I felt alone. I was searching the relationship landscape, wondering when I would find the right person who would make everything wonderful. I walked blind, hoping to hit the jackpot.

Decisions that had been hastily made with women were haunting me and piling up. Instead of feeling free without pesky boundaries, I was sinking in the emotional quick sand of rejection. Anger resided close by at all times, erupting in fits that left holes in the wall and things broken. When the spastic burst of aggression subsided, depression rushed back in, leaving me feeling worthless and alone. I danced between a blast of supposed confidence and a depressive sense of uselessness. There was no balance unless I was satisfying some desire. I was still grasping, hoping to catch hold of the elusive happiness, and I thought perhaps it would come in the form of Stacy.

Stacy and I had worked together for several years. The process of confining young college students in a low-effort job created a tangle of love triangles and issues. I continued to harbor a crush for her throughout the flow of flings and "almosts" with other girls that worked there.

I'd sneak glances toward the concession stand while sweeping up wrappers and dust as she leaned over the counter doing homework or doodling. She was a small, blonde girl with bright steel eyes. There was a sadness hiding behind her smile, and a touch of a "get-back" glare. She had a wall up, and I was ever attracted to what hid behind the iron wall. Growing up, it was that secret vulnerability that had me going for girls I imagined would end up finding the answer in our relationship…like I expected myself to do.

I would saunter past Stacy with the push broom, muttering some snide comment her way. She would react sometimes, while other times she would brush me off.

The game drew me in.

Following a few tries with other girls both in and out of work, I found out she had broken up with her boyfriend. He had been my dealer for a short time, and soon we became casual friends, meeting when one of us wanted to get high.

After their break-up, I took the opportunity to move in. We'd occasionally spend time together outside of work and text sporadically throughout the day.

Before we were having sex, I made it clear to her:

"If I'm sleeping with you, it means that I have feelings for you."

She looked up to me, eyes opening a little wider.

"So, please tell me now if you're just having fun and don't really feel anything for me," I continued. "It's fine if you don't. But I need to know. We don't have to be in a relationship right now or anything, but I really like you, and that's why I want it."

She thought for a moment or two.

"No, I do really like you. Yeah, I have feelings for you."

That was enough of a go-ahead for me. Soon enough, she was sleeping over at my place regularly.

On Halloween, we went to a party together, enjoying our time but never really getting closer. There was a space in between us that was driving me crazy. There were times when she would open up, fulfilling my requests for small, sporadic examples of care or desire. We both lived with desperation, although I couldn't recognize that she was in as much of a struggle of identity as I was.

Her birthday came and I wasn't invited. I was miffed and torn, wondering what the deal was. She claimed it was due to an ex-boyfriend coming, and he would cause a scene for my being there. It didn't sit well, but what could I do? I was doing my best to give her space and hope that she came around to feeling like I did.

Our relationship drove like a jalopy with 2½ working cylinders. It would pull and lurch, fighting to make any ground through the course of the winter. There were days when we had fun, laughter, joking and joy. Other days were filled with silence, frustration, arguments and offenses. We stayed for the occasional physical episodes, which were followed by distance and silence. Things cooled off after a plethora of arguments about where our "relationship" was headed.

Then came spring break, with my intentions to head to Florida to visit Chuck. Alone.

Chuck and I grew up together, meeting in youth hockey. Over the years, our friendship deepened and flourished. We were confidants who relied on each other to speak the truth with sound advice.

My plan was to get away from the debacle in Michigan and run to warm weather and relaxation. Images of palm trees and white sandy beaches danced through my head and encouraged the thoughts of escaping the blast-zone my life had become.

Stacy had plans to have her own spring break celebration with a friend…in Florida. Then her friend bailed.

"I want to go somewhere, but I have no one to go with," she complained.

I thought for a second. Part of me screamed in horror. The other hoped.

"You could come with me to Florida," slid out of my mouth without control. I wasn't sure whether to defend it or let it be.

"No, that's fine. I don't want to impose on what you have planned with Chuck," she said. Some people hide their true feelings with a polite declination, but I didn't believe her reply was merely polite. I watched a face that would rarely look back at mine. The single lamp in my apartment living room pushed shadows up the walls and across her face. The old green, leather couch swallowed me whole as I slid deeper, waiting. Something was playing on the TV, but it wasn't grabbing my attention.

"If you want to go, you can go. I know I would feel bad if I went and you were sitting home by yourself. Either way, you were planning to go to Florida, so might as well come and enjoy the warmth," I offered. I was in full spin mode. The salesman spirit had come out, pitching a Florida vacation with all the perks.

"It's okay," she said.

"It's up to you, but you might as well," I offered again.

After a few moments of silence and a hope betraying me, she eventually agreed.

My desire to cut our connections had been buried under thoughts that I could salvage the pieces of the broken-down jalopy. Romance happened on soft beaches as waves lapped the shore. The fantasy joy of palm trees waving overhead as we held hands was blowing kisses to my hopes, motioning for me to put everything I had into this chance, my chance to break the invisible wall.

I planned our vacation, and booked a hotel that seemed reasonably priced. I gave her the information while we were wasting time at work.

"It doesn't have a pool," she said, a look of distaste dressing her face.

I looked again at the page. "Are you sure?"

"Yeah, I'm sure."

Annoyance fired through neuron channels as I scratched my head. The plans had been made on my own time and dime, yet they weren't good enough? A flash of inner anger toyed with canceling one plane ticket.

"Do you have to have a pool? I mean, I already booked it," I said, hoping this would be easy.

"It's fine, don't worry about it."

I groaned inside. The next day was spent searching for hotels with pools that were still in a decent price range. I found one and booked while canceling the other.

She relented to my siege ramps against her outer wall, giving an honest and sensitive, "thank you" and a smile.

Within a few weeks, we were on the plane to Florida. We sat stiff in our seats with mouths locked shut, languishing without conversation. We were both quiet people, but the invisible barrier stood thick and sturdy. She had her life, and I had mine, and she was content to keep it that way.

We shuffled off the plane and waited for Chuck. There was no heavy, humid heat to meet us at the door. I looked to the palm trees and bright blue sky, wondering who had turned down the thermostat.

Chuck pulled up and we loaded our baggage. The ride to the hotel was long and awkward, so we attempted to make small talk as Chuck asked Stacy various questions. She gave polite responses without seeking out deeper conversation. Chuck and I filled in the vacuum, reliving our old days and resurrecting old jokes. I felt at home with Chuck, despite the weight gnawing at me. I ignored it, and hoped the less I thought about it, the more comfortable things might get.

The room door swung open, and the stubby hallway gave way to two beds nestled against the wall. She took one and insinuated I was to take the other. It stayed that way all week. Frustration was piling up. What was I? Just a path to a vacation? She had been on her own program, and I was fuming. She wasn't agreeing to my terms. And in my self-absorbed state, the situation was all her fault. If only she would open up. If only she would just relax. If only she would like me the way I wanted her to. If only I could get her to be what I wanted.

One day after leaving Stacy at a mall to do some shopping, Chuck and I went to go have our own fun.

"I just don't know man. It gets frustrating that I can't seem to get through to her," I said, watching the cars in the other lane blur past.

"It's hard. Do you guys think you'll stay together?" he asked.

"I don't know. I really like her. I think she's a great girl with a lot of things I look for, but where's the line?"

He paused to think, letting my statements warm in the sun.

"Well, is it worth it? You two seem okay together, but I can tell something's up. If she doesn't want to be in it, she's not going to. You have to do for you what you have to. Like they say, there are other girls out there, and if she's not happy, then you're not happy," he said.

He was right, but my pride argued, "If only I could make her see who I am. If only I could get her to open up." We drove on in silence for a few minutes. I thought over every angle of the relationship *ad-nauseam* and found myself sick with the realistic options.

"Do you see yourself marrying her?" he asked.

"If things were going well? The thought doesn't turn me off. But, this isn't working," I said. "I like her, but this sucks."

It came to a head in the mall later that day. I asked the question that made me feel like an insecure high school girl.

"What is this? Is this really going somewhere or is it just for fun?" I asked as we walked through a clothing store. Mannequins dressed in the latest fashion watched with blank stares, giving no care to who we were or what we thought. People passed by with large bags and cell phones, wrapped up in their own worlds.

"We've already talked about this," she said, slightly annoyed.

"I told you that if I had sex with you, it meant I had feelings for you. I told you that if this was just for fun or not going anywhere, then I wasn't interested. I told you how I really liked you, and that you better not jerk me around," I said. The heat was rising as my fingertips curled towards my palms.

She moved deeper into the store, casually scanning racks of designer clothes.

"You never told me that," she said as she fondled the price tag on a summer dress. She moved forward and cast glances over random pieces of clothing without resting on anything that produced an enthusiastic response. It was as if the clothing was unsatisfying, merely keeping her occupied.

"Yes I did. I told you three or four times!" I said, straining to keep my voice down.

"No you didn't."

"Yes I did. I remember it pretty clearly," I shot back. Curses were tumbling out under my breath.

She tried to season her words with a hint of sympathy, "Well, I don't remember it. But, I'm not sure what to tell you."

I strode out of the store and came to a rest on the railing overlooking the lower floor. A thought fluttered through my head, "I wonder how much damage I could do if I jumped." She finally followed out of the store and walked up to me, realizing I was in some serious pain.

"I'm sorry if I don't remember that. I like you, but I just can't do a relationship right now. I don't want a boyfriend anytime soon."

"Am I supposed to wait around?" She didn't respond except to give a hug and a kiss. The first real physical contact we'd had all week.

That night, we went to the bar and restaurant where Chuck worked. Patrons writhed against each other to heavy bass beats while lights flashed random colors. We stood at a raised platform over-looking the floor. He and I downed high-ball after high-ball as Stacy leaned on the railing, hazily watching people lose control of their inhibitions. She was emotionally absent and complained she wasn't feeling well. My plan to combat the steely-eyed statue leaning on the rail involved getting plastered, and Chuck commiserated with a destroyed friend, passing support and encouragement in spurts of humor or friendly advice.

And then we drank some more.

I stumbled through the hotel room door early in the morning with Stacy slowly coming in behind. I surpassed my goal of being plastered on whiskey, and was emotional to boot.

When I press the rewind button on the memories, pieces of the argument were missing from the reel. There were blurs of me cursing with every word I could find as I let it all fly. I was done beating around the bush, and she wasn't going to escape the destruction I was feeling.

The sad thing was, she played a role in how I was feeling, but only a secondary part. I was crashing my own plane into the ground with a grin, a joint and a snifter. She was just the scapegoat upon which I poured my bubbling wrath. After all the disappointment, I was left clawing air in life, and I wanted to make sure she got scratched for taking hold of my vulnerable spot and demolishing it with her own crashing plane.

"You don't give a crap about me. You don't ask how I'm doing or whats going on. You never once asked how my mom is doing or how I'm handling it. You haven't asked at all. I'm torn up, scared to death that my mom might die, and I don't even hear a peep out of you."

I went to the bathroom and slammed the door. My knees gave way and I crumpled to the floor, tears bursting through the dam. The rejection and embarrassment I felt had all welled up. The loneliness of being in Florida with a girl who wanted little to do with me tore hard. The nagging fear of my mom succumbing to the kidney cancer she'd been diagnosed with the previous fall. It all rushed over me, breaking forth in tears and choked sobs.

She carefully knocked on the door.

"Are you okay?" she asked. It was honest and humble.

"I'm fine. I'll be alright," I responded quietly. I heard the room door shut and there was silence.

The next day was cordial. We didn't talk about the previous night, allowing respect to cautiously hang in the air. She went to the pool, and I stayed in the room to meditate and stretch. My mind was a snarl of knots. So I sought the quiet repose of meditation, forcing myself to allow her to be herself. She was Stacy, and I was Christian. We were two separate people traveling two separate paths. And that's okay, I meditated.

But it was hard convincing myself that it was okay.

We tip-toed out of Florida, hoping the beast named anger would slumber. Few words were spoken as we exited the plane, parting ways into our routine lives.

Chapter 6

Stacy and I didn't talk after the Florida disaster. I had sworn her off and felt officially done with the merry-go-round. No texts. No phone calls. No contact.

After two weeks, the silence broke.

"What are you doing on Friday?" she texted.

The inner debate tore my sensibilities in two. Do I make the wise decision and leave it alone? Or do I decide to wash over the past and try again?

What the heck.

"Not much," I responded.

An awkward silence followed, although this wasn't anything new. Rarely did I receive a text from her immediately after a response.

"Want to go out for drinks?"

A part of me jumped. The other groaned.

I responded, "Sure."

Friday came, and we headed out. I drove the dark, damp streets and sped towards my favorite watering hole. Dull orange lights passed overhead, leaving a trail of where we had been. Rainwater glistened on the roadway and reflected the headlights that illuminated the path ahead.

We arrived and picked out seats towards the front. The bar was a long, wooden building, refined and casual. The lighting was brighter than most beer halls, inviting its patrons to enjoy the faces of their confidants. Most of the bar populace were college students with a twinge of liberal art chic dictating their outfits. An indie rock band played on the two foot riser at the head of the building. The set-up invited a connection between patrons and musicians, offering a sense of unity.

We sat across from each other. The large wooden table formed a chasm between two bodies as they both faced the stage. It was loud and lonely. We attempted to talk over the music, but it proved fruitless.

The band finished and words were sporadically shared. One of the musicians approached and leaned in to her ear. She smiled, and he walked away. I stared at her dumbfounded, while she calculated the best approach to get her way.

"He wondered if he could buy me a beer," she asked. "But it's okay if you say no."

I wanted to be relaxed and confident.

"I don't mind. It's just one beer. Get a free one, why not," I said, assuring myself that she came with me. After all, she had asked me out.

"Are you sure? It'll just be one beer," she said.

She focused on her watch.

"Come get me in 15 minutes. If you feel you're ready, come get me in 10," she offered.

I watched her approach the slender band member. I turned back to watch the next band and sipped my beer. They steered into their set with guitars flashing against a yellow curtain backdrop. I watched hair bob and mouths etch out words in the air. I wasn't going to spy or be jealous. I was going to let her be and play it cool.

A few minutes later, my head turned to check on her. They were dancing intimately, her arm around his neck. Anger flushed my cheeks. She had duped me. I turned back, thinking after their dance I was going to get her and we'd go. I realized I had made myself a fool. I wasn't going to let her make it any worse.

They finished and moved back to the bar. I approached with a hand slightly balling into a fist. He introduced himself.

"Hey, I'm Mark," he said with a smirk on his face.

I stared back, piercing him with a look that spoke louder than words ever could.

"I'll wipe that smirk right off your face," flashed through my head, as I sized him up. I outweighed him by at least 50 lbs and could tell playing music was his only activity. I, on the other hand, had plenty of hockey, drinking and fighting under my belt.

Yet, something deep inside kept me restrained. I turned to her and said, "I'm ready to go."

She looked shocked. "I still have another 10 minutes!"

"No, it's already been 15 minutes."

She shook her head, "No, give me 10 more minutes."

I rolled my eyes and walked away. Every part of me shouted to leave her behind. I longed to get in the car and drive far away from the destruction that followed in her wake. But my feet plodded forward, and I found myself ordering another beer. An older man sat alone next to me. He was curled over the bar with both hands on his glass, eyes casting glances up to the televisions and back down to the rich red wood of the bar below his drink. I hesitated, then leaned in to ask how to get over a girl that tore your heart out.

He thought for a moment.

"It takes time. Women will do that. They'll rip your heart out, and you're standing there wondering what the heck happened. Give it time, and you'll get over her."

"How do you deal with it though? How do you get over it?" I wanted an answer that would instantly make it all better.

"Best you can. Let go and live your life. Don't hold grudges, and time will take care of it."

His countenance was kind and wise. He knew he was helping a young buck get a grasp on the deadly sport of relationships. He spoke with a maturity that bulged with experience and past memories. I tried to cling to his words, but all my thoughts were awash with rage and hurt.

While we were talking over the painful truth of women, I glanced down the bar. They were gone. I searched, wondering where she had gone. Frustration brought me to storming about the bar, searching the thinning crowd of faces. They were nowhere to be found.

I came across a bouncer I knew well and asked, "Have you seen the blonde girl I came in with?"

He shrugged his shoulders, "Nope, sorry man."

"Well, You're about to have a fight on your hands. I'm about to put someone in the hospital."

"Come on, you can't do that. Just stay cool. Don't get yourself into trouble," he said. "Just stay cool," he repeated as he patted me on the back.

Five minutes later, they were back. I strode up, having no interest in looking at him.

"I'm leaving," I said, giving her a cold hard look.

She smiled at Mark.

We walked to the car in silence. I started it up and sped off, hitting turns and banking curves with race-driver efficiency.

"That was unbelievable," I fumed.

"What?"

I swerved around cars who hindered my progress.

"You asked me if you can have a beer with him, and the next thing I know you're dancing and have your arms draped all over him."

"So? You told me I could!" she snapped back.

"I told you that you could have a beer with him, not make-out!"

She paused, "We didn't make out..."

"That's crap. I know what you were doing when the two of you disappeared," I shot back.

"We just went out to have a cigarette," she mumbled.

I swerved around another car.

"Yeah. And you kissed him. Didn't you?"

If she was going to play semantics, I was going to win.

She let out a, "Yeah."

Then her phone rang. Anger burned hot through my whole body. I watched out of the corner of my eye as she debated whether to pick it up. Her fingers traced over the top of the screen as I hoped she'd pick it up.

She answered the phone.

"Hey, how's it going?"

I could hear his voice through the speaker pressed tightly against her ear.

"I had a great time with you tonight," he said.

"Me too," she said with a coy smile slapped across her face.

"I was wondering, you want to hang out next weekend?" he asked.

My hands gripped the steering wheel tighter, turning my knuckles white. I gave a sarcastic grin, making some type of "pssht" sound.

"Next weekend? I don't think so, but I'll give you a call," she said. They exchanged good-nights and hung up.

I blasted back at her with full force. "And you gave him your number?" I said, my voice getting louder.

"So?" she said again. "You said I could have a beer with him. What did you expect?"

"Not for you to go handing out your number. You asked ME out for drinks, remember? I told you to go ahead and get a free beer. Not go and make out with the guy and hand out your phone number."

We arrived at my apartment. I slammed the car door and began walking away. I refused to give her any acknowledgment. "I still want to be friends..." she said to my back.

"You know what, you call me when you decide you want to!" I snapped. She could call, but I wasn't going to pick up.

"No, you can call me!" she retorted as she got in her car.

Soon after, I was at Tanya's apartment, drinking with two other friends who had suffered recent wrongs by significant others. One had been cheated on and blamed for it, while the other had been dumped and trashed for being "too nice." We drank as much as possible, lamenting our sad state of affairs and the tortures women put us through. We shared tales of pain and misunderstanding, grieving at how such kind, gentle souls as we could be chewed up and spit out like refuse. It felt good to have friends with which to lament to about the crimes committed. Misery truly loves company.

The drinking binge continued into the next day and night. We drank at Tanya's, at the bar, at my place, and back to the bar. We slept over and went at it again. It was a blur of wallowing in self-pity and drunken fits of making fun of the people who had caused us to drink. It was all their fault we were in this state. We were supposed innocent victims.

And God waited patiently.

Chapter 7

An observation was becoming clear. The collage of beliefs I tried to claim didn't produce the peace I sought. The Buddhism I studied wasn't dissolving the bitterness inside. It promised a far away answer, like a ship in the mist that never reaches land. I could perceive the answer, but it never actualized.

Love your neighbor as yourself seemed unreasonable. Why should I sacrifice myself for someone who hurt me? Wasn't this rule predicated on whether that person loved you back? After all, Christ seemed to be a good moral teacher, much like Buddha, Gandhi and Muhammad. He was a great man who taught things so similar to the others, that they all must have the truth. Even the horoscopes I read every once in a while never made rational sense. The advice was so general, I could have written the same thing and considered myself a "medium".

Christ's words were merely guidelines in my life, giving a sort of "feel-good" that only pertained to me when I needed it to. Things like grace and mercy became my scapegoat for when I screwed up, keeping me from any true conviction for my sinful behavior. Instead, I continued to chase the gratification of my body, seeking the day by day pleasures I thought made me happy, riding on an understanding that I was already "forgiven."

The Buddhism made me feel in control. I steered the journey, and the more I focused, the better life could be. I sat on Buddhist Sutras and Christian Parables like a sofa—useful only when I wanted comfort. Repentance was the one concept I shied away from. That pointed to responsibility for my actions.

So, I was left with my own thoughts. The barrage of thinking and voices inside my head was deafening. Being in charge of my own life was drawing me deeper into a pit, and the more I dug to get free, the lower I sank. Bitterness was growing roots around my heart as I sought to please myself and throw away the "useless" attitude of putting others first. As the roots thickened and entwined my heart, the drugs and drinking intensified. I focused on enlightening myself and expanding my mind. What I got for my efforts was depression and a hole inside me that seemed tangible.

The next few months were spent chasing women. I scored a record string of failures. One particular night at the bar,I struck out four times in a row. Strike four left me to filch fries from her abandoned plate. I had lost the will to care what anyone thought about me. No one was interested anyway, so I figured at least I'd be full.

I concluded that chasing girls was getting me nowhere, so I gave up. The pain of rejection was too great. The collapse of relationships had come to a head, and women were blind to me. The few with whom I did have a chance, I chickened out on even trying.

There was no confidence.

There was no enthusiasm.

There was no real me anymore.

I was crumbling and wasn't sure where to go or what to do. The complete demolition of my relationship life left me worn out. I had no energy left to chase women. After years of one relationship disaster following another, I was left in the desert. The pain wasn't just in the rejection, but in the loss of my self-image. My self-esteem that had been built on the compliments of others was washing away in a tide of despondency and self-criticism.

The medication by alcohol was getting worse, and I was spiraling downward with drugs. Add in absolutely no career direction, and my world was becoming flat and unrecognizable. The moments were pieced together as if a blind man were painting a picture. In an abstract sort of way, one could consider it a life. But in the real definition of it all, I was a mess.

There's a danger in giving the perception of being put together well. People don't recognize the crisis you've become. They walk past and respond to your smile with their own. I sat in my little shell, crying out for a person to really engage my inner being.

All I had was work at the ice rink after school ended. Finding a new place to live sat atop my priority list. My lease was up and I had a feeling that I wouldn't be sticking around. Life was getting too miserable to bear, and the thought of running from all my problems became cemented in my head.

I manned the front desk with a laptop screen washed in white. I was attempting to figure out some semblance of a life plan. The white template with blinking bar felt overpowering. The various tabs on my internet browser bar offered the perfect escape from planning a new life.

"How's it going Christian?" Tom asked.

"Not too bad, how about you?" I responded automatically.

Tom was a former minor league hockey player who always showed up for our open ice time.

"What's new?" he asked as I took his money.

His long black hair was matted down, and he smiled with a gaping hole where a tooth used to be.

Tom was an enforcer with a scorer's touch, however; he didn't lose a single tooth to an opponent's fist. The only loss of chompers was to a badly placed shot.

I hesitated. Tom was a great guy, and I enjoyed talking with him, but I was tired of giving the truth about my life. I wanted to stay shallow with everyone while I figured things out.

"Well, I'm moving out pretty soon, so I'm just looking for a place to live," I said, the words spurting out. It wasn't what I wanted to say, but my mouth had already vomited truth. I looked up to bright eyes and a carefree grin. Somehow this grizzled, retired hockey player was wearing down my resistance.

"Come live with me. I've got a spare room," he said.

I groaned inside. I knew him, but not extremely well. How was I going to just move in with someone I didn't know?

"Thanks, I may do that. I'm not exactly sure what my plan is though, so I don't want to just move in to move right out." I hoped he would rescind his offer.

"That works. This way you don't have to sign a lease or anything. And if you take off in a couple months or a couple weeks, it'll be easier," he said, persisting.

My wall was crumbling. I was exhausted from fighting things and trying to do it my own way.

"Maybe I will. I'll let you know," I said. Could I really be considering this? What made me say anything but "No, I'm good"?

A week later I moved in.

It was the best thing that could have happened to me. Tom was a 42 year-old, laid back guy who kept a clean house with a relaxed atmosphere. It felt great to have a stable, consistent person with whom to live. He was a friend who had walked through the crush of life and come out the other side.

Since school no longer contended for time, I took a job at the local park, which was owned by the same township that owned the rink. Several days a week I worked 11 hour shifts at the park, while a few nights a week I'd work at the rink. When I wasn't at work, I lifted weights. Tom took no part in drugs or alcohol, helping me to sober up. With no influences keeping me in that world, I was slowly finding some pieces to fit together.

One day while off work, I headed to my hometown to meet with a former teacher. We met occasionally, talking about every subject possible while the sun ran its course through the sky. The sound of a coffee grinder along with a steamer blasting away spoke comfort to my ears. It blanketed me like the soft singing of a mother, lulling a child to safety in bed. I was with an old friend, drinking coffee and feeling at home.

"I'm ready to get out of here," I said.

The cup radiated warmth in my hands. "I can tell. You're anxious to get out. Some people do fine with the white picket fence and the 2.5 children. But I don't think that's what you want, is it?" he smiled. "And it's okay if it is. For some people, that's all they desire in life. But I don't think that's you."

"No, it's not. I want to go exploring. I want to drive the country. I want adventure and excitement. Maybe someday I could handle the white picket fence, kids and dog, but not right now. I'm too young. I've got to get the most out of life," I said.

My teacher grabbed a notepad and set it on the marble-swirl tabletop. He took out a pen and looked me in the eye.

"Alright, let's begin," he said. "If you could go anywhere, where would it be?"

I thought for a moment. "I'm not quite sure. Somewhere other than here?"

He scribbled quickly, while one hand briefly combed his short, graying beard.

"So a trip then? Going somewhere on an adventure?" he asked.

"Yeah. I love to be in nature. I love hiking, camping…really anything like that. But you're right: I want adventure. I want stories to tell my kids when I'm older. 'When I was in my 20's, I went here. And I did this…'"

As if my teacher were crafting a new idea for a novel, he cobbled together ideas that could have comprised "The Story of Christian: His Life and Times."

People bustled in the coffee shop. I looked out the window at a few cars cruising main street, while idle shoppers strode along the sidewalk. We were in small-town U.S.A. A home for the suburbanite family just trying to etch out a serene existence. I felt like a foreigner visiting a far-away, strange country. Just ten years ago, I had rollerbladed up and down main street with a burrito in hand.

Scribbling, he continued, "Okay, so you're going to drive the country. Do some camping, that kind of thing." His eyes were attached to the paper. He was focused on my life, maybe more so than I was. His heart was in it, seeking to find what interested me. Since I had no clue what I wanted to do with my life, it was the perfect moment to brainstorm. His excitement was bubbling over, splashing me with a new sense of hope.

"And what are you going to drive on this trip?"

Now I was filling with enthusiasm. "I've always wanted an old truck. Like a '55 Chevy pick-up or something. I want to build the motor, and make it a street rod," I said. "And it has to have a 350. I've always wanted a 350," I added.

He smiled and wrote it down. "Perfect. So you have an old truck. Maybe with a topper on the back, so you can pull over and sleep. You could put a mattress back there, and camp out in nature."

I liked the sound of this.

"And would you have a companion? A friend or significant other? Maybe a dog?" my familiar friend wondered.

"I've always wanted a big dog. Like a Presa Canario or something," I said.

His chin came up, an inquisitive look in his eyes. "They're a really big dog. Presa Canarios can grow to be 150 lbs and stand higher than your waist on all fours," I said with glee as I dreamed about my brute of a dog.

"Alright, so you've got your '55 Chevy truck, with your dog and you set out for adventure. You could journal as you travel, writing about your experiences," he said.

"Like Jack Kerouac," I smiled.

We spent the next half an hour discussing my desires. I felt a hope in being free. My mood changed, recognizing that I was no longer happy in this little area. I had used up the resources, squeezing what I could out of West Michigan. I wanted to come back some day, but this was the time to go out and find some clarity in life. My heart had left a while ago, I just never realized it. The plan felt refreshing.

And God was paying close attention.

CHAPTER 8

My job at the park was relaxing. A soft breeze usually blew through the trees and provided a slight relief from the sun's dry heat. I could look down the grassy slope to a small inland lake surrounded by bird-inhabited trees. The lake was just big enough to bother with canoeing or kayaking.

It also fostered boredom.

I was the only attendant on duty, working in a 5 by 5 cinder block booth at the top of the drive.

There were no doors or windows, only gaping holes. I sat atop an old wooden stool, my cell void of the comforts amenities provided. If the bathroom called out to my bladder, I made the quarter mile drive down to the restrooms, and quickly returned to my faithful stool. The summer heat was stifling, so I brought water bottles and food to hold me over for my 11 hour shift. Despite the inconveniences, I could look out at the inviting grass, the waving leaves that surrounded the lake, and the small sandy beach. It was a peaceful place to be, and I was grateful for the chance to be in nature with no distractions. God placed me on a desert island, (literally, my ticket booth was an oval, raised plot of concrete that split the driveway in two), and I knew I needed to sort things out.

I made various books and writing my companions. Several times, I even brought my guitar, practicing in between cars coming to use the park. Most patrons were friendly, and some of the female patrons were extra-friendly. The sun was shining, and I enjoyed going nowhere.

But the problem of life-direction lingered. My spiritual walk was broken. Christ and Buddha were not getting along like I wanted them to, and in the recesses of my heart, I knew there was a decision to be made. For so long, I took what I wanted from the Bible, and left the rest. I chalked it up to "changing society," "meaning something other than what it says," or "doesn't apply to me." My own excuses couldn't keep me convinced. So I made a self-agreement to read the entire New Testament, and either accept it all…or be done with Christianity.

I began with the first chapter of Matthew.
I finished with the last word of Revelation.

And that summer—after all my flailing about and a childhood raised in the church where I thought I was good—my Lord and Savior Jesus Christ introduced Himself to me and saved my life. He is the Alpha and the Omega, the beginning and the end. He was and is everything, the only thing, the center, the focus. In the pages of the New Testament, my eyes were opened to a man that no longer just spoke words which gave comfort and conviction, but these eyes saw God in the flesh who became man to save me from myself. His words were alive. I dove into those words, not allowing myself to argue or discredit because I didn't like what He had to say. I refused to once again take the buffet approach, picking and choosing which slices I thoroughly enjoyed, and which I wanted to spit out. I read each word with discretion and decided whether I could step into a life with Him. My heart finally saw the difference between my life and what He taught. I was hit hard with how screwed up I'd become without Him. In an instant, the equation balanced, and I saw clearly how my flailing about was the result of my sin. I accepted Him wholly, and He began to make me whole.

The conviction I felt over all my bad choices was the pressing of His Holy Spirit, the counselor He said He would send to guide us. I was so thankful that Christ worked through His most powerful asset – His word – to change my life. When I humbled my pride to accept what He was saying and to finally agree with the conviction He brought, my life changed. I was a sinner. I needed a savior. He was the only way to be reconciled to a just God who loved me dearly, but must punish sin that had not been paid for. That punishment is eternal death. And Christ died for me, so I wouldn't have to. If I didn't choose that gift, I would be forced to make the payment myself.

I praised God that by His actions I was kept from Hell, a punishment that had been reserved for the devil and his angels, unless I chose to follow the devil instead of God. With our free will, we as man chose destruction, but the loving, graceful God above gave us a second chance to make amends, knowing full well our inability to save ourselves.

I had a mind full of Bible knowledge. There were pieces loosely stitched together from my laid-back faith exploration. But it was time to put all that aside and just follow. So I vowed my life to Him, and that's when things started changing.

The mountains of Colorado were my lifestyle fantasy. I loved the dreamy escape into nature, and knew I'd be happy into the backwoods. I longed to escape into the land where life seemed so care-free.

The internal pressure to leave West Michigan was getting fierce, so I posted my resume on some websites and searched for anything that piqued my interest. I prayed, asking God to bring the right job. I knew He provided, so I did my best to have faith that something would come along. After a few weeks, I was contacted by a company in Colorado of all places. Perhaps this God thing was working out after all. I traded phone calls with the company, who was looking for a person that could be molded into a management role. I was excited about the prospect. But the more we talked, the clearer it became that I was just a number. There was no offer to help me come out for the interview. There was no urgency to meet me. And soon, that possibility fell through.

"Okay, I'll trust He has something else," I said to myself.

A friend suggested trail-building work on the Appalachian trail in Maine. "Lord, is this where I get to go?"

I applied and put everything I had into the resume and cover letter. My mind, body and soul were ready to forsake the creature comforts of suburbia and become a rugged forest man, swinging a pick-ax against the mountainside. I kept the hope that God was fulfilling my desire to connect with Him and nature. The pay wasn't much and the work was hard, but I was excited.

The email response came a few days later. "We're sorry, but due to the limited number of positions and the number of candidates, we've chosen to go a different direction and...blah blah blah."

My heart sank, but I was determined to trust in God If I was going to follow Him, I had to trust He had a place to settle His disciple.

"He isn't going to leave me starving and without work..." I kept telling myself.

The next opportunity was to teach how to use a medical program for a company out of Madison, WI called Epic. I researched the company online and fell in love with it. The website said the company cherished creativity, and showed it by building a vast campus with different themed buildings, tree houses to work in, and offices that yearned to be decorated. They encouraged their employees by giving the freedom to be creative without a micro-management culture that strangled individuality. They prided themselves on bringing out the best of each person in a nurturing environment. I worked hard on the application, checking and re-checking my documents. Clicking the send button, I sat back satisfied.

A few days later, I received another rejection. Fighting depression, I opened up the resume and cover letter I sent to see where something could have been changed. Horror struck. The cover letter spoke about a desire to "build trails in the back woods of Maine" and how the "scenery reminded me of my love for Michigan." Embarrassment barreled all the way through. What a fool I must have looked like! The thoughts of, "This guy wants to work for us, yet can't even send a coherent resume?" flooded my mind. I had screwed up my biggest opportunity so far because I hadn't properly save my edits.

I look back to that moment and recognized that perhaps the Lord had planned for such a mistake. And while I decided Madison WI was not my destiny, God quietly worked His plan together for my life. All He wanted was for me to not fight and obediently go along for the ride.

On the ride of life, there are those who say that God is their co-pilot. This notion is wrong. When God is in our life, He's not just in the front seat...He's in the driver seat! And I will warn you: the ride may get wild.

I kept praying He would get me to the right destination, and I was learning patience in those times when my world was whirling. There were moments when the hope would fade into pessimism. Doubt crept in bringing questions of whether He could be trusted. But Christ kept me going. Random opportunities came along to sell insurance, but a tiny pressing in my heart, a little quiet voice said to keep waiting. My faith was in trusting that voice and that God knew the way.

With my family, there was a positive development in those uncertain days. Mom was doing well after chemo had beaten back her cancer. Her energy was returning along with a new vigor for life. She had stayed strong, never complaining or succumbing to any recognizable depression. I saw a woman who put her faith in God, trusting He was there with her. I however, had kept myself slightly separated from the whole event. I checked in on her through it all, had prayed for her, and visited. But I had built a small wall to protect myself from the whole scenario. She was winning the battle when Stacy and I were struggling in Florida, and now Mom had won. I just didn't know how to handle the possibility of losing her. I didn't want to confront the fear of losing the woman who had loved me so deeply. My mother had been my best friend. She was the one whom I could trust with anything. She was let in on the truth of what happened to the car mirror 2 months after I got my license (it wasn't a deer like I told them, but a mailbox…as I was being pulled over….for doing 80 in a 55). She knew the secret about the bumps and dings of my dad's car. She knew about the pregnancy scare with Hannah and the broken hearts with Ashley on through to Stacy.

My mom had wiped away my tears, embraced my smiles and calmed my fears. This woman had raised me with a driving focus of love that I feared I might never be able to give or find. To wake up with the realization that I might not have her with me during my best years was a scary thought. I didn't want any part of it, but Mom had beaten cancer, and she was healthy now. She was working full-time again, and doing all she could to get my dad to retire.

And as I fought with job applications and attempted to step into the next stage of my life, I watched my parents go through a similar battle of transition. Their wishes tussled with the ticking of time. Dad's heart was filled with responsibility and worthy motive, sacrificing himself for his employee's welfare and to provide for his family. But, while he worked, both of them were eager to begin their new stage together.

Mom's war had brought realizations to the forefront, and they both felt trapped by the crush of responsibility and desire.

CHAPTER 9

I hadn't visited Mom and Dad in a while. Life at Tom's was a good one, and things were looking positive for a change. Regret filled the tank to full, bringing about the conclusion that it was time to visit after a month of not traveling the 45 minutes to see them.

I stood in the doorway of my old bedroom which had been converted into an office. Mom sat at her desk, pouring over tax returns while a small TV atop my old dresser played *Law and Order.* Boxes of paperwork were stacked along the walls, but most of my stuff was still where it'd been left. A shelf behind her desk displayed a hockey stick signed by a local minor league team along with various pucks I'd collected from highlight games. She had pictures of me in hockey equipment or football pads strategically placed in her line of sight. I never doubted my mother's love for my brother and me, and was thankful to have been blessed with that foundation every child deserves.

"I don't know what to do," I said, lamenting the Madison resume failure. "I still can't believe I didn't save it right. I feel so stupid and embarrassed."

"Hey, I want to work for you," I mocked. "So here's a resume that doesn't make any sense!"

She looked up from her work with a small smile. A warmth of love poured out. "Have you found anything else?"

"No, not really. I keep getting those insurance companies offering me a sales spot, but I really don't want to do that."

She continued working on the tax return taking up desk space. "I don't blame you. That's not something you'd be happy doing," she said. She paused for a second, and then asked, "What about calling your friend Stephen? I think he's working out in the oilfields right now."

"He is? He's working on an oil rig?" I asked, a little shocked that this kid I had loosely known all my life was now working in the rough and tough life of oil.

"I believe so. Maybe you could work out there. It sounds like there are a lot of jobs," she said.

I thought back to a conversation I'd had with another friend's dad. He'd been talking about the tar sands oil boom in Alberta. He told us the money people were making and the work guys our age were doing. The adventure of the idea thrilled me, so I quickly looked into working in Alberta, but couldn't find much that was offered without being a Canadian citizen. Soon, my laziness took over and I scrapped the idea.

Mom persisted, "Would you like his number?"

I normally would have said sure, thought about the idea for a few days and then decided it wasn't worth the trouble. However, for some unknown reason, I asked for the number and called him right away.

It rang.

"Hello?"

"Hey Stephen, it's Christian. My mom said that you were working out in North Dakota or something."

"Yeah. I'm working on a workover rig. They're like moveable rigs, and they do maintenance and stuff," he said.

I was pacing up and down the hallway.

"Are there any jobs out there? Or do you think you could help me get a job?" I asked.

"Definitely. There's all kinds of jobs out here. The biggest problem is housing. Right now I'm going to be living with a couple of guys, so I don't know that there would be room. But, I'm sure we could figure something out," he said.

"Well, could you maybe check and see if there's any jobs with your company, or some place I could look?" I asked. I was surprising myself. This attitude of asking and getting things done immediately was not normally how I approached any decision.

"Sure. I'll talk to my boss tomorrow and see if there's something you could do. I'll give a call and let you know," he said.

We said our good-byes and hung up. I was amazed at how easy it was, still understanding it might not lead to anything. Most likely I would continue searching on-line, looking for any job that would take me. However, the seed of thought of an adventure began to nourished itself and grow. Nothing felt better than having the opportunity to change my landscape.

I waited the next few days to see what was going to happen.

In the kitchen of Tom's house,we sat eating dinner. The table was small and square with a faded top. A single light hung low, illuminating our faces as the sinking sun shown through the slider behind him.

"I think I'm headed to North Dakota," I said.

"Yeah? I thought you might be headed to Maine or Colorado," he responded.

A gentle pause took over the conversation as we forked dinner into our mouths.

"I thought so too, but I guess this is where I'm headed. My buddy is asking his boss and is going to get back to me."

Tom smiled, "That's good. I know you've been itching to get out of here. I wish you the best of luck. Maybe I can come out and visit."

"Heck man, come with me. You've done your time logging and stuff; I'm sure you could get a job out there no problem," I said smiling. I would have loved for him to come. He was the easiest roommate I'd ever had.

"So what are you going to be doing?" he asked. His hands had left his dinner, entertaining themselves with a smart phone.

"I don't know, I guess working on a rig. I'd be up in the derricks. He said not many guys like working up there, and I could make a few extra bucks. I figure why not."

Tom shuffled a little bit and set his phone down. "That's awesome. It'll be a cool experience for you. I'm sure you'll have that adventure you're looking for."

He knew I was raring to go places. As a man who had lived on the road and in many different places, he knew the call the road could have on a person. Especially when they're young and ready to leave all they know. Tom spent most of his life as a hockey player traveling on buses and planes to different cities. After years of such a lifestyle, he took off the skates to start working for his uncle logging in northern Washington. Tom fit right in as a rugged, of-the-earth type of guy. After some time working for family, he moved on to working on cargo ships. He never became the menial desk-job, tie and button up middle class drone that so many of us morphed into after college. He lived the life I wanted, but felt I'd never have.

With the successful phone call to my friend, there was a chance at living a less than normal life. Working the oilfields of North Dakota was not the path I had envisioned, nor dreamed of, but the fantasy of it sparked my spirit. The idea awakened something deep within. My heart beat a little faster at the notion of packing my car and leaving the familiar beaches and roads for the wilderness of the northern plains.

God was nourishing my desires, eager to lead me to where He could teach me best.

And the first thing I heard from my friends was, "Are there any girls in North Dakota?"

I paused at their question, "Um...I'm not quite sure. I don't think so," I said with a laugh. It didn't matter. I didn't need another girl in my life for a while. They laughed and teased, but were sure to wish me the best and then remind me that I better come back.

Friday came and Stephen called.

"Hey, I talked to my pusher," he said. I waited, holding on to a hope. "He said if you can be out here by Monday morning, you've got a job."

There was silence between us. The adventure might actually become a reality?

"Alright, I'll be there," I said trying to play it cool.

"I don't know where you're going to live, but we'll figure something out. There's a couple of us in a small camper right now. I'm sure we can get something though. I was thinking about buying one anyways."

"Well, if you need help with it, I can split it with you once I get working," I responded. He agreed and we both stated we'd see each other soon.

Then, it hit how quickly I had to pack. I went through my room, slinging clothes into a pile on the mattress and discerning what could be brought and left. Tom, was more than happy to let me leave some things in the spare room in case I returned, either with my tail low or my chin high.

Thankfulness radiated from my soul for Tom's position and timing in my life. I felt as though the Lord had sent him to give me a solid place to live while I was in transition, allowing a solid starting point for my next phase.

Bags of clothes and random necessities were packed tightly in the back seat of my car. It was my version of a hobo's checkered bag on a stick. I felt like a true adventure seeker, living life on the road with only what I could carry. I had the bare essentials and that was all that I needed.

I waited impatiently for morning. Fantasies of life in the oil frontier bounded about in my head, while the most prevailing thought that floated among the splatter of ideas was, "I'm really doing it. I'm finally moving forward with my life". My heart leapt with excitement.

Even amidst plenty of happiness, a bitter thought seeped into the edges of the moment. Many people were being left behind, and who knew when we would see each other again. God had used so many people in my life to get me where I was, and to Him the credit was deserved. Leaving my friends and family behind nagged, pulling on my coat sleeve as I turned west. They had been there for the best and worst.

However, Christ comforted my worries. This was His path. If I had followed my own trail and not submitted to waiting for Him to work, I would have continued to obsess over women, look for fulfillment in directions that only brought emptiness, and chased my tail in finding a career or path in life to follow. God loved me enough to put me in the desert and wait for me to finally say, "Okay God. Show me."

CHAPTER 10

As I stood in the driveway, I reflected upon how invaluable of a friend Tom had been. We never struggled nor fought. He opened his home wide and blanketed me with security as God moved pieces in my life to lead me out of Michigan. Tom was a lighthouse, directing me away from the torrent of drug storms and alcohol waves.

"You take care of yourself out there," he told me, seeming to understand the sadness of the moment. I shared the sentiment.

"I will. You too. Thank you so much for everything you've done. Thanks for giving me a place to live for the summer, and opening up your home," I said.

"No problem. As long as that room is empty, consider it yours. Please keep in touch."

We hugged tightly to let the other know that this wasn't just a casual friendship easily left behind. It was a connection that would remain a lifetime.

I drove and the rearview mirror reflected my own eyes off center to a fading driveway with a waving figure, as if I were a character of a tear-jerking Saturday afternoon special or maybe a country western. Perhaps I was the cowboy riding into the horizon, turning my back to all I knew for the exciting prospect of adventure and black gold.

My travel itinerary included an overnight stay at my parents' retirement house in Upper Michigan, then I'd make the rest of the journey on Sunday. The Honda floated onto the highway and the city gave way to trees and fields. Mile markers climbed higher and left a trail behind, showing the bread-crumb path of where I'd been. Not all of me was committing to the new reality though. Part of my heart was still with Tom at the house. Pieces of me were being left with the guys on a Thursday afternoon at the pub, enjoying talking to the staff over burgers. My hands still tingled from the warm embrace of close friends or the cool, crisp shaft of a hockey stick during free skate. Complimenting the bittersweet taste was the anxiousness of being out on my own. I would soon be responsible for myself in an unknown land, surrounded by the pressures of an industry about which I knew nothing, and new people with whom I had no intimacy.

I took time to pray. I don't remember the prayer itself, but I asked for protection and understanding. The only thing I could do was to pray the Lord would keep and guide me. I longed to know more about Him and to become a better follower. The prayer included seeking strength to trust in His plan, and it reflected an abrupt honesty that felt cleansing. I was recognizing that a chanted prayer seemed like checking a box of 'daily tasks done', while a humble and contrite prayer bore a person's soul and faults, refreshing me with a deeper fulfillment of creating a personal relationship with my God.

My mind wandered from the start of the vertical green mile-markers, past my present location driving up the middle of the mitten, and into the land of oil. It was as if I were dancing with two partners at once, switching in the middle of the mental waltz from one beautiful, graceful young lady I'd known for quite some time, to a mysterious and mesmerizing stranger. The young lady of the mental waltz was familiar and joyful, a presence that brought comfort followed by longing and emptiness. The mysterious stranger seemed so fresh, providing a new sense of excitement that my heart desired.

As the dreams of what might be intermingled with the memories of what was, I crept closer to my parent's house. The end of the six hour segment saw me pull in the driveway mentally exhausted from the dance between where I had been and where I was going. Both partners floated into the shadows. The music wasn't finished, and I knew they would return – ready to continue the mind-exhausting tryst of old and new.

But, for the moment, I carried a small clothes bag through the house and collapsed into a chair to visit with my parents. We shared our thoughts about the trip, but I noticed hesitancy in Mom. Our conversations were fluffy, keeping sentimentality at bay. She saw the great opportunity and knew it was best, but I could tell it wasn't an easy task for a mom to send her son off into the unknown.

As I lay down in bed that night, sleep skittered away, escaping as soon as I thought it had been caught. The thoughts were beckoning to have another round at the waltz, while I wanted to sleep deep and escape all the thinking. Despite the tussle, I could sense a new peace transcending, budding from my new faith in God's plan.

Meanwhile, God was guiding, waiting for me to get to the destination He was preparing.

The darkness of Sunday evening spread, and I was exhausted. I was ready to get to the end of my travel. It had been a long day of driving interspersed with short stops. As I headed into Western North Dakota, little orange glows popped up in the darkness where supposedly expansive meadows lay. Right next to the highway burned a huge fireball, shooting 20 feet into the air. It shook and danced with a fearful beauty. I wondered if this was something terribly wrong that needed to be reported. The closer I looked, the more it seemed the fire was contained.

It was on the edge of a flattened out space, located inside a square with dirt piled high creating a berm. There were tan tanks halfway down the cleared area, and in the middle was a horse-head shaped structure moving up and down. I recalled images of such a structure, pumping without rest in the great outdoors. The light from the flame illuminated the entire site, bouncing off the pumping unit and tanks in a bathing warmth.

A little farther down the highway stood a tower lit up like a Christmas tree. Surrounding it were trailer houses and tanks, trucks and machines. Pipes, buildings and equipment seemed spread in a chaotic mess around the tower of lights and cables. The entire site was well-lit with huge fluorescent glows seemingly everywhere. Here was the first drilling rig I had ever seen in person.

I was officially in "The Bakken".

Excitement pushed away the exhaustion from a 14 hour drive. As I crested the hill, burning orange against a cloudy night sky gave way to city lights sprawled wide and thin. The highway curved and slanted downwards into the spill of soft luminescence, splitting the sea of lights down the middle. I had made it. I was now about to enter Williston, North Dakota.

The traffic was heavy, and getting busier every mile. For a tiny town in North Dakota, it seemed as though the whole world was there. Semi-trucks lined the highway and pulled huge machinery or tanks. Vehicles fought for position coming into town and the rules of the road didn't seem to exist. As I approached the edge of town, I saw Wal-Mart to my right interrupting the darkness. I turned in, noticing that if I didn't have my head on a swivel, it might just get taken off. Vehicles had no organization, tearing past each other in every direction. A whole section of RV's and campers sat at the back as if a camp ground had vomited into the parking lot. I dodged vehicles coming from every direction and recognized Stephen's car. I pulled up and rolled down my window.

"Dude, this place is crazy," I exclaimed.

He smirked. "Yeah, this is how it usually is. It's a mad-house around here. Let's go back to the camper. I'm sure you're probably ready to relax," he said.

I agreed, ready to follow him out of the crazy collage of cars and customers.

Thoughts of the oil boom in North Dakota, or images on television of the massive growth, are most likely drawn from the Western area. The first oil well in North Dakota was drilled in the 1950's in a town called Tioga, which sits about 40 miles from Williston. Oil had left its mark in the 70's and 80's, again in the 90's, and finally this boom that started around 2008. The town itself was small, but growth from the industry had spread fast and sporadically all around it. Structures of thin steel and dirt lots popped up in a spastic fashion, filling in the holes and spaces along the roadways. As the demand for workers grew, people flocked to stake their claim in the black gold rush. Combine this phenomenon with a recession in the rest of the country, and the product was a recipe for a great big mess. Many people lived in campers, whether they were located in campgrounds, people's yards, company lots, the streets, or even out on country roads. Other people lived in man-camps. These huge camps were row after row of FEMA-like trailers. If you were lucky enough to know someone who had a house or an apartment, you might be able to squeeze into a room for a price. Some houses had 7 or 8 people sharing a few bedrooms. And because of the shortage of available housing, apartment prices were sky-high. As I write this, an advertisement is tacked to a bulletin board for a two bedroom apartment. The asking price is 3400 dollars a month.

A town, normally home to 12-15 thousand residents, now had anywhere from 30-60 thousand estimated people in the surrounding area. I followed Stephen into a fenced-in industrial lot with a shop and old equipment scattered on the edges. As we drove around the end of the building, the back opened up to a yard with equipment on one side, and a row of 8 or 9 old trailers and RVs parked against the wall of the shop.

Stephen's car came to a stop in front of a small, brown trailer. It looked to be 30 years old, with jagged edges and faded two-tone brown paint. We stepped up to the door and it easily swung open. The reason was obvious: it didn't latch in the first place. Stephen took me up the steps made of wood pallets, through the door that wouldn't latch and into a cramped space. The trailer was 10 to 12 feet long and 6 feet wide. There was a bed in the back, and a bench that had been fashioned into a bed in the front. A small counter space was home to clutter and random boxes of food, along with a small TV. Stephen's trailer-mate, Anthony was sitting on his bed.

"He's here! Yo man, how's it going?" Anthony said with a wide smile. He was small and wiry, with thick dark hair tussled upwards and a bright smile beneath sparkling eyes.

"Pretty good. It's been a long drive," I said plopping myself down on the bench/bed next to Stephen.

"I bet. You ready to work?"

"Yeah I think so. I'm excited to get working and get on the rigs," I said.

"Dude, it's a blast. I love working on the rigs. One of these days I'll be working in on the floor. Right now I'm in the derricks."

I nodded, doing my best to keep up with his erratic pace.

"That's what I'm supposed to be doing too," I said.

He sat back petting his cat. The cat was dark brown and seemed full of as much energy as he was.

"For sure. You're supposed to be on Stephen's rig, right?" he asked. "That'll be cool. If he and I were on a rig together, we'd be killin' it..." He quickly traveled off into his own world of conversation. I tried to pay attention despite the exhaustion, but he talked with blistering consistency. Words blended together, and I did my best to take pieces and form meanings. All I could really comprehend was the need for sleep and being ready to go tomorrow if they wanted me right away.

"Did you hear what happened last week?" Anthony asked.

I perked up, "No, what happened?"

"Dude, there was a rig last week that had a blow out. I guess it caught fire and 3 guys died. One guy jumped from the derricks because he was on fire and hit the ground and died," he said, eyes wide.

"Holy crap," I commented, wondering what kind of world I was coming into.

"I know man. Word is that he jumped because he was on fire, and yeah, the three of them died."

"Does this happen a lot?" I asked.

"Once in a while, but most of it doesn't get reported. They try to keep that kind of stuff on the down-low."

I thought about the men and their families. One morning they walked out the door for another day of work. And in a split second, their lives were over. I had never worked a job where death was a plausible way to end my work day. Slivers of doubt nestled into my thoughts.

After more conversation dominated by Anthony, we settled down into our beds. I rolled out my sleeping bag and squeezed between the counter and the small built-in dresser on the opposite side. I crashed into unconsciousness.

The next sound I heard was an obnoxious alarm wailing as if a nuclear spill had happened in the trailer. It startled me, and I took a second to realize that it was Anthony's alarm. It took him a minute to wake up, and gather enough coherence to turn it off. I tried not to move, hoping blissful sleep would come back from the shadows. He stumbled out of bed onto my legs, forgetting that the cramped space had collected another human. I heard shuffling and finally the slap of a trailer door, pushing a blast of cold air in. The door shifted ajar to leave the usual two inches of open space. I grasped for my phone: 4:45am. I couldn't believe they got up this early.

Soon Stephen was up and out the door, leaving the trailer in a peaceful quiet. I took my sleeping bag and scrambled up onto his spot, enjoying the cushions as opposed to the floor. The cat came and snuggled up next to me and we rested for a few more hours.

That day I sat. I played with the cat at random times, petting her as I stared into space. I searched the camper for a book or something to bide my time. I found a book Stephen had about crab fisherman in Alaska, written by one of the captains on a famous television show. It was an interesting book, highlighting the hardships they experienced and noting the dangers they faced every day. After a few hours of reading, I went to my car to see what I could find and see if anyone was around. The row of trailers and campers sat silent. So back into the camper I went, playing with my phone to speed along the sun.

Stephen clambered through the door as early evening approached. He set down his gear and plopped onto the bench.

"How was work?" I asked, happy to have someone to talk to.

"Not too bad." His response was withdrawn and curt. His work clothes were covered in oil and dirt, grease and dust. I watched hands painted a few shades darker by a fine mist of oil push themselves through matted hair. The smell of grease and sweat soaked the stale air of the trailer. Hesitant to ask, but excited to know, I finally popped out the question.

"So? What did your boss say?" I was ready to work.

The words dropped hard in the camper, "Yeah…I asked him about it today. He told me that he didn't have anything for you." A hint of frustration threaded through in his voice.

I stared. I'd just driven 20 hours to a town I had no clue existed, slept on a camper floor with a door that didn't shut, and now I was being told his boss didn't have any work for me?

"I thought you said he told you if I was here by Monday morning that he'd have something for me," I said with exasperation.

"He did. He told me you'd have work, and when I asked him today he said he didn't have anything for you, and he didn't need you."

Confusion wound through our emotions.

After a diatribe of choice words directed towards his boss, I finished with a pause and a "So what now then?"

"I don't know, but there's lots of jobs here in town. I'm sure you can find something," he said.

"I know, but can I live here if I don't work for them? Where am I supposed to go?" I asked quietly, wondering what was going to happen now.

"We'll figure something out. I can't believe he did that. I'm sorry man, if I had known…" he said, eyes full of truth.

"It's okay. It's not your fault. Thanks for trying for me," I said.

Stephen grabbed his towel and went to take a shower in the only spot that had running water- the shop bathroom. As he showered, I sat dumbfounded at the situation. I couldn't believe someone would do that to another person. To act so nonchalantly, when a person was depending on their word, was incredulous to me.

I wondered where God was. I thought He had provided a job that I needed. I thought work had finally come that would provide financial support and stability. God had brought me out to North Dakota, and now I wondered. Was He leaving me high and dry? Did I do this wrong? Did I not listen to Him when I should have? Did I hear Him wrong?

The next day I stewed and tried to figure out what to do. Anxiety clawed at me, and I was trying my best to hold it back. Part of me just wanted to give up and go home. I would have felt defeated and embarrassed, but I began to think maybe I just wasn't meant to be there. The other part of me decided that going to find work at another company was the best option. Maybe one of them would treat me a little better than this place had.

There was a knock at the door. I opened it to find a guy about my age looking up at me.

"Are you Christian?" he asked.

"Yeah…"

"Kyle wants to speak with you," he said, backing up so I could exit.

I muttered an "Oh," wondering what was next. I followed him down the row and through a back door into the shop. The cavern was massive, with four big bay doors open to the front lot where we drove in. One bay down, a gigantic red truck was parked. It had a front like a semi, and a big cab on the back where a worker sat and did whatever they do with those trucks. A long slender pipe arm jutted out towards the front over the top, and appeared to be able to swing to the back, where the cab faced outward.

A few guys stood around talking and eyed me as I followed the young man. A man, who appeared to be in his early 40's, approached. He had a bushy mustache and carried his extra weight with a look of comfort. It seemed to be his armor. His eyes were tired, but kind.

"Are you Christian?" he asked.

I scanned the group of men circling me. All eyes were focused, analyzing as I shifted nervously.

"Yeah," I responded.

"I heard you're looking for a job," he said, appearing to make judgments in his mind.

"Yeah, I am," I said. I kept my mouth shut, not wanting to talk bad about my predicament. I wanted to let this guy know how frustrated I was, but something told me to be silent.

He stared for a second, then asked, "Can you talk to people?"

"Sure, I can do that," I answered tentatively, wondering what he was driving at.

"You think you could chat with someone for 20 or 30 minutes if you had to?"

"Yeah, I could do that. I like talking to people," I said. I felt awkward, realizing that even though I said I could hold conversations, I'd only spoken a few words to this man.

He looked me over again as if trying to make up his mind and seemed to come to an agreement within himself.

"Well, one of the other divisions needs a salesman. So, let me make a call to Don and see if he wants to talk to you," Kyle said.

My heart began to pound a little faster. So it wasn't the rigs, but this opportunity would be a job.

"Sounds good, I can do that," I said.

He nodded. "Come with me."

I followed Kyle through a door into the offices and slid into a tall, leather chair as he dialed Don.

"Hey Don, Kyle. Are you still looking for a salesman?" he asked. He was quiet as Don responded on the other end.

"Alright, sounds good. I'll send him your way," Kyle said as he hung up the phone.

My eyes widened.

"Go ahead and see Don tomorrow morning. He runs the rental shop over at the other office."

I nodded.

"Do you know how to get there?"

I tried to focus. The way it was working out seemed amazing. I couldn't help but wonder if I'd be content, though.

"Nope. Honestly I've got no clue," I laughed.

After he gave directions, I thanked him profusely, trying to be as polite and earnest as possible. I walked out of the office, curious as to what God was doing. I prayed, "Was this the path you wanted me on, Lord? I didn't really want to be a salesman, but if this is your will, who am I to argue?"

Back in the camper, I pondered. Decent pay was necessary, at least enough to buy a truck. My little Honda Accord couldn't plow through a Dakota winter. That fact I knew. I worried about how much I would or wouldn't make in a sales position. The guys on the rigs made good money, and that was what I wanted. Turning down a prosperous job on the rigs was difficult, but if it was a job God provided, I'd give it a fair shot. I spent the rest of the afternoon prepping myself for what might come at the interview. I had no clue how to sell. The best work experience I could offer at an interview was running tournaments at the rink back home, along with heading some coaching programs. Those would be my go to accomplishments. I hoped they mattered.

When Stephen returned home, I was excited to tell him the news. I gave him the full scoop about Kyle and the sales job. He and Anthony listened carefully, showing more excitement at the prospect than I did.

"Dude, that's a good gig. You don't have to do much. It's really a cake job," Anthony said. "You get to sit in a truck all winter, and you get paid to drive around and talk to people. It's much better than freezing your butt off on the rigs!"

"That does sound pretty good. I guess I was just hoping to get on the rigs. That's where the real work is. I like doing hard work. I like manual labor," I responded.

He smiled. "Yeah, but it's rough when it's the middle of winter. When it's -20 and you're standing at the top of the derricks, you'd sure wish you were in a warm truck."

They both continued to congratulate me on the opportunity, and encourage that it was a good job. They really hounded excitedly on the fact that I'd be getting paid to drive around. I agreed for the most part, but longed to be outside on the rigs. I had come out to do the hard work, and to have a job I could boast of back home. Not many people worked the dangerous, rough jobs in the oilfield, and I wanted that adventure, and to be able to tell my kids about how their dad worked in the patch during the oil-boom. But, I was also clear-headed. If this job was from God, it was what He wanted me to do.

So I struck a personal deal. If it didn't pay enough, didn't have benefits, or didn't at least provide enough to buy a truck, then I could always find something else. I lay awake that night, thinking about the interview and the job. Every image of being in the oilfields was going up in flames, and I only hoped it would rise from the ashes better than expected. I fell asleep praying, "God, I'm going to trust you. Your will be done, not mine."

I arrived nervous, but eager at the shop the next morning. I passed through an outside door into a dingy, old shop and went on through an old wooden door adorned with an "office" sign. Inside, an older man with a thick, shock of white hair and large glasses sat at a desk across from where I stood. He wore an old shop shirt with the name "Don" on it, reminiscent of a car mechanic. He smiled and motioned me in.

"Hi, I'm Christian. Are you Don?" I asked. He gave a firm, long handshake.

"Yup, that's me. Go ahead and have a seat," he said, motioning to the old leather chair to my right. I sat down and did my best to look professional and confident. My hands played together, attempting to figure out where they should rest.

He leaned back in his old rickety chair and intertwined his fingers.

"So, where are you from?" he began, continuing the friendly smile and inviting tone. I was already liking Don.

"I'm from Michigan. My friend said they had work out here, so I figured I might as well come out and see if I could get a job."

"Michigan. I've lived a lot of places, but I haven't lived there," he responded.

"You haven't lived here your whole life?" I questioned, trying to show how beautifully I could converse.

"Nope. Well, I grew up here," he said thinking back, "but after I got out of the service I lived in a lot of different cities before ending up back here. I lived in Los Angeles, New York, St. Louis. A lot of other places too."

"I like to travel. I'd love to live plenty of different places too. Maybe some day return home," I grinned, "but right now I want to get out and see more of the country."

"That's a good thing," he smiled. "So, I take it Kyle explained the job?" he asked changing gears.

"Yeah, he said a little bit about it. He said it's a sales position and asked if I could hold conversations with people," I responded.

"Do you think you could?" Don asked. I felt as though he was already pleased. I sensed that he could read people well, and so far I hadn't been shoved out the door.

"Yeah, I could do that. I like talking to people, and my last jobs where I ran tournaments at a hockey rink and coached had me forming relationships with a lot of people," I said.

He listened as I spoke, agreeing with everything. His eyes were focused. The man looked as though he had lived a rough life and was tired, but possessed a spirit that didn't want to quit.

"Basically what you'd be doing is keeping customers happy. You'd go out and visit them, get tickets signed, bring them a bucket of chicken or something. You'd drive to site, deliver equipment or pick it up, and help customers with any issues they might have," he said. "Does that sound okay to you?"

"Yup, sounds great. I can do that," I said.

He climbed out of his chair and motioned for me to follow. "Here, I'll show you around the shop."

We left the office and turned the corner. Big pieces of equipment sat in various forms of readiness as shop hands rushed to finish tasks. He pointed out the different pieces.

"Most of what we do is workover rig equipment. I want you to be able to tear it down, and put it back together. That way you'll know what you're selling."

It made sense. I wanted to know all I could about what the shop had. I didn't want to be 'that guy' stuck fumbling for words when a customer asked a question I didn't know how to answer.

We walked back towards the office. He turned to face me.

"So is it something you might be interested in?"

"Definitely."

"Any idea what you're looking to get?"

I had no clue what to say. Go too high and you sound greedy. Go too low and you've low-balled yourself.

He continued, "We usually start you out at 60. Does that sound okay?" My jaw dropped a little. "And you'll get a company truck. You drive it wherever you need to go. If you need to go to the grocery store, or out to eat, then you take the company truck. Now, it's not supposed to go on long trips like to Minot or anything, but as for anything around town, don't drive your own vehicle."

I immediately thought about all the times we're told that God provides. Here I was, becoming a living testimony to those words.

"Yeah, that sounds great," I said, perhaps a little too quickly. "I was wondering how I could afford to get a truck, and honestly the company truck is what really does it."

"Yup, you'll get a company truck, benefits and then $60,000 a year. Some days you might be done at 5, other days you might be done at 3 or 4. As long as you see who you need to see and get your work done, that's what counts. Does that work?"

"That works." I looked at him for a moment, then asked, "How long of a commitment are you looking for?" My fear was the lack of an exit strategy out of town.

"How long can you give me?"

I thought for a moment.

"I can give you a year and a half to two years," I said.

"If you can give me a year and a half to two years, that works for me," he responded.

We shook hands.

In the oilfield, two years was a long term commitment. The revolving door was spinning so consistently that employers loved to hold onto anyone who would give them a couple years of service. And with that handshake, I had become part of the industry. While I wouldn't be slinging pipe on the rigs, I would be driving around in a company truck with company gas, paid salary and doing a job that kept me warm and independent. God may not have given me exactly what I wanted, but He gave exactly what I needed.

Don had to get approval from the CEO, so we trekked to the main office and plopped down in Chris' office.

"I found my guy," Don started out.

Chris looked at me.

"This your man?" he asked Don.

"Yup, he's the full package. I want him. And I want Darryl out," he said.

I shifted in my seat, taken aback. I hadn't realized I was replacing someone…

Chris nodded. I studied him. Chris looked worn out and didn't seem interested in what was going on. His words were spoken to pacify and appease, not to dictate and direct.

"He doesn't do anything. He doesn't visit customers, he doesn't bring them anything. I drive past his house and he's home by 1 or 2 in the afternoon!" Don continued.

I took mental notes. I never wanted a meeting like this going on behind my back.

Chris nodded again.

"Nope. Well, if you want him," he pointed to me, "and Darryl gone, that's fine. Get him an app and down to be drug tested."

The shock of the truth brought a small damp feeling to the celebration, but I wasn't about to let it bother me. Obviously, Darryl hadn't been doing his job.

"Good, I'll get him started then," Don said getting up from his chair. As we walked back, he filled me in on the situation with Darryl.

"I need to replace him. He doesn't want to work. He does as little as possible and doesn't have any interest in helping the company. I just can't do it anymore," Don said, getting visibly agitated by the thought of Darryl's lack of effort.

"I won't put up with it," he added, speaking to himself.

We covered the specifics, and I left dumbstruck. I drove on auto-pilot somewhere to eat lunch. I was ready to cry at the provision God had just given. I wouldn't have to worry about buying a truck, on top of getting paid $60,000. I mulled that number over. I never would have expected to make that much right out of college. My eyes welled up at the overwhelming feeling of being taken care of. I ate my lunch with full focus, enjoying the savory bites that tasted sweeter than they would have the day before. This was a celebration of all that God had provided. I came out here expecting work, had been mislead and left broken, but through a random questioning, had been given a job. I also realized: he had never even asked me for a resume. I was never asked where I went to college, or even if I had graduated. He never questioned, "What was your GPA? What was your major?" Instead, Don got to know me as a person. We conversed and he made a call based on his initial reactions.

If my plan to finish the teaching degree had succeeded, it would've taken 1 ½ to 2 more years in order to finish. That would have been seven total years of education, in order to net perhaps $30,000 to start my career. This opportunity wasn't about making more, but a good salary was being gratuitously accepted as a blessing. Immediately, the doubts barged in, trying to make me discontent with what the job offered, compared with how much the rigs paid. But, I refused to allow those thoughts safe passage through my mind. This opportunity was God's blessing, and I was determined to cherish it.

My perception of God was changing through the course of my days after being born again. For so long I had heard of others who had received God's blessing, but I never understood how I could win such favor. Stories were illustrated in online testimonials and books by wet-behind-the-ears Christian kids. Other people always told the stories of miracles and how they received great abundance. I felt like I fought for everything and had always been left stranded. But, now that I decided to do my best to trust God with everything, I was seeing that even when things seemed bad, He provided. It may not have been what I expected, but He gave what was necessary. And what excited me most was that God was beginning my own personal testimony to His greatness. It had started with a job on a cement island and now, despite the obstacles faced, He gave me a job that fulfilled every need and more.

I had no clue to the benefit the job would provide for my relationship with Christ. All I knew was I'd be making money, driving a truck, and living in the land of adventure. God was preparing me to let go of more than I ever thought I could.

And as if I had forgotten my face after leaving a mirror, I went back to the camper and celebrated with my old ways. Alcohol flowed. I wanted so badly to enjoy the night with my favorite drug, but something tugged at me to stay away. I ignored it and grabbed the pipe. I had passed my drug test, and now it was the time to follow the theme-song on the row: get loaded and buy some fake urine in case of a random drug test. I drank and smoked, enjoying the freedom of being a working man on his own time.

We were independent young men. We had no authority over us, plenty of money in our pockets, and endless opportunities; yet, I could feel God watching, wondering why I hadn't given up the vices that had caused so much pain already. I rationalized my actions by misplacing the encompassing power of grace and holding onto a willful ignorance of who He was calling me to be.

Chapter 11

I walked into the break room where faded red coveralls sat on a shelf. The walls were dingy, stained with years of dust mixed with grease. The floor was pitted concrete worn from boots and oil, creating a surface resembling the moon with its crevices and cracks. Chairs sat in a row along the wall. The first was a recliner that had seen better days twenty years ago. Then there was an old swivel computer chair, and on to some random fold out metal chairs. Everything about the break room was mashed together in a collage of items one might find at a yard sale. They all looked cast out, picked up by hands who saw their worth despite the exterior. I watched the men sitting in the chairs pushing their feet through red pant legs and their arms through red sleeves.

We matched our break room perfectly, dressed in faded, well-worn coveralls. Each face reflected a glimmer of hope, obfuscated by weariness and the malaise of another work day. I didn't see sadness in their eyes, but rather a languishing in life. They were watching another day drift past before it had even begun. This instantly brought back thoughts of the 9 to 5 desk job I feared so deeply. Was this the same? Would I be like this when I was twenty years into a job?

My nose stayed pointed just below the horizon as I walked around the shop. It wasn't out of discontent, but bore witness to my feeling out of place. These guys knew what they were doing, and I didn't. They shuffled about, talking and joking as the morning sun rose. Some held a cigarette while trying to figure out which project to begin. Others scoped out the yard to see what equipment had been brought in over night.

One employee was given the task of instructing me on the basics. His name was Jason. He had a friendly face inviting me to be a part of the crew. As he spoke, he would laugh just a little harder than the jokes justified. I didn't mind. It was calming. I was a fish out of water, and I got the feeling both of us knew it.

"Jason, I want you to show Christian how to tear stuff down. I want him to be working on them with you," Don instructed as workers milled about.

"Sure thing," Jason responded, turning to me.

We set to work, hoisting the bulky piece of equipment with an old lift that swung in a half circle. It bobbed as the hoist groaned from the weight of the cast iron with one of us pushing and the other pulling. We placed the equipment on a stand and used an air wrench to undo bolts that held parts in place.

Jason pointed out various pieces and described what they did. He spoke fast, as if he wanted to catch the thought with his mouth before it passed into oblivion. I could see him working things out in his head. He moved like his words and jumped at the opportunity to complete a job.

I moved like a slug on a hot day for fear of making a mistake. If he asked for a part, I would search the pile he pointed to, trying to figure out what looked like its name. He remained patient, kindly stating that the part I had grabbed had nothing to do with the job. On the off chance I did do something right, he gave some affirmation and kept on going.

By the end of the day, I felt like I had gained a little knowledge. The coveralls came off, and I scrubbed my hands viciously under the faucet. I caught my reflection in the mirror. Surprised, I saw my face was covered in the same dirt and dust shading that had painted Stephen and Anthony. And I was satisfied. I was a blue-collar, grease-neck worker just like the wild spirited men of the past. These men had built, shaped and honed our great country. Each night they wiped away the residue from making a superpower nation, and tonight I joined their ranks. This wasn't washing cars at the dealership back home. This was the oil industry. We made the world turn, and I got to claim my own investment in keeping it spinning.

I got home and started the ritual of showering, waiting for the guys, eating and doing drugs. Since the only shower was in the shop bathroom, it was always a rush to get in before the hot water ran out. Those of us who held in-shop positions had the advantage. We were usually off work at 5, whereas those who were out in the field might not get back until 7 or later.

I grabbed my shower gear and headed through the massive garage towards the back. No one was around, and I enjoyed the brief moment of being alone. The bathroom was a small single-toilet closet with a stand-up shower. I locked the door and immediately felt a flush of peace and privacy. The day had been long, and I felt overloaded from meeting new people and learning a new job. After washing away the day, I was ready to return to the world of people and don my extrovert hat.

Anthony and Stephen returned at different times, and after their own showers, we went out to eat.

"How'd your first day go?" they asked as we sat in an overcrowded restaurant. I smiled and tapped my fingers against the table. "It went alright. I've got to get used to how to do everything, but it wasn't too bad." Anthony began talking about what happened on the rigs that day. Stephen and I listened, interjecting occasionally. I tried to follow the oilfield slang that made no sense. Terms like "Running string in the hole", "elevators", "tongs,", and "rods" flew with ease.

They were well-versed in the lexicon of the field, and I felt like an alien. I nodded and kept quiet, just trying to absorb it all. We ate and they continued the conversation, at moments throwing questions my direction. I wanted to be one of the guys and that meant pushing past one word answers. I did my best to give five words where three would have sufficed. I tried to speak three sentences instead of two. As they continued talking about work and the field, I found myself trying to stay afloat in a sea of unfamiliarity.

Such effort made it obvious to me that I was fully committed to my western adventure.

Pictures and trinkets plastered the walls of the restaurant. Loud voices laughed and cawed from the bar area, while groups of people crushed each other in the booths lining the walls. The vast majority of people were men in a wide array of ages. The servers were mostly women, with a spattering of different accents and looks.

It felt like the wild west saloons, only with televisions over the bar. Gruff, dirty men surrounded us everywhere we went, and the few ladies that lived in town were working the bars, restaurants and service industries. Word was the strip clubs were doing quite the clean-up on profits. Women were coming from Vegas because they could make more in the Boomtown. Stories of violence and wild events permeated conversations. Meth houses popped up in close-knit residential areas. Rapes and murders, shootings, stabbings and break-ins were the topics of conversation always on people's tongues. It didn't matter if the words were true or not, they tasted juicy and satisfying, as if we were savoring a delicacy of gossip found nowhere else. No one knew how much of it was true or false, but nobody cared either.

The freedom and obscurity complemented the jobs prospects. Men with criminal records that other companies would run from, gained employment making six-figures. Here, the only question was if you could do the job. The boomtown environment was at, or just moving past its peak when I arrived. The drive-thru wait at fast food joints could be as long as an hour. Yet people still sat in line. The wait at restaurants was easily 45 minutes no matter where you went. Entry-level positions at burger places paid 15-17 dollars an hour, and the main supermarket paid its overnight workers in the area of 21 dollars an hour. Help was so hard to find that one place in a nearby town had only its drive-thru open, and that was from 11am to 8pm.

The history making phenomenon of which I had become a part was difficult to grasp. The rest of America was in a recession, where long-lines cornered city blocks, waiting for unemployment checks. People scoured job postings and competed against hundreds of others for a single job opening. In Boomtown, it was the opposite. Companies were swamped with applications, but even more job openings. Since 98 percent of those coming into town had no prior oilfield experience, the companies had to take a chance on a person.

Stephen and Anthony came to town the same way. They knew someone back home who spoke of the opportunities. On a whim, they came out and found jobs with a workover rig company. After working for a little while, Stephen went home. Later on, he came back and got on with another company doing the same work. Both boys were determined to make some cash, put it away and begin a real life.

Stephen gave me my shot, and for that I was truly grateful. He opened up his arms and offered to help a friend get his start. He housed me and made sure I lacked nothing. We connected quickly, enjoying each other's friendly company. Later on, he and I were sitting in the camper talking out our plans.

"We need to get a camper soon," he said. "and I was going to get one anyway, so we should get it this week."

"Well, do you want to go half on it?" I offered. Campers weren't priced like packs of gum because of their high demand.

"No, if you don't mind, I'd rather pay for the full thing. That way I can have it for other stuff after this. I'm kind of thinking I want it for camping or something."

I pondered the offer. "If that's what you really want. I mean, I'm more than happy to pay half, and then if you still decided you wanted it, you could pay me off for the other half."

"No, it's fine. Problem is though," he said, "I don't have all the money right now. I don't know anybody with that kind of money to spend right now either."

The thought struck me as odd. Here in a town of flowing dollars, no one on the row had enough to loan for a camper? The cat jumped up, looking to be petted. I stroked her a few times, thinking about what we could do. We needed a camper. I couldn't keep sleeping on the floor, and it was too cramped to fit three of us. Plus, I could tell the state of cleanliness was getting to Stephen. He'd mentioned that prior to coming out, he was fairly OCD about things being clean. He learned to relax, and by Anthony's own admission, "I got him to not be so uptight on that kind of stuff."

But, this mess was more than Stephen could handle.

"I'll make a call, and see what I can do. Maybe my parents could loan you the money if you want to own the thing, and you could just pay them back," I said.

"If you're sure that's okay…" he said hesitantly.

After the pleasantries with Mom, I tried to push the question out.

"So, Stephen and I really need a favor," I started.

"Yes?" she said, already knowing this was probably going to be a request for a loan from the Bank of Momma.

"We really need to buy a camper, and we were wondering if you'd be willing to give a loan, so we could get one this week. Stephen will pay you back. He wants to own it outright," I said as relaxed as possible. Inside, I was hesitant. This wouldn't be the first time I had referred a friend to the loan department. Unfortunately, another friend also received approval, and had never really paid her back. What hurt her most was the lack of contact. I felt bad putting her in this situation again, but I was determined to pay it back if he didn't. Then I could try to collect on my own.

"I think we can do that. How much would you guys need?" she asked, unfazed by the request.

"Probably $3,000."

"That's not too bad. When would you need it?"

I gave a thumbs up to Stephen. "As soon as possible I guess. We'd like to get the camper this week. We're probably going to go tomorrow and check them out to see what we can find. He doesn't want to spend more than $10,000 on it."

"I'll put the money in your account. You just let me know if you guys need anything else," she said.

I couldn't believe how generous my mother always was. If someone needed provision, she was there to give it. If they needed work or guidance, she was always open to helping. Tanya had done some work at her office, and commented on how she loved being around my mom. The words "wise" and "so loving" were used to describe Mom regularly when she came up in conversation. I was proud to be raised by such an open, Godly woman.

Stephen and I went to find a camper the next day. The sun was out, but a chill ran in the air. The camper company had a monopoly on the market in a town where most of the "residents" lived in such accommodations. We checked out one that was 19 feet long. The salesperson said it had just come in, and they hadn't even cleaned it. Stephen fell in love right away. The master bed was huge and plush, the back had bunk beds, and it was priced right.

After a short discussion, we decided to buy it. Since Stephen was working and didn't have all the money to pay up front, the dealer agreed to payments. I wrote my check, and he paid what he could. We went back later to pick up our new home and transported it to the row. As we leveled the stands, others came out to admire the new addition.

Anthony immediately jumped up the stairs into the trailer.

"This is sweet man! I need to get a camper like this," he called out. "You guys want another roommate?"

Stephen and I looked at each other. I knew that deep down a reason Stephen wanted his own camper was to get a few degrees of separation from Anthony. Stephen shrugged off the comment as if he hadn't heard it, and we kept balancing the camper on its stands.

After a trip to the store to buy supplies, we cleaned our new home. Finally, the two of us settled down. It felt cozy. We were making headway on our new life, and were doing it together. Since it was going to be his camper, I offered to sleep in the back on one of the bunks, and Stephen took the master bed. I put my bags and trinkets on the empty bunks as if they were shelves, laying out my clothes in arranged stacks. I spread my thick cloth sleeping bag and blankets on the bottom left bunk. It was my own room with a curtain I could pull for privacy. I was pleased and finally felt settled in a new territory.

God saw that I was settled into my place, and soon He would be working to remove the sin that still unsettled my life.

CHAPTER 12

Living on the row was a time of work and play. Drinking and drugs were part of the normal daily procedure. After work, I usually found a camper that had a supply to offer, and we would relax and chat about the oilfield, women and life. Once I was high, I would find my exit to go back to the camper and tinker on my guitar.

Despite the high, with the drugs and drinking returned the nagging of despair into which I had fallen in college. I had accepted Christ, but wasn't ready to completely give up on my lifestyle for His. Reading and praying were a part of my life, and I was becoming more confident in my beliefs, but the addictions were hard to break. It was apparent the Bible didn't condone these actions, yet I told myself that God gave me grace. I occasionally attempted to quit for a week or two, and then would fall back into the same pattern. I wondered, "Where is the strength I'm told I'm supposed to have? Where's God's power that makes it so I never desire any drug or drink again? Wasn't He going to instantly cure me of this stranglehold of substances?" I looked for God's voice, and there were times He led me with the Word, the press of the Holy Spirit, and the voice of others, but I couldn't feel the supernatural power I thought was supposed to be there. So I continued on, trying to do it myself In order to please Him.

And I failed miserably.

Day after day, week after week I ended up smoking, drinking or lusting. God was patient with me, as if He were setting up the next phase of my life, allowing me to get some behaviors out of my system. God was not condoning what I was doing, but there was grace given in order to get me to the spot where He wanted me.

As the days passed, Jason and I became closer. He invited me to his house for lunch a few times, and we shared some late nights and long weekends working. Once we had become comfortable with one another, we began to enjoy some smoking and drinking together.

One night he stopped by the camper. I had offered for him to come by for a visit, and one night he showed up on my stairstep. He came in, eyes glossy. Energy coursed through him and he spoke quickly without pause.

After a few beers, the talk slid into drugs and money.

"Yeah, I used to deal a little weed here and there," I offered.

"Me too. I make enough to support myself," he said.

As the beer took effect, I became more boisterous. "Well, if you ever need help or need to collect, just let me know," I asserted. My inner self stood shocked. Where did that come from?

"I do have a guy who owes me money. I swear he keeps dodging me about it, and I'm getting sick of it," he said, looking off into space.

Ah, man.

My inner self swore at my own stupidity, while my outer self kept the braggadocio flowing.

"Well, lets go get your money back," I blustered. "I know how to handle myself, and I wouldn't mind pounding someone right now. I need a little release."

Who was I? My attitude of swagger and testosterone was shoving at the seams, trying to break out of the cage I thought I had built around it with faith. Conviction hit me over the head as I listened to what was coming out of my mouth. This wasn't Christ-like. This wasn't the Sermon on the Mount.

The alcohol argued against the Holy Spirit, strangling conviction until I rationalized that it was okay, and that a little compromise didn't matter too much in the grand scheme of life.

And my mouth continued to spout idiocy.

"I've done some things before and gotten in some scrapes. It's been awhile, but I'm not afraid to take a bat to someone," I said. I must have watched too many gangster movies. The words falling out of my mouth were appalling. I thought I was past all this.

Jason took another slam of his beer to finish it off, and he stood up.

"Why not? Let's go see if we can get it."

My inner self groaned, my outer self jumped up and finished my beer.

As the SUV's headlights bathed the road in dim yellow, Jason's cigarette smoke curled up and through the cracked window. He was talking fast, jumping erratically from subject to subject as the cigarette twirled in his fingers.

"This guy has owed me money for a few months now, and every time I bring it up, he dodges me," Jason said. "He's a good guy, and I really like him, but he thinks of himself first. You know, if you're going to borrow money, I expect you to pay it back."

"Well, hopefully he's willing to just give you some money, and there won't be too much of a hassle," I said.

"I'm sure it'll be alright. But I gotta do something," Jason said emphatically.

We pulled onto a middle-class neighborhood street with newer townhouses. I put on my game face, ready to do a little intimidation and pressuring if need be, not wanting Jason to think I was a wuss. We knocked. The town house looked a little too nice and cozy for someone who owed money for drugs, or loans or whatever. The door opened and a middle-aged woman answered. A little yappy dog barked and hopped at our feet. The guy lived with his mom? Go figure.

My shoulders dropped an inch and my back relaxed. This wasn't what I had envisioned. I pictured coming into a run down trailer, trashed with bottles and random baggies. I pictured a guy on a ratty couch, scared something would happen if he didn't pay up. Instead, I walked through a suburbia comfort-zone portal.

"Is John around?" Jason asked the lady.

She looked uninterested, caring only to get back to what she'd been doing. "Yup, he's downstairs," she said as she turned to head back to the kitchen.

We took the staircase to the basement. Black painted walls intensified the lack of lighting. Neon paint adorned a back wall with stylized graffiti illuminated by blacklights. We found John lying on his bed watching TV with his daughter. My back relaxed more. Now I just felt stupid.

"Hey man, what's going on?" Jason said, offering his hand out to John. They shook, John not moving from his spot on the bed. John's head was shaved on the sides with a draping strip down the middle that resembled a long Mohawk. His gangly arms bent behind his head, fashioned as a fleshy pillow.

"Not much, just chillin' with the kid. What are you guys up to?" he asked looking at me and then back at Jason.

I nodded and examined the basement. I felt out of place and wanted to be back in my safe camper.

"We were just driving around, thought we would stop in and say hi," Jason said. At least he was in the same mood as I. Neither of us was comfortable with barging in with a baseball bat and breaking kneecaps.

"Ah, that's cool," John said, petting his dog and gazing at the television.

"But I was wondering man, do you happen to have some of what you owe me? I could use it right now," Jason asked.

John looked up, slightly miffed at the question. "Yeah, yeah. I'll get it to you this week. I had to pay child support and all that stuff. You know how it goes," he said.

I could tell he was giving Jason the slide, but they seemed to be friends beyond a couple of drug deals.

"That's cool, just figured I'd stop by and see what was going on," Jason offered.

"Yeah, I'll get some to you this week. I'm not ducking you; I just had some stuff I had to do and all that," John said. His daughter played on the bed with her toys. She was maybe 5, and seemed oblivious to what was going on around her. We stayed to talk for a few more minutes and then said our good-byes.

I breathed a small sigh of relief as the vehicle made its way out of suburbia back into the guts of the city.

I had escaped a situation I hadn't really wanted to be a part of. My mouth's boasting had placed me squarely into a spot my conscience and heart did not appreciate and the offers put me in a sore place: put-up or shut-up. Had the bravado won, I would have held strong regrets. Jason had a similar approach to such moments. He didn't want to harm anyone. He didn't want to play tough guy, but put us together, and we fed off the macho-ism, becoming collection thugs.

Jason drove to the edge of town. Soon, we were driving through a field and kicking up dust, before coming to rest overlooking the lights of the city. Jason opened up the center console and pulled out a lightbulb without the metal at the end. Something clicked, and I knew it wasn't for weed.

"Do you want some?" he asked, slightly tilting his hand towards me.

"No it's cool. Thanks though," I said. A deep pressure from my spirit allowed no curiosity. The rejection came naturally and flowed as if God had drawn a strong line in the sand. While a tiny part was interested in what meth was really like, I knew I would never come back above surface if I started.

"No problem," he said.

He started the lighter, moving it around and around the bottom of the bulb. The contents bubbled and turned black, smoke swirling inside. Soon, he sucked in a couple of small hits, and let it sink in his lungs before slowly blowing the smoke out. His eyes didn't bug out of his head. He didn't eat a random stranger's arm. There was no babbling about demons on the front doorstep or ninjas in his cereal. His energy dipped a bit, and he spoke in a more even manner.

"I don't do it too often, but every once in a while I just need something to relax," he said. As an afterthought, he added, "We should probably get out of here before someone calls the cops."

Sitting in a field with a lightbulb full of meth was not a low-key activity.

We drove back through town like any other normal vehicle. We didn't drive down the sidewalk or blow through stop signs.

"It's not something I like to do....well screw it, yes I do," he laughed. "But not too often. I've quit before, and I'll quit again."

"I've never tried it," I said.

"Don't," he added.

"Yeah, I won't. I tend to stick to pot and pills, alcohol, shrooms. That kind of thing," I said. My thoughts jumped to my time with Tanya. What a wonderful escapade that ended up being, I thought sarcastically.

"If you ever need anything, just let me know," he said. "I've got weed and pills and stuff. I can hook you up. But I'm glad you'd rather not get started on meth. I don't want to get other people hooked on it." And he kept to his word.

We pulled back into the shop lot, rounded the building and stopped in front of my camper.

"Thanks man, I appreciate it," I said. "Do you want to come in for a beer?"

He shook his head. "Naw, I think I'm going to head home. Thanks for chillin' tonight though," he added.

I gave a small wave while opening the trailer door. The couch sitting inside brought sanctuary. I wasn't sure where Stephen was, but it didn't concern me. People ended up in every other trailer on the row.

I battled with what had transpired. My first reaction was to cut ties with anybody who had an issue, but it was a hard solution to accept. I had my own problems and considered myself a normal person. If I were to be an example, shouldn't I be involved in their life? I tried to avoid thinking about the contradictions of a life lived and a life spoken. Jason's kindness was true. He gave anything he had in order to help, and in a odd way, I knew I could trust him. My pride told me I could handle outside influences, and so I pushed the events of the day out of my mind. I wanted to connect with people, and this was the first logical step, ignoring the burgeoning thoughts of being a hypocrite.

Things fell in place at the shop over the next few weeks. I became comfortable with what I needed to do, and enjoyed the independence the job afforded. Even though we were all working together, each person had his own project. Since my task was cleaning, fixing and prepping equipment, It was easy to zone out. I went to and fro, occasionally making small talk with the other guys. Jason and I would test parts together when they were finished. We'd peer down the top with a flashlight, looking for leaks of pressurized water between the big iron rams that fit snug around the pipe. We would twist nuts and turn valves, open doors and throw levers. By now, I felt mechanically competent beyond the minor car repairs I'd done in my garage. One day, I decided, "Why not get high before work?" I smoked down that morning, arrived to the shop and prepped for the day.

Nothing went the way I thought it would. Instead of enjoying the time, I found myself losing focus. I moved even slower than usual. Paranoia that my boss knew crept into my thinking. He had shown confidence in me and handed out plenty of compliments in my direction. I didn't want to disappoint him. So after that day, I vowed never to come to work high again.

Even though salvation was mine, the drugs controlled my desires. Getting high and making music or hanging out remained the daily goal, and God wasn't impressed. He was speaking to me about it, warning me in my spirit that this wasn't where to find life's meaning. I tried to do it less, but the substances never fell away. The struggle technically continued. Grace had me, I rationalized. I didn't have too much of an argument with the drinking, but the weed was a different story. It never said anywhere in the Bible not to smoke weed. It was a plant. It was natural. It felt good and didn't do any harm, or so I told myself.

And the arguments I touted in college reared their ugly heads once again. Some day I figured I would be done with the stuff. Just not yet.

CHAPTER 13

After a month and a half, Don called me into the office.

"We're going to start training you for sales," he said. "Do you think you know the equipment well enough?"

"Sure. I still have some things I could learn, but I think I've got most of it down," I responded.

"Sounds good. Here's the keys to your truck."

Don leaned back in his chair and I relaxed in the deep, comfortable leather chair facing his desk.

"We're going to have you train with Darryl, since Wes doesn't want anybody riding in his truck with him," he started.

I thought silently, "Wait, what? I'm going to be training with the guy I'm supposed to replace? How is that going to go?"

"Is that okay? I know it's not a great situation. It's not how I wanted it, but it's the only thing we can do. So are you alright with that?" Don asked honestly. I could tell in the creases on his forehead and clear eyes that he knew it wasn't the most comfortable situation.

I shifted in my seat. If that's what the job called for, then how could I say no.

"No, it's fine. Not my favorite idea, but I can do that."

Don leaned forward and put up his hand. "I know I know, and I wish we didn't have to do it this way."

"It'll be alright," I said. "So start training sales tomorrow?"

"Yup, go ahead and just come in the office tomorrow morning, and we'll have you go with Darryl."

Later that night, Stephen and I chatted about the new training situation.

"They want you to train with the guy you're going to be replacing?" he asked, surprised.

"Yup. They want me to keep it down low, since Wes is going to be retiring sooner or later. I guess Darryl thinks that's the reason they hired me," I said.

I watched Stephen's face at the news. He looked at the table and then at me.

"That sucks. Are they going to have you fire him too?" he laughed.

"Maybe. I better get a raise for it though," I said chiding back. "Oh well. I gotta do what I gotta do."

My leather chair welcomed my nervous body the next morning. Wes wasn't in yet, and Darryl sat with crossed-legs at one of the other desks.

"Want some coffee?" Darryl offered, holding a coffee cup.

"Sure, I'll take some," I responded. He poured the coffee and handed it to me with a smile. I sat back down wondering, "How am I going to do this?"

Darryl was mid 50's, tall and a blonde of Norwegian descent. Then again, just about everybody in North Dakota was Norwegian, Finnish or Swedish. He flashed a kind smile that relaxed its witnesses and reflected a confidence I'd seen before. It was the confidence of a guy who had an easy time with girls and enjoyed living the good life.

"Wes isn't feeling good today, so he won't be in," Don said to Darryl.

Wes was old, but still had no thoughts about retirement. From what I had heard, he was one of those guys everyone liked, but who would never back down from putting you in your place. Don told me how much Wes loved to work, and the sense was he would die doing what he loved.

"That's too bad," Darryl said, blowing on his coffee. Tickets were separated out into two piles on his desk, One being his group of clients, and the other Wes' stack. "I hope he feels better."

After an hour of waiting for the sun to come up, Darryl turned to me, "Well, should we get going?"

I shot Don a look and stood up. "Sure, let's get this show on the road." All I could think was, "Here we go."

We left the parking lot and started down the road, my body held rigid and uncomfortable. I searched for the right line of words, but nothing came to mind. Could I handle spending all day trapped in a truck with someone I didn't know?

Darryl made light chit-chat, asking where I was from, how long I'd been in town, what I thought of it and all the rest. We talked about our pasts and our history of playing sports. Turns out Darryl played sports in college. He moved to the area after a stint of living in Montana and worked a couple of jobs before settling in with this sales job.

We stopped at a gas station to fill up and prepped with snacks and coffee to head out of town. He chatted with the cashier, flashing the familiar easy-going attitude. Even though I could tell he'd known her for a while, a charisma flowed from him to her that most people never showed.

One of our main tasks was getting tickets signed. Once we finished a job for a company, our company wrote up a bill. We brought the ticket to the customer, they signed, and the sales staff turned it into our office. Some tickets needed to be dropped off at offices, while others needed to be signed by someone in the field. Darryl took the easiest possible approach to this task. Go in, drop the ticket off, walk out. Maybe talk to the secretary for a few moments before leaving. If it had to be signed in the field, he would chat with the company man for a few moments, and then be on his way.

After a few stops that morning, we pulled into a cafe parking lot.

"Want some coffee?"

I shrugged, "Sure, sounds good." In my head, I knew this was probably his standard operating procedure, but most of me doubted it was company policy.

We walked in and found a table. The diner was faded from floor to ceiling. The yellow walls had seen years of farmer talk and oilfield banter, while the waitresses carried years of pounds and make-up. The tables and chairs were cheap, as if picked out of a restaurant bargain bin, but the décor made the place comfortable. It was a small-town diner with friendly faces and many large laughing plaid shirts.

We ate our sticky rolls and read the newspaper. I was getting antsy with wanting to do some real work, but uttered no complaints. How could I be irritated with getting paid to drink coffee? Besides, he was driving; I wasn't. After an hour, he folded up the newspaper.

"Well, ready to go?" he asked.

"Yup, might as well," I said, rising to push in my chair.

The rest of the day was spent stopping at offices on Wes' route and introducing myself. Each time, Darryl would say, "This is Wes' replacement. He's working into the position since Wes will be retiring soon." And each time he said it, I cringed. I couldn't correct him, but how was I to explain it to folks when Wes was still around and Darryl wasn't?

We pulled back into town about 2:30. A few minutes remained on the work clock, so Darryl drove through town to the car wash. As we sat in line, he offered his perspective on the work day.

"My paycheck says 8 hours. I get paid for 40 hours a week, and 80 hours a pay period. They tell us our day starts at 7:00am. So, as far as I see it: I'm working what I've been paid for when I get done at 3-3:30." His passionately spoken words showed resentment about unfair treatment in the employee-employer relationship.

"If they want me to work those extra 10 hours," he continued, "then they're going to have to pay me for them. When I first started here, Wes told me, 'I work my day, and I'm done at 3:30.' So that's what I do. I work, do my job, and I'm done at 3:30."

I thought back to what Don said, "...I drive past his house and he's home by 1 or 2 in the afternoon!" I wondered who was embellishing his point, or if perhaps they both were. I also remembered Don telling me, "...And some days you might be done at 5, other days you might be done at 3 or 4. As long as you see who you need to see and get your work done."

So I let Darryl prove his point and nodded in silent agreement. He had a point with the paycheck. If we were getting paid for 40 hours, why were we told that our work day was 7 to 5? That was an extra ten hours that wasn't being recognized. The philosophy made sense and the laid-back approach appealed to me. I figured, when my work was done, my day was done.

Darryl turned into the shop yard with another day behind him. We walked into the office and plopped ourselves down.

"How'd it go?" Don asked, smiling at me as Darryl sat down at his desk.

"Pretty good," was all I could muster. I wasn't going to give away our little stops and laissez-faire approach to working.

"We stopped at a bunch of offices and he introduced me to some people. I think I'm going to like this job," I added.

"Good, good," Don said, putting on an act with Darryl in the room.

Once Darryl left, Don turned to me, "So how did it all go?"

He was searching, looking for something else he could put on the list against Darryl. I wasn't going to be the one to throw him under the bus.

"We made some visits, stopped for some lunch and stuff. It went pretty well," I said, trying to be vague.

Don pried a few different ways, but could tell I wasn't going to rat-out Darryl. He settled back into his seat, looking satisfied.

I left torn. The job would be a great job, but I wondered how to do the actual sales. We didn't do much selling, and only introduced ourselves to one or two company men.

The approach for the next week was the same as the first day. We went out, visited with some secretaries, met a couple of company men in the field, and ran several rounds through the car wash.

During our travels, we discussed life, politics, faith, relationships, our past, our future, our goals and our dreams. Darryl was well educated with a strong outlook on life, and he was a conservative man that had an entrepreneurial spirit, from whom I could learn a few things. The few times we talked faith, I did my best to be a representative of Christ.

"So do you go to church?" I asked, nervous but knowing I was supposed to share my faith and get people saved. I determined that if I was going to follow the Bible, I was going to have to speak about Christ. Little made me more uncomfortable than sharing the gospel as I thought about how awkward it felt, how people might respond, and the reactions of those who were against Christ.

"I used to, and we still go every once in a while," he said. "Do you?"

"I've been thinking about finding a church out here, but haven't found anything yet." It was true, the thought had crossed my mind. But I was nervous about getting back into the church scene. It had been several years since I had stepped foot in a church, and I wasn't sure where to start.

"I've heard that there's a good one near the highway," he said.

I tried to picture it and thought perhaps I knew which one he was talking about.

"The big white building?" I asked.

"Yup, that's the one. I hear it's a good one. We've gone there several times, and I think my son used to go there. He's a lot like you…a faithful guy and stuff."

I felt the label didn't quite fit.

"I'll have to check it out."

We were driving somewhere in deserted North Dakota. Farm fields stretched to the horizon, freshly cleared of their crops. Clouds hung in the blue ocean of sky, lazily crawling as the sun bleached them to bright white. The cold air of a North Dakota winter was starting to creep in.

"You don't go to church anymore?" I asked.

"Not really. I still believe in God and everything, but I haven't had much time. I probably should get back to it," he said, thoughtful.

"No time like the present," I added.

"That's true. I believe in God, and feel that I don't necessarily need to go to church in order to believe," he said, leaving the conversation hanging.

I didn't say anything. There wasn't much else I could say. I wasn't going to church either, and I was doing the drugs and drinking routine. How could I give this guy a lesson on following Christ? My life didn't model that of a disciple.

We let the words fade into the distance, and drove towards our next destination. It wouldn't be the last time we talked about God. It was my mission to bring God up, and I was feeling a burden to speak His name.

Christians get it beaten into their head to share the gospel, and it's usually called The Great Commission. I felt ashamed for my lack of sharing. There were so many people that I hadn't offered the free gift, and I wondered if this negligence made me a horrible Christian. It'd always seemed like the passion to speak His name was supposed to be supernatural, as if once you were saved and re-born, life took on a whole new meaning and you were a completely changed person filled only with Christ. I didn't feel that way. I didn't feel any of it, which brought forth the shame. I lived a life that was not filled with Christ and I was embarrassed to bring up His name. To make it worse, I'd read too many passages in the Bible that talked about people who shrank away from giving the word of Christ, and it wasn't in a kind or positive light.

I decided it was time to start saying no to the drugs. The change in me needed to occur in honor of what Christ had done for me. I began driving solo for work, and saw that life's schedule needed changes. One day, I came across a radio station that played sermons. I didn't want to listen to dry, stuffy pastors droning on about "do this and don't do that."

The oldies station was comfortable, like a cool iced tea on a warm summer's day. It made the day pass by and had me reminiscing of my college days. The thought of replacing that music for listening to people piling on conviction was not my idea of fun, but I determined to force one sermon a day through my ears. I felt ashamed that this resource was available and I wasn't using it. I kept asking myself, "What is number one in your life? You and what you want? Or God and what He wants. If you were to stand before Him, what would you say you did with what He gave you?"

This thought started the journey of learning the Lord's Word. The first day was one or two sermons. That wasn't enough. There was so much to learn. I started fading out the music stations and focused on the truth. Pretty soon, I was listening to messages for 8 to 10 hours a day. I learned who came on when, what pastors I liked, and which pastors I wasn't as fond of. At first, the pastors who were hard to bear were ones who made me feel convicted and lackadaisical about my faith. I pressed on. I wanted the faith of Moses or Paul.

The days took on a dependable schedule.

- Get to work in the morning and have coffee with the others.
- Get my day organized.

- Listen to sermons while traveling to see customers and go to sites.
- Get home and go lift.
- Try to read some of my Bible and pray before bed.

This process molded itself into my routine in a seemingly natural manner. I wasn't perfect, but faith grew more important in my day to day interactions. An eagerness grew to share Christ with others, and while this didn't always happen, I worked to step out and try, even when my comfort-zone screamed against it. Swearing fell away from my vocabulary, and no longer did I entertain conversations about women as objects. Honesty and care were tantamount in my dealings with other people.

But the substance abuse lingered, and I avoided the problem. The town was full of dark escapes, and it appeared everyone used something. I had worked to curb all the other sins in my life, but my hands were wrapped tightly around the pills, bottles and pipes. My grip wouldn't break.

CHAPTER 14

About two months after I started work, God introduced me to a man who changed my life. We met one night when he was extremely drunk. Stephen, Anthony and I were hanging out in Anthony's trailer, relaxing our weekend away. The man stumbled in and stood looming in the doorway. He wore a dark t-shirt and faded jeans with a chain attached to his wallet. Soon the atmosphere grew tense as he spoke his mind.

His name was Doug. He lived on the end of the row in an old '78 ford RV. One tire was flat, so the thing leaned forward and to the right. Anyone who came around the shop to the row saw his RV first. It sat separated from the rest of the group. Doug lived a life that matched his camper. He was tall with thinning blonde hair and his back hunched a bit with shoulders rolled forward, as if he were protecting himself from the world in front of him. He worked in the shop we lived behind and kept to himself both during and after work.

"I don't like your cat," he observed as he watched the cat bounding around the trailer.

"It's a good thing it's not yours then," Anthony said.

Doug continued to watch the cat with amusement. He turned to look at us and thought about whether to say what was on his mind. I saw a complete lack of care in making impressions. More so, I saw eyes that were there to stir up trouble and see if he could produce a challenge out of someone.

"Well it better not come around my place..." he trailed off as if talking to himself.

We looked at each other, trying to play nice and just wait him out. Our hope was that he would get bored and find something else to do.

"What are you guys doing tonight?" he asked.

"Not really sure, probably just hanging out," I responded. Stephen had gone silent and watched the whole event transpire. Anthony chose his words wisely. I got the feeling he didn't want to do anything to provoke Doug.

Doug eyed the contents of the trailer and its inhabitants, made a few more incoherent comments and finally sauntered off.

"Who was that?" I asked.

Anthony grabbed his cat.

"That's Doug. He lives at the end of the row."

I was curious what his story was and got my chance to find out a few nights later. Doug and I were introduced while sober. He invited me over for a beer or two, and I obliged.

"You're not like the rest of them," he said, his eyes zeroing in.

"No?"

"No...the rest of them are...well..." Doug tempered himself, trying to hold back what his heart wanted to say. He settled on "You seem smarter..."

I drank a few sips of beer and returned the compliment. "Seems like you're not like the rest of them either. You've got more going than you let on," I posited.

"Don't try that stuff on me," he said laughing. "I see what you're doing."

"And what am I doing?" I asked. I could tell this guy was smart, and a lot keener than his drunken self showed with that little visit to Anthony's camper.

"You're analyzing me. You've got a psychology background or something, don't you," he said, becoming wary.

I nodded. Doug was more observant than I had expected.

"I was a psych major for a while, but ended up with an English degree," I responded, knowing that trying to hide it wouldn't do me much good.

"I took psych in college too," he said.

The conversation was intriguing. I found myself in a complex game of wits. We weren't discussing how hot a certain girl was, or what kind of car we'd purchase with our bundles of oil money. He was delving into psychology and analyzing behavior. It'd been a long time since I had met somebody with that style of perception, and I wanted to find out more about the man behind the thoughts.

He had fashioned a shell of hardness and tough action that steered most people away, and like a porcupine, he sat comfortably in his own little zone, not wanting to be prodded. It was refreshing. Doug had substance, even if he did seem off-kilter. His eyes focused and his mind worked the angles. Instead of being entranced by his own thoughts, he examined the environment.

"Who do you think I am?" he asked.

"I'm sorry?"

He shifted.

"Use that psychology. Give me a profile of who I am."

"Well, my guess is you've been burned several times by close friends. Probably a few girls as well. I'm thinking maybe ex-military? You're college educated, so you're not dumb. You probably know how to use your fists and you don't trust easily." He showed surprise at the list of traits.

"How about me?" I asked.

"You're college educated, so you're not dumb either. You can read people pretty well, and you sit back and observe. My guess is you use your psych background on most people, but you're fairly open. I think you're hiding more than you're letting on though."

I was impressed with his accuracy. The game of analytical chess came to a draw. We saw each other as a respectable acquaintance, able to hold conversation beyond the banal.

"Let's go get a drink," he offered.

"Sure, why not."

I probably should have been nervous. However, something told me he was more trustworthy than most of the other people around here. We took his small pick-up to a little building at the edge of downtown. It was one of those joints with the locked door and a slide at eye level. He vouched for me with the keeper at the gate, and we were allowed access. The decor reminded me of an Elks lodge or VFW hall. Several styles of wood covered the entire interior. Patrons ranged in age from what appeared to be 35-80. Cowboy hats and plaid pushed back drinks next to sweatshirts and baseball caps. The music was low and the televisions broadcasted the regular football fix.

The atmosphere released the tension in the back of my neck. This was not the type of hang-out for someone who murdered people for fun. This was where a person found sanctuary.

We talked lightly, and he started to open up while another side fought to keep the wall intact.

"I was in the army and got out," he said. "Then I went to college and got that finished up, and now I'm here to make some money."

"How long do you plan on staying?" I asked.

"Not sure. Long enough to get things paid off and get a good chunk of savings to live off the grid. I want to be self-sufficient."

"Me too," I said. "I don't want the government sniffing around everything I do."

He smiled.

"I knew you were smart."

He continued, "It's hard to meet people out here. It gets difficult dealing with the crap people pull, and at some point you just want to be left alone," he said.

The drinks flowed and the emotional layers continued to fall to the swept floor. Details were shared that I wouldn't have expected in our first encounter, and soon he caught himself.

"Quit it," he said.

"Quit what?" I asked.

His eyes narrowed, and immediately he put mortar to bricks on the personal wall. His shoulders tensed, and his face twisted to protect his emotions.

"I don't know how you're doing it, but you're getting me to say stuff. I don't know if I like it. I don't know if I can trust you," he said.

"Well, I could tell you that you can trust me, but we both know words don't do a lot of good. It's up to you to figure it out. But, for what it's worth, you can trust me," I said with a chuckle.

"I feel like I can, but..." he trailed off, warring inside.

"Besides, I'm not quite sure if I can trust you either," I said. "But here we are, and you know things about me that not everyone gets to hear."

The drinks eventually washed down our fears and slowed our minds. We paid the tab, got up and sauntered back to his truck. Arriving at home, we said good night and headed towards our separate campers. As I walked back to my camper, I thought about the fierce defense Doug had over his life. I wasn't sure why I was the one to open him up, but then again, he had done the same to me. My own hidden struggles had let themselves out.

I was aware of what the others thought of him, which brought another skirmish within. They considered him crazy and not to to be trusted. I saw the machinations of a man in pain. They viewed him as the guy who might one day snap with a shotgun and a cigarette. Perhaps they weren't that far off, but I saw him as a person with great potential.

The more time we spent together, the more they referred to him as my "buddy Doug". It wasn't the classification of being his friend that made me uncomfortable, but his own interactions with the rest of the row. He would waltz in drunk, looming over everyone and talking trash or looking to pick a fight in a covert, psychological, tactical strike. I didn't want to be in the middle. It was hard to know who he really was since he showed a different person to the others. If he didn't like them, he didn't hide it. He had no patience for most people, but he enjoyed a few on the row. Those people also spoke well of him. As for Anthony, Doug had no love.

"I just don't like him," he said one night as we were working our way through a case of Coors' Original.

"Well that's not hard to tell," I laughed. "But why don't you like him?"

"I don't know," he said. The wheels turned. "I can't really put my finger on it. I feel like he just represents everything I don't like. He's just a hyper, little frat boy or something."

"God tells us to love our enemy," I said. The words felt hollow coming out of my mouth. They had no depth, giving a surface cover that never got to the root of the issue. It was easy for me to say to love someone, but acting on it was much more difficult.

"Trust me, I'm loving him the best I can. I do that by just staying away."

"That works." I didn't want to press the matter. If he wasn't going to throw his arms around the kid, who was I to change it? The issue slid away from our conversation and we continued on.

Thanksgiving was a few days away, and going home wasn't an option. Some of the others decided to ditch us for family, and we figured we'd stick around. Before the travelers left, we all came together for a final night before the troops split.

Anthony grew sick of his camper, so he and a friend named Sam bought an old RV. They fixed it up and added little touches to the 80's throwback. The game of musical-campers was never ending among all of us, as new residents bought out old residents all the time.

Sam was a young guy about 19 or 20 who came out from Idaho. He was like all of us–eager to cash in on the black gold rush. Sam was friendly, a little energetic and harmless. Sam and

Anthony rented a movie, and the group coalesced in their trailer when word spread of a movie and drugs.

A new craze called "Bath Salts" was catching on in the US. A friend of a friend told us how it was scientifically engineered, so such a drug must be safe and legal in most states. Moreover, it provided a high similar to coke while lasting longer.

"This stuff is safe. It's made in a lab, so you know what you're getting," the guy said. "The best part is you can buy it online." We mocked him for the comments, yet there we sat.

He poured the bag onto the table and we circled around. Within a few minutes lines were stacked on the table and each guy took his bump. It was a quick kick, and soon we were all talking at once. I felt the rush of being on top of the world. The camaraderie of being with guys in the same spot of life replaced the emptiness. We all spoke with energy, letting rest the foul moods and insults. Four or five different conversations happened at once, and without any lapse we could track what others were talking about. The lines continued to be cut, and more noses were left with white powder dusting.

In a small RV, on an industrial lot in an oil boom town, sat 5 guys with "Crazy, Stupid Love" playing on the television and bath salts on the table.

I never thought I'd end up in North Dakota watching a chick flick with a bunch of oil workers.

Sam played on his computer, and brought up a picture to show off.

"This is my girlfriend," Sam said, proud of the catch. We all complimented him in a way only guys could.

Terry pulled out his phone to show us his wife.

"This is my wife, I love her to death. I haven't seen her much because she's back home and I've been here for the past two years. I really miss her and my kids," he said.

"Sorry to hear that. How many kids do you have?" I asked. His face grew solemn at the thought. "I've got 5 kids. I don't know, I'm not sure I can handle being away from them too much longer. But I couldn't find any work back home, so I had to come out. I'm making good money, but I'm not sure it's worth it."

Words of sympathy flowed. The RV became a circle of support, missing only the fold-out chairs and donuts.

"I don't blame you, but is there any way you can bring them out here? Or are you planning on moving back home any time soon?" I asked. The story was common, and it blew my mind as to how someone could be away from his family for so long.

"No, I don't want them out here. We have a good house back home." He eyed the picture of his wife, "And I'm not sure how much longer I'll be out here." Premonition wavered in his voice and planning brought shadows across his face.

"Anybody want some more?" A voice called out. Bodies quickly crunched together in the small booth. More lines of white powder dressed the surface of the table. A couple of dollar bills sat rolled, waiting as people grabbed for their turn. Once the round of snorting and sniffing subsided, people continued showing off former girlfriends or current ones in a game of 'the best prize'. Congratulations were offered up as we bragged about our exploits. Voices blurred together around me. The boundaries between each word became fuzzy, and my thoughts grew louder as I started to draw into my shell. I sat with the razor, chopping lines of white and putting them back together over and over. I was obsessed with the routine. Twenty minutes went by without stopping, and when I finally set the razor down, Terry commented.

"I wondered when you were going to stop. You just kept going with that stuff," he laughed.

I didn't have an explanation. The conversation amongst us all continued at its blistering pace, but I fell out of the verbal race. I curled up inside myself, and the motion of refining the powder soothed me as thoughts rambled at light speed. The struggle of introversion took over and I found the right opening to excuse myself. I left the camper and went back to my bunk with plans to get some sleep.

The bath salts had other plans. I left the camper about 2am and sat in bed playing guitar. I soon realized I didn't have the focus to play, so the guitar returned to its resting spot and I lay down. I was wide awake. My body turned like a chicken on a rotisserie. I spun, hoping one side would be comfortable enough. There was no slow down of the thoughts, only a hazy lethargy that hung on amidst my racing mind.

I dozed off around 7 or 8am. It started out fun, but the high gave way to the same emptiness I tried incessantly to avoid. No matter the drug or drink, escape from the haunting depression proved impossible. It wasn't a serious, deep depression that some people faced, but it distorted my view of myself and what my life was. The only time I felt full was when I focused on God or helped others in His name. Whether it was taking someone for lunch or bringing a person food and water, I actually felt full then. It was obvious that we were all trying to solve the problem of emptiness by exacerbating it, and we were failing miserably. We acted in the play of happiness, but our eyes confessed the truth. There was no contentment. This town was supposedly a rest stop on the path to joy, and it felt more like a prison term than a life.

Everybody always talked about what they would do when they had some money saved up. They predicted how long they would be in town before moving on, or they reminisced about the people they left behind. There was no passion for the present moment. Just fulfillment of fleshly desires.

After thanksgiving, Terry disappeared. He went home and never came back. No one was surprised. He was good friends with several guys, but never returned their phone calls. His wife never picked up or returned phone calls either. We were stumped, and a little worried something had happened. But in the Bakken, people disappeared into the fog all the time. I talked with Kyle about it one day.

"I had a guy who swore up and down he was in it for the long haul. It costs a lot of money to get these guys trained, and he promised me he'd be around. So we trained him. Told me how much he loved the job. Then he went home for Christmas, and never came back. Wouldn't return my calls or anything."

It was a rough scenario for the businesses. They needed people, but the workers were flaky because of the easy opportunity.

I wanted to stick my commitment out no matter what. There were better opportunities, but I also knew my word mattered, and I wanted Don to know he could count on me.

A week or so passed, Terry's absence faded into oblivion, and I found myself in Doug's trailer. Pots and dishes were stacked in the little nook called the kitchen. His TV seemed to lean with everything else in the camper, and we both sat as if we were on a ship stuck half-way over a crested wave. When we were drunk, our feet battled to grasp a footing and we stumbled down to a seat. The angle of the environment played with our senses and the flow of alcohol magnified it. The decline may have felt like a five percent slant at the beginning, but by the end of the night it was Mt. Everest.

We were discussing politics with an air of superiority. To us, America was on a downward spiral into immoral debauchery, cronyism and under the control of wickedness. A government established by the people and for the people was now a government of the rulers over their subjects.

After tiring ourselves out on the dire situation of the nation, we stumbled to our pasts. Both of our lives were led in a rebellion against God to varying degrees, and while we were faithful and spoken lovers of God…there were still demons hiding in the corners.

"Mushrooms are really easy to grow. And I can get the stuff we'd need to grow them ourselves," Doug said.

We calculated the options. A small voice in me cried out that once again I was not making the choices God called me to. Instead, the alcohol magnified a voice that said, "don't worry about it, it's not that big of a deal." That voice continued to win out, with no end in sight. Every choice I made concerning drugs or alcohol was in the interest of self-gratification. I shoved my conscience out and focused on what I could get. I couldn't seem to retain the fear and respect of God the sermons told me to hold. Those pastors pushed the importance of becoming more Godly again and again, yet I wasn't listening.

My idols were holding me down.

God knew the consequences would soon become a reality.

Doug pressed harder on my background during our discussion of slinging mushrooms.

"Yeah, I used to deal," I said, opening up even more.

I watched Doug's eyes crunch the angles. The row sat quiet. We huddled in our little spot on the edge of civilization.

"So did I. I did for a while, and I know we could make some good money out here," he said.

"Definitely. This place is a gold mine, and I know plenty of people who would want to buy stuff if we sold it," I said. It felt like a bad drug movie which starts with two characters living in a dilapidated camper and ends in a climactic shoot-out with the cops.

"See, I don't know many people out here. You've got the connections, and I've got a background in dealing," he said. "But the thing is, we have to trust each other. I can't trust most people, and I need to know that if I'm going into business with someone… I can trust them," his voice lowered. A serious look washed across his face. The atmosphere started to change.

Were we this serious about dealing?

"So the question is: can I trust you?" Doug asked. "And can you trust me?"

I could relate to his worry about trust and dealing. My own experiences had taught me that it was a hard line to tow: make money and keep the chances of getting caught low.

Doug searched through a few things stacked to the side. I watched him and continued talking.

"I know how it goes. I have a hard time trusting with this kind of stuff too. I've worked with some stupid people in the past, and I want as few knowing about it as possible."

Doug pulled out a .45 and worked it over in his hands as he examined the dark steel. I watched carefully, wondering what all this was about. My eyes glanced towards the box of empty beer bottles sitting on the floor. We had downed all but a couple of lonely ones waiting for our hands to retrieve them. Doug pulled a full magazine from the carrying case and slammed it into the gun. I was calm, but fully aware.

"We have to be able to trust each other," he said again. And with the clip in, his hand raised the gun to my forehead. With the barrel between my eyes, he asked, "Do you trust me?" After a thoughtful moment, he added, "Can I trust you?"

The barrel was deep, lined with smooth steel. Everything else became fuzzy while the gun came into sharp focus. His fingers were wrapped around the handle as his index finger hovered near the trigger. It hadn't pressed into the crescent moon shaped lever, but I could tell he was keeping his finger at the ready. No nervousness ran through me. Thoughts floated. "Well, if he shoots me, then he shoots me," along with "nothing I can do, so might as well stay calm." A part of me wondered if he was going to end it right there. I had no way of knowing what a person on the edge of the world might do to quiet the demons.

Reminiscing of our first night out drinking, I gave a similar response to his query, "Well, I can say you can trust me, but it really comes down to what we already know about each other. We both have a stake in this, so we're both putting ourselves out there. I've got something to lose too."

He lowered the gun. The magazine was nonchalantly pulled out and he placed the gun back in its pouch. It had been a strange test to observe what I would do or how I might react. And the fact was he could trust me, and I knew I could trust him. Even with a gun in my face, there was no doubt. He wanted at least one person that wouldn't run him over the first chance he got.

I finished my beer to wash away the image of a gun barrel making my eyes cross. Suddenly, my bladder over-flow light illuminated. I got to my feet and stumbled uphill towards the door.

"I've got to take a leak again," I said, recognizing it was already the fourth or fifth time.

"I'll come with ya, I have to go too."

We stepped down onto packed snow and faced away from the campers towards a field behind the shop. A few houses sat twinkling in the dark distance, but there was enough space to present the mirage of freedom. Our heads tipped back to the clear nighttime sky. The moon was a beacon, with little night lights spattered around it. I was amazed at how easy it was to see the stars outside, even in town. The sky was massive and overpowering, covering us like a soft blanket.

"I love the sky out here," I said as I watered the snow and looked towards the heavens.

"I do too. That's one thing I like about out here. The sky is huge," he said. For a moment all you could hear was sprinkling against the ground, while two bodies stood motionless and peered upwards. We finished making ice and immersed ourselves in the night time sky.

"God made such an amazing universe, and I love looking at the stars and seeing all that He created." I said. "It's such a spectacular creation, and He knows each and every star in the sky." I paused for a moment, then added, "I wish I were a better person."

"Me too. I don't know how He loves me after all the things I've done, and I want to be better," Doug said quietly. "We should start a Bible study or something. I need to get back to reading it."

Heads sank and bodies turned. My hand reached for a handle to climb back into the warm cocoon. As I pulled my body up the stairs, I responded, "We definitely need to. I need to start reading more too."

We agreed to start that week.

As the dim lighting in the camper threw shadows on the walls, I recognized a face that found solace in the light, and it reflected my own comfort. Normally, a person would not find companionship with a guy who held a gun to his head, but Doug was growing on me, and I commiserated with a bit of the pain he was holding in. Choices made took a toll along with a life that set its face against all others. After getting out of the military, Doug didn't feel as though he fit in anywhere. When we spent time together, we were able to open up to each other in ways not possible with anyone else.

"I know the Lord will provide and protect. I just wish I could be better for Him." I said.

"Me too. I know He gives me everything I need, but there are some things I'm really struggling to trust Him with," he said.

"Such as?"

"It's hard out here, being by yourself. I'd like to have a girl, but there's none worth having in this town. I just want someone," Doug said, "But I don't even know if I'm ready for that."

I could relate. I was beginning to feel the same way, but I wasn't going to push it. God was doing work on a worn-out soul, and He would bring the right lady when it was time. The phase of abstinence had been refreshing, removing the pain intimacy always brought. I wondered whether Doug was ready. The right woman could make a huge impact on him, and I prayed plenty of times the Lord would bring him the perfect person, but was this the time?

Stephen went home for Christmas to visit his family. I stayed behind since I was still new to the company. Having the camper to myself felt like a pleasant retreat. Instead, I found a struggle in being alone for Christmas. Loneliness attached itself like a leech to memories of my parents and friends. I missed the morning celebration with fresh coffee cake and sweatpants. My family would bask in gathering together, and soon wrapping paper would be in balls on the floor, while stacks of gifts grew next to each person.

I spent my morning in the camper playing Xbox. It wasn't long before a neighbor was knocking. His name was Jim. He lived with his brother in the camper next to us. A rough history followed Jim, and most of his time was spent languishing in the world of substances. Christmas was only different because he was out of alcohol. I decided it might help him feel better if we went and found some lunch together. Two lonely souls drove around trying to find a place that might be open, and after a while of searching, Jim started wondering about an open liquor store.

"You don't need it today," I said, not wanting to be a step to his problems.

"No no, it's fine. It's fine. Let's just check one or two places. I'm sure somebody has to be open right now," he said. He was getting antsy, shifting in his seat.

"Nothing's going to be open today. It's Christmas," I said. It was a fool's errand, but he wasn't letting up.

"Just one more place, one more place." There was a desperation breaking through in his voice.

We stopped at several places, noting they were all closed. I sighed with relief. My habit was bad enough, but a deep conviction came with the notion of enabling an addiction that destroyed Jim.

"Jim, you really should try and quit. I know it's making things worse for you." I said.

He longingly looked out the window. "I know, I know. I should," he said. The battle was quick, and then he gave in, "But not today. Just one more day and then I'll start trying to do that tomorrow. I know I should, and I will."

Finally, Jim conceded the search for an open store and we drove back home. I made small chat for a few minutes, then took to my comfortable, warm shell in the camper.

Even though I took people out for food, spent time listening and giving advice, or just being a light—I struggled with a lack of true passion. It was as if a hand pushed me towards them, while I wanted to be in the camper watching TV or playing video games. My heart was not completely in it, but I knew deep down Christ asked me to sacrifice myself. I was supposed to love others over myself.

I attempted to solve this problem by making love an action. I approached my feelings and actions in reverse order, allowing the action to shape the emotions. God used the needs around me to bring the withdrawn Christian out of his selfish-shell. It was a slow process, but I grew through opportunity. He showed me the need that was all around and reminded me that while I may not ever know what effect I had on these people, it was my responsibility to do my best. They were all around me in a town where self-destruction came so easily.

This battle of sacrifice gnawed at my selfishness. I had no issue telling Jim that drinking was causing big problems in his life, but I had a harder time just loving him by being a true friend. We spent several dinners together, conversing about his past life and where he was at the moment. I tried my best to show love, but I was still figuring out what it looked like. Was it found in not talking? Was advice the best love? Did I share the gospel or leave it for another day?

I figured I'd try out all the options. Jim admitted one day that he knew he needed God, and that Christ loved him, but just like others I talked to, this was as far as he was willing to go. It was rare to find a person who understood the necessity of God. Moreover, it was rare to find a person willing to give themselves up for God. Soon, Jim faded into the backdrop of the world. A dangerous accident crushed his hand and brought on a drug test. It resulted in a positive, forcing the company to fire him. I watched a man who was making six figures have to borrow money to buy a truck to pull his camper away. We're not sure where he went or ended up.

Most people I ran into in Williston faded into the tapestry of the world. My thoughts occasionally drifted back to Jim and the life he was scratching to get through. It always brought on a depression in the pit of my stomach fueled by the sense of hopelessness I saw within him. The saddest part was: how far was I from the life Jim had been leading? I could have been in an accident and put in the same spot. My clean record could have been wiped out in an instant, leaving me to try and find work.

The drug use was running on a limited clock, and the choices I made threatened to overtake me, just as they had Jim.

Chapter 15

The necessity of sharing the gospel became evident not long after Christmas. The urge to go see Anthony hit me that weekend. I knocked on his door and climbed up the stairs. He sat on one of the benches in front of the same table where we pulled white powder through dollar bills into waiting nostrils. He sat, staring into the distance.

"What's going on?" I asked, wondering if he was high.

"You haven't heard?" His face was torn up.

"No, I haven't. I haven't really talked to anybody today. Why's that?"

"Sam was on the way back and crashed in Montana. He died, man," Anthony said with a distant look on his face.

"Seriously?"

"Yeah." He was quiet, the energy completely sapped.

I shuddered. There were nights when Sam and I picked up food, nights when we sat and chatted, but the gospel never came up. I never spoke the good news of Jesus. The thought of a 20 year-old kid gone from the world hit hard in my gut. And what had been his big focus? Money, girls and having fun. All I could think was, "Here I sit. I'm saved. As far as I know he had no relationship with Christ. So most likely, Sam isn't in heaven with Christ, which means..."

Anthony and I talked for a few minutes, but I was empty. My stomach churned with the pain of the truth. Someone, with whom I had delved into self-destruction, was most likely gone for eternity. I couldn't make a conclusion on his soul, but the odds didn't look good. It made me reflect, "How many people do I come in contact with that need to hear this message, but don't get to because I'm too afraid to give it or giving the wrong testimony?"

I would love to say that a singular moment in time, namely this one changed me forever. It would be wonderful to say that after such a day, I became a wild evangelist on a mission, giving the gospel to every single person I saw. It didn't happen. I was affected but not transformed.

But, it woke me up enough to keep my heart open to the Holy Spirit. When I felt the press of the Holy Spirit to do something, I tried to make sure I did. Whether it was giving a meal to a homeless person, sharing the gospel with a few people, or speaking to someone–I did my best to follow through. I failed plenty of times, and a few times I felt success. My heavenly Father slowly shaped me.

He was also protecting me.

A day or two after the news hit of Sam's death, sickness crawled in. Stephen was still back home, so I was on my own. The symptoms of illness were light, and I figured it was just a lack of energy or maybe a small cold. However, It worsened, until the night before New Year's. I tried to light the stove to make a pizza. The flame was gone, refusing to dance and flicker. The next night, I lay awake extremely sick as slight hallucinations and a racing mind pounded at my consciousness. My heart beat against my ribs, and I couldn't get comfortable. I felt dizzy, nauseous and achy. Not being able to handle it, I called Jason.

"Are you home?" I prayed he would take me in.

"Yeah, what's going on?" he responded.

"I'm really sick, and I think I know why," I said.

"Why's that?"

"I looked up the symptoms on my phone, and they all point to propane poisoning. I think I've got a propane leak in the camper," I said. My body shook from the pain and aching.

"Dude, come over. You can lay out on the couch. Stay here as long as you need," he offered.

"Thank you so much," I said, gratefulness oozing from my heart.

I wrapped up, grabbed a few things and somehow made the drive to his house. The couch absorbed me and I rested my eyes, already starting to feel a little better. A few hours and a nap later, my energy returned. The shaking ceased, and thoughts weren't battering my skull. Soon the sickness dissipated; I was devoid of symptoms.

"You could have died. That's serious stuff. There's people who die every year from things like that," he said.

"Yeah, and I should have known something was up when the stove wouldn't light. But it never even occurred to me that the two were connected."

"Well, if you have a leak in the camper, there's no way you can live there. You guys are more than welcome to move in if you want. I can give you my boy's room since he's not here very much. We can figure out something with rent." His words picked up in pace over the prospect, "You guys should come live with me. It might be kind of nice to not be on my own here. I think I need some roommates to keep me out of trouble, because, well, you know how it gets when you're alone. You start thinking and all that stuff. Not that I don't like being on my own, because I'm pretty independent, but it might be nice to just have some people to talk to."

I was amazed. We could live in a house and not have to live in the camper? How could I turn that down?

"I'll talk to Stephen, but yeah, we would love to live here," I said.

As soon as Stephen returned to town, we met at a small cafe. A few truckers with bellies spilling out of their pants took up the booths around us as a blast of cold wind battered the windows.

"I went to Jason's, and I started feeling better almost right away," I said, recounting the close call.

"I don't know man, you sure you weren't just really sick?" he asked.

"Yes, because the stove wouldn't light either. I looked up the symptoms, and they were point for point. As soon as I laid down at Jason's for a few hours, I felt better."

He didn't seem to believe that it was a propane leak, but the offer to live with Jason was enticing.

"So he said we could live at his place?"

"Yup. We'd get his son's room which has bunk beds. We'd get to use the kitchen, living room, all of that stuff."

Stephen suddenly looked eager. A chance to get off the row and into a nice warm house was hard to turn down.

"Sure, why not," he shrugged.

A day later we were hauling the camper and parking it on Jason's property. His family owned farm land a few minutes north of town that sat on a hill overlooking the highway, with the city to the south. It felt like an island, up and away from the crash of the oil tidal-wave slamming into Williston.

I was relieved to be living in a house, and it was nice to know I had made some connections. Jason was a good guy, his house was clean, and the room offered privacy. For a moment, there was relief from all that swirled since I arrived. I reflected back upon everything that had happened. It was a roller-coaster throwing me for loops each time I felt on stable ground. Even though I understood living in an oil boom-town had its wild moments, the waves blindsided me. It was as though I'd been placed at the center of the merry-go-round, and as it spun, the force pushed me closer to the edge.

A bunk bed with a TV on the dresser had never felt so wonderful. We had a kitchen where we could cook meals and a living room where we could relax. I thanked the Lord profusely for not only providing the house, but keeping me alive long enough to get there. It was also a better situation for Jason. He knew being alone could get him in trouble.

"I just want some other people in the house," he admitted to me one night, "because I know how I get when I'm alone. I like having my privacy, but I don't think it would be the best thing right now."

"Well, I'm always here if you want to talk or hang out. It's not like I have a whole lot of places to go," I said.

"Yeah, thanks," he responded. "And I don't know, but Marcy might be moving in with the kid. And if that happens, I'd like to have some people in the house. Maybe things wouldn't get too bad between us,"

"Do you guys fight a lot?" I asked.

"Sometimes. She doesn't do a whole lot, and it gets frustrating. I'm at work all day, and all I ask is that she cleans up after herself, or makes a meal once in a while. I get home and have to cook and clean. She's not doing much since she quit her job," he said. "And I know she's watching the kid, but I come home, and I pretty much have to take care of the kid too."

I listened, wondering what to say. We would make eye contact while talking, and then he would nervously look away. I curiously watched him. I wasn't sure if it was the drugs or just his nature, but he was a skittish and a distrusting person. However, the care he showed to his friends was center stage, and he always held out a helping hand.

"If you need anything, just let me know," I said. He thanked me and excused himself to his room.

Jason led a life that was part open, part secret. He was a smart guy who had a laser-like focus and vision for various projects and plans. The issue was, he would get easily distracted or lose his way on a business idea when an obstacle came up. He was always coming to me with ideas for businesses, and I genuinely wanted to join in.

These ideas would come and go just as Jason would. Sometimes I saw him all day, and other times I wouldn't see him for days. There were times when he had amazing energy, and others when he was too lethargic to move. Usually, he was on top of getting work done around the house. I was impressed, considering I didn't possess that type of work ethic.

CHAPTER 16

One night in April, I searched the kitchen, wondering what to do for food. The bit of food left was not appetizing and my go-to meals like tacos, spaghetti or Hamburger Helper all required one thing I didn't have: beef. I did the calculations. To get the beef, and get back would have taken 20-30 minutes. After browning the beef and draining it, I would've had to spend 10 to 20 minutes preparing the food. Then I'd have to eat and clean up. Nuts to that! I stood in the middle of the kitchen, eyes losing focus, wondering what to have. The thought hit with brute force: "pot-pies! I haven't had a pot-pie in forever!" I weighed the time it would take against what I was willing to dedicate to the adventure. At the end of my journey waited flaky crusts and thick gravy smothering delicious fake meat and processed vegetables. How could I turn down the opportunity?

"What are you doing?" John asked as he came up the stairs. Jason had opened up his basement to John after he was kicked out of his mom's basement. From debt collectors to roommates. One of his co-workers named Manny joined him in the basement. The house filled up fast, containing five oil-land men.

"Wondering what I want for dinner. I'm thinking pot-pies, so I might go to the store to get some," I said.

"You should go to the Supermarket. They have a sale on that stuff," he said.

I declined the idea in my head. I could go, but there was no desire to switch it up. I liked going to the other grocer, and that was all I needed to shoot down the alternative. I thanked him for the suggestion, told him, "Maybe I'll do that," and went out the door.

I had no intention to take his advice, and I'm not sure what made his suggestion undesirable. Perhaps the thought of changing it up that night just did not hit my fancy. No matter what it was, I chose what did hit my fancy. I pulled into the lot of my favorite grocer and got out of my truck. I started the long walk toward the door, wearing work-out shorts and a sweatshirt in the midst of a cold North Dakota April. A fold-out table was situated to the side of the door, with two people standing bundled up beside it. I always felt uncomfortable walking past the makeshift set-ups with literature and people asking for donations, even though I felt a sense of sympathy for their plight, since I'm sure they had better places they could be. However, their plight didn't outweigh the call of pot-pies.

"Hey man, how's it going tonight?" the guy nearest me asked as I approached the entrance. I sighed. I was caught.

He was Mexican, a couple inches shorter than I, a little rounder and full of life. I noticed piercings and tattoos. It was obvious he wasn't your typical fundraiser. He spoke with a down to earth approach, yet was filled with exuberance. Coupled with the piercings, I found myself a bit more willing to hear him out. Something drew me to give him my attention.

"Not too bad, how about you?" I asked.

"Good man, cold though. My Mexican blood doesn't like standing out in this," he said. He looked me up and down, and added, "I can't believe you're wearing shorts in this stuff!"

I smiled, "yeah, I'm used to the cold."

He laughed and added a,"No kidding" before continuing with his presentation.

"So, we're with a ministry that goes around speaking to schools about the Constitution, our Founding Fathers and the state of our nation," he said.

Suddenly I was listening very closely.

"And we're also a band, so we play shows and speak about the Founding Fathers and God's love," he continued. "I'm sure you like music, right?" he asked.

"Of course."

He pulled out an Ipod with some headphones, "I'm guessing you like hard rock?"

"Yeah, I like most kinds of music."

He offered up the headphones, "We're a heavy metal band, and this is some of our stuff. You want to hear some?"

I donned the ear caps. Heavy guitars throbbed through with drums cascading in the background. A singer rapped at a blistering pace, complimenting the empty spaces left by the staccato-style riffs of bass and guitar. It was driving music, good for that last heavy set of squats or before you jumped out of a plane. I've never jumped out of a plane, but I believe I'd need something like this to psych me up for such a leap. After a minute of taking in the music, I set the headphones down.

"That's some really good stuff," I said. "And that's you guys?"

"Yup," he said. "I play bass and I'm the lead singer."

"Really? I play bass too," I offered. I could feel the connection strengthen.

"You do? That's crazy," he said thoughtfully. "I've been praying about needing a new bass player, because I want to be able to focus on singing. I can do both, but you know how it goes—it's so much easier to focus on one or the other." My eyebrow raised. "Who knows, maybe the Lord brought you here for a reason," he said.

We continued chatting, delving into the Constitution and where we felt our country was headed. We fed off each other, passing knowledge of what our country was intended to be, and how it was sliding downward with the decisions being made in the government, media and schools.

"We're trying to make people aware of the truth. So much is being taught to kids these days that just isn't true. If our kids are lost, our next generation is gone," he said. "We need to stand up and give these kids the whole truth, and give them the opportunity to make a difference and change things around."

I was sold. It was unique to meet a guy about my age who was so passionate for the moral, conservative way of life. He and I connected, feeling the Holy Spirit flow through both of us as we talked. I wondered, "Lord, why did you have me meet this guy?"

After a half an hour of discussing everything from music to God, he noticed I was still wearing shorts in the middle of a cold April night.

"Dude, I better let you go inside," he said. "But my name is Massey. Let me get your number so we can talk some more. I don't know why, but I feel like we need to."

"I'm Christian, and that's cool," I said. We exchanged numbers, talking briefly about the his band's need for a bass player.

I walked into the store, stunned at the random meeting. Like an automaton, I carried out the procedure to buy my pot-pies.

Thoughts swarmed about Massey. He wasn't like anything I encountered before. His looks and demeanor spoke of a rebellious spirit, craving to put his energy into something. The sentences he spoke were intelligent and complex, filled with confidence, passion, facts and history. He could quote any of the Founding Fathers, speaking of their wisdom in how the country was shaped and what it could become – good or bad. A sense of loving God radiated out. There was a commitment to the truth that had been lacking for so long from many of our pastors and speakers.

I walked out of the store and we spoke for a few more minutes about the surprise of our connection.

"I feel like this is just the beginning. I feel like we were supposed to meet," he said.

"I have a feeling God had me wanting pot-pies for a reason," I said, smiling. We said our good-byes, and I settled into my pick-up.

"Lord, I'm not sure what this means, or what you have planned," I prayed. "But thank you. I don't know if you're going to use my passion for music, or if this is somebody you want to mentor me, but thank you for leading me here. You're always watching out for me. Please lead me on this. I'm not sure where you want me, or what you want me to do, but I trust you."

Realizing it could mean a huge change in life, I sent a text to a close friend. "I met a guy tonight in a Christian heavy metal band, and they're looking for a bassist. I'm not sure if that's what the Lord wants, but can you please be praying for me that He will lead me in the right direction?"

She responded, "Of course! That's really exciting! I'll be praying for you, and keep me updated on what's going on."

God was just getting started in answering my prayers. I asked from my heart for Him to shape my life, and I had no clue how much He would be pressing and molding the clay that was named Christian.

Spring time rolled on into the beginning of summer. The air began to hold its warmth, and the sun stayed to visit a little longer each day. I enjoyed my busy work schedule and the evenings at the farm. Stephen and I spent the few hours we had each night hanging out in our room or going to the row to visit friends. Occasionally, I was able to get more out of him than surface level conversation. When we weren't talking about work, girls or other people around us, we would touch on our goals or our past.

We knew each other through family, but hadn't spent time together in a long while. This loose connection made me clueless about his past. I tried to learn more about who he was, and we opened up about the things in our history that had brought us to the present. I loved hanging out with him because he was relaxed and drama free. We both felt the same way about many things, and wanted to make some money in town before leaving.

I bounced between hanging out with Jason and his friends, or with Stephen in our room. He spent most of his time in the room, and was quiet when hanging out with Jason or other people.

"You're welcome to come out in the living room," I said. He sat on the bunk bed, playing a hockey game on the Xbox.

"I just wasn't sure if it's okay to be out there, or if that's more of their area or what. I don't want to get in the way," he said.

"You won't," I offered. "Trust me; you're more than welcome to come hang out with us. Jason's a good guy, and I know you'll have fun."

"Yeah, he seems pretty cool. I just didn't want to be a bother," he said.

"Nope, you're fine," I said. "Feel free to come on out."

Over the next few weeks, Stephen opened up a lot more with Jason and the rest of the crew. He was speaking up, cracking jokes and spending time with the guys. I wanted him to make friends, since having connections was vital to not going crazy in such a town.

While Stephen was growing with Jason and the guys, I was spending a lot of free time with Doug. Even if I could avoid drinking at the house, it was a different story in his RV. We would inhale a case of beer while discussing whatever came to our minds.

"I've been looking for a truck," I said.

"Yeah? Finding anything?" he asked.

I had been keeping my eyes open for a project truck, hoping to score the old truck I described to my former teacher in his game of "imagine your life".

"I've found a couple different trucks. There was one that looked really good at that junkyard on the way to Watford City,"

I said. "It's a white '55. It'd be a perfect truck, but I have a feeling God didn't want me to have it."

"Why's that?" he asked.

"Well, when I drove past, I was praying about it, asking, 'Lord, is this what you want me to have?' When I approached the junkyard to check it out, it started to lightly drizzle rain. As soon as I got out, the rain started pouring, and I could just feel the Lord saying this wasn't the truck. When I got back in my work truck and pulled back onto the road, the rain quit completely. It was sunshine and lollipops," I said.

"Yeah, my guess is that isn't the one then," he laughed.

I wasn't the only one who made a discovery either.

"I've been talking to a girl from back home," he said. His face brightened with the thought.

"Really? How'd you meet her?"

"A friend from my church back home introduced us. He was talking about her and how I should get in touch with her. We connected online and on the phone," he said. "I think I really like this girl. She's cool. She's not like other girls."

"That's awesome Doug, I'm really happy for you," I said. I was being honest. Doug had been on edge since the first day we met. The only thing keeping him alive and going was God, and now God placed a lady in his life. Doug was rough around the edges….extremely rough, but his heart wanted someone worthy to love and cherish. He wanted a person that could connect to him and understand him on his level. It sounded like God might have brought that girl.

I asked him, "So you guys are talking on the phone then?"

"Yup. We've been emailing back and forth too."

I pushed to see if he was going to see her soon.

"We'll see," he responded.

We relaxed in the drab yellow camper with a tilt to the front. I was completely comfortable around Doug and enjoyed the close camaraderie.

"How are you enjoying living at the house?" he asked.

I hesitated. I didn't want to rub it in. I knew how blessed I was.

"It's pretty good so far. We've got our own room and have some privacy," I said.

"That's good. I'm glad God blessed you with a good situation," he responded.

"And God blessed you too!"

I was thrilled for him even if it was hard to see another person meet a girl when I was feeling ready to move back on the market. But, I accepted God had control. I would find a girl when He knew I was ready.

The process of looking had begun though. I put myself on a Christian dating website, feeling in a good spot and ready to try again. If God determined Doug was ready, maybe I was too. It was difficult though, since the supply of faithful Christian girls was rare in the area. Even fewer girls were Christian AND single. I set-up a profile and dove in. There weren't many ladies, and I found no connections to pursue. After a few weeks, there wasn't much activity.

I became frustrated, wondering if this was where God wanted me. I prayed on a Friday, "Lord, I want what you want for me. If you don't want me to be on this site, or it's a waste of my time, please show me. Otherwise, could you please show me a sign that this is where you want me? I promise I'm not testing you, but if there's no activity by Monday morning, I'm going to get rid of it."

By Monday morning, I had plenty of activity. There were girls who looked at my profile and several messages sat in my inbox. So I kept at it.

A few weeks later, the activity dropped off again. There were no strong connections or any interest. I prayed once more, "Lord, could you please let me know if this is where I'm supposed to be? Could you possibly show me a sign that I'm where you want me?" By the end of the weekend, I had several messages and responses from women.

When the activity dropped off a third time, I adjusted my profile, because the words didn't reveal who I was in a real and natural way. I sat wondering how I could make it portray the true me. I made the edits a third time, settling upon on a line that I felt described me perfectly. It read, "I want a girl who loves the Lord more than she loves me."

A few days later, I received a message from a girl in Madison, Wisconsin. She sent a simple message, stating, "I hope you have a great day." As any sensible person would do, I went to her profile, realizing she was a beautiful college girl I had seen before.

One of the perks to the site was a "Secret Admirer" feature. A person could use the app and get a picture of a person as well as a link to his or her profile. Underneath the link were buttons that read "I'm interested", "I'm not interested" and "Maybe". If two people pressed the "I'm Interested" button on each other, a connection was offered by the site. If you pressed the "I'm not Interested" button, a new profile would randomly come up. I remembered seeing her picture scroll through several times when I spent bits of free time playing around with the app. I never thought much about her since she was in Wisconsin, though she was good-looking and intelligent. Yet, here she was, sending a message to the lonely guy in the middle of nowhere.

So I responded.

Her name was Michelle, and she was a few years younger. She went to school in Madison and was studying to become a nurse. She was a farm girl with a matching outlook on life. The trait that drew me in was her faith. She held a love for God that was powerful and attractive. We emailed once a week or so, letting our messages grow in length and depth. I felt relaxed, not wishing to push anything with someone who lived so far away.

But, I wondered if God was starting a new phase for my life.

It wasn't a battle being single. I didn't feel it necessary to have a girlfriend, but was open to the prospect of Michelle, which revealed the growth I had experienced over the last six months.

The joy of it all was not having the option of physicality. Without that temptation, I was able to focus on getting to know her, as opposed to giving in to my lusts.

Overall, the single life was good. The hard part had been the cleansing stage, which took months of being invisible to women before I finally threw my hands up and said, "I quit trying!" Soon after, I was enjoying becoming more of who I wanted to be.

I read more books. I played more guitar. I worked-out consistently. I prayed and read my Bible. I took time to go on walks with friends and see people. I made sure to say yes to offers of activity. Without a girlfriend, I was able to say yes to a job in the oilfield for as long as I wanted.

The most important part of it all was my relationship with God. The time that passed in Williston had been fraught with drugs and alcohol, but I could see their influence declining. The pull of the drugs weakened while the strength of wanting to do what God asked was growing. He was placing within me the desire to be more like Christ. This fire grew through listening to sermons, praying and reading. As my relationship with Christ deepened, I began to recognize the troubles suffered at the hands of my addiction.

I continued to do my best to enjoy time with those whose habits gravitated towards drugs, and despite God's commands, I occasionally slipped into indulging again. The times where I politely turned the offer down became more consistent, and I stayed sober to talk with those who didn't. When I did decide to hit the bowl, snort the crushed pills, or drink the alcohol, God threw up reminders that this was not His will.

First came a random drug test for Anthony. He used fake urine and passed the test, but I could see the stress in a face that assumed such a test would never come. Another time I decided to get high while I was taking phone calls for the weekend. There was a situation with our equipment and a customer who wasn't sure what to do. I felt lost, scrambling to figure out how to solve a problem for which I had no answer. I called Darryl, and found myself fumbling words. I was embarrassed. My pants had been pulled down in front of the classroom, and smoking weed put me there.

The next time I smoked, my boss was drug tested. Up to this point, I had assumed that management, sales and the like were off-limits in an unspoken rule. However, Don had received a phone call that morning letting him know he was randomly selected. His selection hit close to home. The truth of random drug-tests was scratching my hard-headed surface. I wasn't watching random people on random rigs get random tests, but it was my own division and my own boss that had been selected.

I was finished. I kept a bottle of fake urine just in case, but I was sick of the worry and stress. I convinced myself that weed wasn't a big ticket item on God's do-not-do list, but "Do not make an idol" was. I recognized smoking pot had become such.

Not long after, the real warning came across my bow. I was standing with Jason and a couple of his friends outside on a warm June day. The wind tussled with my shirt as the sun jumped to hide behind passing clouds. We were relaxing, enjoying a Saturday without any responsibilities. The pipe shifted from hand to hand, until I reached out and brought it to my lips. I'd stayed clean, but automatic reactions moved my hand without a thought. I took the lighter, lit the weed and pulled in a nice big breath. I did it again. As soon as it left my hand, the realization hit me: What had I done? After ten minutes, I was high and saddened at the choice, but I cast it aside, figuring it was a light mistake that would soon be forgotten.

Monday morning Darryl and I sat waiting for Don to arrive. The phone rang. It was our CEO Chris on the line.

"Is Don there?"

"Not yet," I said. "He'll be in soon."

"You guys are getting drug-tested. Have everyone come over to the other shop to do their test," Chris said.

We hung up. Two days ago, I thought nothing of smoking weed, and now the consequence was staring me in the face. There was nowhere to run, and nothing I could do. In a moment of clarity, I relaxed.

"Well, If I'm done, I'm done. If this is the lesson I have to learn, so be it."

Don arrived and we let him know. We walked over, took our tests and handed over our samples. I signed my name and left the table, feeling numb. That day as I worked, I prayed.

"Lord, I know I screwed up," I said out loud in the truck, "and if this is how you want to punish me, I accept it. I deserve to lose this job, and I'm really sorry I did it. Lord, please have mercy. I vow never to smoke weed again. I will never again smoke weed, and that is my oath to you." I paused, shocked at what I just said. I'd read in the Bible to be very careful about speaking an oath to God, who held you to your words and expected you to make good on the oath set before Him. The words had been spoken and sealed before the King of the universe.

Part of me screamed, "What are you doing??"

The other part decided it was a necessary step to take. Such a choice cemented a line I knew I couldn't cross. There was no more compromise. No more talking myself into one more hit. This was the last time, and I had put it in concrete.

So I continued, "Lord, I may not be happy with it, but it's what you deserve, and what I need. I just pray you'll be merciful. I pray you'll watch over and take care of me, no matter what happens. I know you will, and I'm so thankful you provided me with this opportunity. I'm sorry if I screwed it up, but thank you for giving it. If you choose to somehow let me keep my job, I would be thankful, and will do my best to honor you with it, but Lord, your will be done."

I got back to the shop at the end of the day, and felt I needed to warn Don. I placed myself in the big comfy leather chair where I had first sat when I was hired.

"So, I have to be honest with you Don," I said.

He smiled and leaned forward, "What is it?"

"Well, I got high on Saturday. It rarely happens, and never will again. You need to know though, the drug test I took might come up positive."

He thought and put up his hand, "We'll see what happens with it. You should have told me before you took the test."

I nodded, happy in knowing that God provided a boss who could see past a mistake.

He continued, "But it's done and over with, so we'll just wait and see what happens. We'll figure it out from there."

"Thank you Don. I'm really sorry," I said.

"It's okay. That stuff happens," he said. "I had my time where I did that stuff."

We chatted for a few more minutes on random subjects, which he did in an attempt to ease my worry. I drove home, mulling over what would come of the mistake. How was I going to explain this to my parents? How was I going to find a new job with a failed drug test on my record?

I got home and sank into the couch, zoning out with the stress that was eating me.

"What's going on?" Jason asked, recognizing something was amiss.

"I may have failed my drug test," I said. I tried to speak with a light, joking manner, hoping to cover up my regret.

"You guys got drug tested?" he asked. He would've been part of it too, but he made money renting out spaces and rooms. He decided enough money was coming in, so he quit working to figure out what he really wanted to do.

"Yeah. Remember how we all smoked on Saturday?" I asked.

"Oh, dang. Well, you might be okay, but otherwise, there's plenty of work out there," he said.

I faintly smiled. He tried his best, but the cheering-up routine wasn't working. Stephen did the same thing when I told him.

"I'm sure you can get a job somewhere else if you want," he said. "There's always work in this town." He had quit the company himself, and was working for another rig company across town.

The next day, I headed across the border into Montana. My job gave to me the freedom to choose where I went and when, and a favorite destination of mine was Sydney. It was a little town located a few minutes inside the state line. The road led right through town, with small shops and antiquated buildings lining either side. It felt like an escape from the rest of the oilfield, and all the stops I had to make were next to each other. As I drove through town praying and wondering if this was going to be my last day, a blue flash out of the corner of my eye caught my attention.

Sitting at the corner of a drive-thru car wash was a lowered, dark blue Chevy truck with a "For Sale" sign. Immediately, I thought, "That's it. That's the truck." I pulled a u-turn and parked next to it. The body was in great condition, and while it was a 1970 as opposed to a 1950's truck, I was in love. It looked classic, yet built to be a hot-rod. I scanned the info on the sign.

The truck had a 350 in it.

It was a manual transmission.

It was low-mileage.

I went into the shop attached to the car wash and asked the attendant if she knew whose truck it was. She smiled and said, "Yup, just a second. I'll go get him." Soon after, she came through the back door with a kid who looked no older than 18. He was tall and skinny, as if he outpaced the growth of his own body.

He smiled politely, "You're interested in the truck?"

"Yup. What can you tell me about it?"

We walked out to take a look. I scoured it over, trying to appear as if I knew what to look for.

"I bought it from a guy who goes to my church. He was the original owner and just used it to tow his camper around once in a while. It mostly sat, so I bought it from him and now I'm selling it because I've got my own project I'm doing."

The word "church" hit me. I immediately felt a connection with a fellow brother. He was genuine, speaking with a humility that spoke volumes about his character.

"I'm really interested in it," I said. "How much are you looking to get?"

"About $5,000."

I peered in the window, falling deeper in love.

The old bench seat with its cloth cover. The tall shifter and old time knobs. It looked unique and classic with a bare interior except for a few accessories like a grip style shift knob and aftermarket CD player. The sun danced off the blue paint, sparkling as I walked around the truck to drink it all in.

"Alright, can I get your number? I'm working right now, but I'd love to set up a time to take it for a test drive." We exchanged numbers, and I drove away feeling blessed.

"Lord, I've been praying and seeking a truck, and while I'm going through this tough time, you set this truck in front of my face. If you don't want me to get it, could you please let me know? I really like it, but I'll wait a few days."

In the midst of the waiting game and storm of mistakes made, my heart was softened by the truck. It was an oasis in the middle of an ocean, and I was happy for the possibility of such a blessing.

The days came and went, yet I never received a phone call. There was no letter or sit down with my boss. By Friday, I knew it wasn't a mistake. I passed the drug test. I couldn't believe I tested negative, but thanked God profusely for the mercy He showed.

"Lord, thank you so much for what you've given me," I prayed. "I screwed up, but I will stick to my oath. I know it probably wasn't the smartest thing for me to do, but I will stick by my word and honor you. Lord, you've given me so much.

You've provided me with work, you've given me this work truck, you put the '70 Chevy in front of me after I'd been praying for a project truck, you have always provided housing and food. You've given me second chances over and over again. I can't thank you enough for how much you've done and how much you've loved me despite what I've done and who I am. I thank you so much for the gift of your Son. Thank you for your death, Jesus. Thank you that I can live, and thank you for loving me even when I was still an enemy to you."

Even if He had blocked the truck, or never placed it in front of me, God showed me His love by always bringing me through the roughest moments.

It was becoming apparent more needed to change in my life, so I made sure to make consistent prayer for a few needs, "Also, Lord: could you please send me some leadership. I need someone in my life that can lead me and mentor me. I want to be raised up as one of your children, and I know I need a mentor or an elder in my life."

On Saturday, I took the truck for a test drive with the owner's dad. As we started it up, I could hear the growl of the v8 under the hood. We got in and pulled out of the parking lot. The motor felt smooth as the truck rumbled up the street. I put a little gas into it, and she came to life, slapping a smile across my face as we cruised and discussed the truck and project vehicles.

When we pulled back into the lot, I got out and looked the truck over once more.

"I'll take it," I said.

I wrote the check for the full amount, wanting to help a fellow brother out. The truck could have easily been bought for less, but I knew in my heart it was better to give what he was asking. We finished the paperwork and I shook hands with both father and son.

"Thank you very much for the truck," I said. I looked both in the eye with a smile. "I'll be back in a few days to pick it up." They both agreed.

"Thanks and God bless, guys," I said as I got in my work truck. I was now the official owner of a dark blue, 1970 Chevy C20.

A few days later, Stephen and I retrieved the new purchase. As I pulled out of the gas station, heads turned to catch a glance. Tires squealed as I shifted, and the tail-end swung slightly. When we arrived home, Stephen seconded the observation, "People were looking at the truck all the way home. It's a pretty sweet truck."

"Thanks. Yeah, I'm really happy with it. The motor runs well, and it looks good. There are some minor fixes, but overall it's a great project truck.

And I was thankful the Father kept me from a project truck that would have sunk me. This one fit my skills. There were things to do that could keep me busy, but not enough to bring on frustration.

Soon after, I was drag-racing up and down the trail on Jason's property. Dust kicked as the tires spun hard then caught after a slight swerve from the rear-end. I hit fourth gear and let off the gas, slowing down to turn around and do it again. I loved playing with the pick-up, and was excited to start buying parts.

Despite the stumble with drugs, I was making headway in every area of life. The conversations between Michelle and me were growing. I would spend a night typing up responses, making sure to address every point or question asked. The message was proof-read with careful eyes, and sent with giddy fingers. A week later, a reply would show up in my inbox. My heart would quicken as I opened the email and read her message. It was carefully crafted and thought-out. She weighed the words I had used and dove into the topics without reservation. Every conversation went deeper into what God was doing and the daily struggles; while from the beginning it felt natural and easy. Not only was this girl not blind to me, but against all odds was enjoying our conversations. I didn't even need to ask for some of her french fries.

Doug was having his own success in the field of courtship. He traveled back to his hometown to meet with Sarah and came back with an extra person in his truck. Instantly, they were living comfortably and intimately. At first, I was skeptical since they hadn't been talking for too long before deciding the best thing for their relationship was for her to move to North Dakota, but as I got to know her, I realized they were a perfect match.

She was patient with Doug, seeing past his rough exterior and grabbing hold of a heart that needed the golden touch to soften it. Doug gave her the undivided, pure attention and love she deserved, not for a second under-appreciating who she was and how lucky he was to have her.

"If I lose her man, it's over," he said one night as the three of us sat in the camper.

She laughed, "It's the same for me. So we better not lose each other!"

I basked in the joy of the moment. A guy who a few months ago saw little hope in life, was now blessed by the presence of a woman who needed to be honored and appreciated. Doug had gone from blank-stare womanizer to romantic, trying his best to love Sarah with all of himself.

At times they would fight or snap, but as they grew closer, the impatience and anger faded. Doug began to cautiously relax and Sarah remained her ever patient self. They were two stones, chipping and grinding eachother's edges. Progress was moving slowly, but two smooth gems was God's goal.

"We need to do Bible study," Sarah said. "I know you guys have, and we should keep going."

"I would love to do that," I said.

I was thankful God provided a woman who kept Doug's faith growing, and I wanted to support it any way possible. We did our best with the Bible studies, taking the book chapter by chapter. Some weekends we forgot or missed, but a new appreciation for the Word built in the three of us. I could see a live relationship beginning to grow beyond just reading words and following mantras.

My own faith was flowering. There was a push from within to find a church, so I started with the place Darryl suggested. The building was modern, and the people friendly. I tried to connect myself to the social pipeline by making friends and spending some time with others my age.

As a new self formed and the old was dying, Doug's RV became my favorite place to enjoy solace and intimate friendship. I sensed he played a strong part in the growth of my faith and the death of my former wanderings. We would spend weekend nights hanging out, eating at our favorite Mexican restaurant, and enjoying close companionship.

Soon, I found out it was going to get harder to enjoy those times.

"I'm quitting," Doug said one night as we were enjoying the summer warmth under the stars. The buzz of traffic played in the background as the row sat quiet. The afternoon air was thick, exhaling the last stand of heat before fall took control.

"You're done?"

"Yeah. There's actually a position about an hour away I think I'm going to take. He's offering me housing and pretty good pay. I'd be supervising a few wells, and he's going to let me do it my way," Doug said.

"That's awesome, congrats on the job. It's good that you can get out," I said, finding it hard to let a friend leave me behind.

"It's time. I can't handle being there anymore. It's better for everyone if I leave. My boss is a good man, but when he's gone, it gets hard to deal. This job sounds a lot better...if it's true. If it happens like the guy says it will, I'll be independent and overseeing things."

Doug struggled in his shop, butting heads with another worker. He liked to keep to himself and do his job, but the other employee saw fit to give him trouble and make his life unbearable.

"I'm done with this place. I was about to kill Gary the other day, so it's time."

"At least you'll still be nearby. I can come over on the weekend and see you guys. Plus, you'll be out of the RV!"

"I know. We can't wait. These places aren't real big, but just about anything beats that thing."

I asked him where their new home was, and he told of a huge expanse of campers, trailers and FEMA style shacks.

"We're in one of those small, mobile home style sheds. It's got a small kitchen space, a bathroom and a spot for a bed, but anything is better than what we have now," he said.

"That's for sure. Although I'm going to miss our nights hanging out."

I had met so many people behind the shop with different stories. They came from all over the U.S., each seeking a new start. Some were young men looking to pocket cash and build a future back home. Others were transients that bounced all around the country and found work in the one place where there were more jobs than people. A few were middle-age and looking to put away a little retirement cash and make up for lost time. I watched people come and go, lives go up and down, friends connect and friends break apart. I watched as drugs and alcohol cut a path of destruction through the lives of my friends, as well as my own. The choices I had made didn't make me different from anyone. Instead, it set us all on the same level. Thankfully, I started to climb out of that hole without serious repercussions.

"After I'm done next Friday, we're going to be moving, so we could use some help if you're around," Doug said, snapping me back to reality.

"Sure thing. Give me a call and let me know," I responded.

"We'll make some dinner and relax," he offered.

I smiled at Doug, "Here's to the new job. Congrats on the blessing God gave you. He's always watching out for you."

"He definitely is. He's given me a lot lately," Doug said.

"He's given both of us a lot," I said.

Doug led the way back into the camper, climbing the steps and then bracing against the slant. As the three of us sat, they asked about the church I was going to.

"It's not too bad," I said. "The people are pretty nice and everything. You guys are more than welcome to come some time."

"We should do that, just to check it out," Sarah said. "We need to find a church, and maybe this will get us to look into one once we're settled."

Sunday came, and we went. The service was its usual comfortable pace as a few scriptures were presented and a life lesson was wrapped around them.

"It wasn't too bad," Doug said. "I think I like it more when the pastor gets deeper into the Word, but it was good."

"Yeah, I thought the same thing. It's not a bad church though," I said, trying to convince myself.

Something just didn't satisfy with the church. The people were nice, the teaching wasn't bad, and I made some friends, but it felt slightly empty. I figured perhaps I wasn't involved enough, so I made a mental note to approach the pastor next chance I got, to find out what other opportunities were available.

"We'll have to find one that we like. We've kept our eyes open, so there's a few we can try. I know we need to have a church and get some community around us. We can't do it on our own," Doug said.

I agreed wholeheartedly. Too often I heard people talk about not needing a church, yet they had no support system or role-models to give them guidance.

As we spoke and talked of being close to God, a passion from within bubbled. Each day, my thoughts came to center more on God. Instead of going to church on Sunday and calling it a victory for life, I paid attention to the words the pastor spoke. My days of listening to music were gone, replaced by the voices of men seeking to be a vessel for the Holy Spirit, who was speaking loud and clear. There were times when I had a question or struggle. I would park my truck on a deserted dirt road, far from people or civilization and cry out, yelling for answers about why there was still so much pain inside. When the fervor of emotional explosion faded and the tears dried, a sermon—many times the next one—would answer my prayers. Other times, prayers that were said the night before were answered the next day. The more I hungered and thirsted for his guidance, the more I was filled.

With the answers flowing, boldness urged me to share with others. I saw small changes in Doug and Sarah as we spoke about Christ. Words given in encouragement had a lasting effect, while words of instruction were treasured. They would ask my advice on a situation, and would lean in to hear my answers, and I knew they could provide me with reliable guidance when there was a dilemma I was facing. A fire was being stoked, and I had to figure out how to fan the flames higher.

The next chance I got, I approached the pastor at church. I was nervous, and not sure why. A flurry of people filled the lobby after the service, and the pastor was a pillar in the center, shaking hands with various people and smiling. He conversed with confidence, speaking and laughing as regular members approached him to catch up and thank him for a sermon well done. I inched closer and waited for an open opportunity. As soon as the person he was talking with left, I inserted myself.

"Hey Pastor, I was just wondering if maybe there was something I could do for the church. I'd really like to get involved and was wondering if you could help me out," I said. The words were soft and careful, hope cushioning my uncertainty.

He quickly glanced at me and craned his neck to look above and behind. I fought the urge to look behind me and see what grabbed his attention.

"Yeah, you can go over there and talk to that guy at the desk," he said, pointing behind him as his eyes continued to scan the room. He gazed past again, muttered an "excuse me" and walked away. I stood miffed. I felt stranded in a sea of people. As the waves of faces and laughter crashed against my self-worth, the empty feelings produced words within. This was not my church. I need to find a different place.

I didn't hold it against him, but I needed a shepherd that could make time for one of his flock. I was an obstacle to his plans, and I left the church knowing God had somewhere else in mind.

"Lord, I don't hold it against him," I prayed. "But, this is not the church for me. I really need a church and home where I can flourish. I need a place where I can grow. I need a leader who has time for his flock, since that's what he's there for."

I was trying to find where I belonged. I wanted a church in which I could have a spiritual leader. Massey and I talked regularly, and there were rumblings of me working with his ministry. We became good friends so quickly, but I wanted to go where God wanted me. I wondered, "Was this why God wanted me to meet Massey? To bring me into full ministry?" The passion to serve bulged, and I was lost as to how I could satisfy the desire.

The search was on, and little did I know that God had already chosen the place I was to go. I just had to say "yes" and respond to his calling.

Chapter 17

Part of my job's perk package was an expense account that covered lunches, so when in town, I attempted to eat at places that weren't complete grease-pits or major fast food joints. One in particular made great Mexican food. I went in so often that the girl behind the counter could rattle off my order as soon as I opened the door. A craving for a big burrito burrowed into my stomach, so I stopped in. I wasn't going to argue with the hunger pains.

As I sat munching on the thick beef burrito, I noticed two men sat at a table behind me, speaking of politics and faith. I caught bits of the conversation and couldn't help but listen. Soon, I was being pushed hard by the Holy Spirit to interrupt. I fought it, trying to pass it off, but the feeling grew, and deep down I knew I was supposed to talk to these men. After a bite or two, I worked up the courage to turn around.

"Excuse me, I couldn't help but overhear your conversation," I said.

Both turned to look. A slight surprise shot across their faces, and instantly smiles opened up.

"Here, pull up a chair," one man said. He was blonde and looked like he was mid 40's. He spoke with exuberance, exuding energy all over the room. His motions were grandiose, but never forceful.

"I'm Mark, and this is Ray," Mark said.

His eyes were keen, driving straight into mine. A welcoming smile put me at ease. His skin was weathered, showing he lived a full life under the sun.

"I'm Christian," I said.

"So are you a follower of Christ too?" he asked.

I took a second to digest the question. I wondered how he made the connection so quick.

Ray smiled, allowing his companion to take the lead.

"Yup. I couldn't help but overhear your conversation, and just felt like I had to talk to you guys."

"Awesome! Glad you could join us," Mark said. "Are you from the area?"

"Nope. I'm from Michigan originally. I've been in town a little less than a year now."

There was a sense of understanding that there was a difference from natives and long-timers. One rarely met a person who had spent his whole life in town. One could easily pick out most of the nation's license plates in the Wal-Mart parking lot.

"Came out for the oil work?" Mark asked.

"Yeah. Came out for a job, and God ended up providing what I needed," I said.

"He tends to do that," Ray commented. There was a calm that surrounded Ray, as if he possessed an inner wisdom ready to be tapped.

Mark leaned in and motioned towards Ray, "I work for him. God gave me a job by introducing us. He owns some oil leases, and I take care of them. You know the pastor that comes on the radio here in the patch?" Mark asked, excitement infusing his words.

"I've heard it a couple times," I said.

"That's Ray."

"Really? That's cool, nice to meet you." I was already meeting celebrities.

"So do you have a church?" Mark asked, continuing the barrage of friendly questions.

"Actually, I had one, but I just didn't feel it was the right church for me. Just didn't feel like the pastor there was the type of shepherd I needed."

They both looked at each other and back at me.

"Is it a white church?" Mark asked, already sniffing the trail of where I had been.

"Yeah, that's the one," I said.

His shoulders turned towards me and his hands opened. "You should come to my church. It's a great place to go," he said.

I pondered the suggestion. Was this the reason God wanted me to talk to these men? Or was there something else I was supposed to do here? I thanked Mark for the suggestion and agreed to try out the church.

"Come next week, and I'll show you around," he said.

"And if you'd like to come to a BBQ I'm having, you're more than welcome," Ray said speaking up. He handed me his business card, giving directions on how to get there.

I left the restaurant filled with joy. I couldn't believe the connection God presented. Perhaps the Lord was bringing more mentors into my life, just as I had been praying for. To top it off, I got a suggestion for a good church to be a part of. Could it be that He was answering prayers like believers say He does?

The next Saturday I went to Ray's BBQ. I conversed with his family and friends, getting to know people who were strong and passionate about their faith. I wasn't used to the new atmosphere of faith they had. Their beliefs didn't find shape in the church they went to, or the offering they put in the plate. It was animated by their relationship with God, and permeated their being. Some were eccentric, while others were calm and relaxed. There was a tangible difference between the love they expressed and that of many other Christians I'd met.

Despite the love, despite the passion and the faith, I left the BBQ feeling lonely. They were wonderful hosts, piling the mashed potatoes on my plate and pushing another burger toward me. People were curious about who I was and how I was doing in my new life. They were gracious and loving people, but I still felt lonely. I sat in the circle watching others jovially chide each other and jump into conversations. My face hurt from keeping a smile, and the aching within to get back home grew more intense throughout the afternoon. A sigh of relief came when I was driving away, even though my heart and voice thanked God for at least introducing me to good and godly people.

The dissection commenced as I drove down the sunny subdivision road. Trees leaned towards the road, fanning out their leaves in an attempt to shade my truck as it passed underneath. Why was I feeling lonely? These were brothers and sisters in Christ. They welcomed me with open arms. Why wasn't I snuggling into the warm embrace of a family in Christ?

My inner dialog settled on a point being unearthed from the dirt of confusion. This was family, but I wasn't truly a part of it. I still craved to become one with a faith family. I wanted to know the inside jokes and the details of the souls surrounding me. I desired to be connected not just by food on a grill and a sunny summer day, but by the rigors of a faith built through struggle and hardship. It was obvious: these facets could not be fashioned in a single day, no matter how good the bratwurst tasted.

The day after the BBQ, I buttoned up a dress shirt, spread the wrinkles out of my cleanest jeans and climbed into my truck with my leather-covered Bible. Today was the day I took Mark up on his offer and tried out his church. I followed his directions, seeing several churches line the left side of the road. I came to a single story, long building. As I pulled into the parking lot, something didn't feel right. I looked for some type of sign or indication that this was the right place.

I found the sign. It read, "Church of Jesus Christ and Latter Day Saints." Oops.

I pulled through to the far exit, not embracing the idea of becoming a Mormon for a day. I looked to my left, and the next property was a church building marked by a tall white sign near the road, "Williston Assembly of God." Found it!

I eased my hulking truck into a parking space. Nervous hands and feet kept still for a few moments, looking for the strength to get out, while in seeped the typical fears and apprehensions. Despite the intention of a church to be a welcoming place, there were always worst-case scenarios that ran through my head. Am I worthy? What if they shun me? What if they're weird? What are they going to think? How is this going to go? Will they sacrifice a virgin on the alter? I took a deep breath and hopped out. As I reached the door, a bright, smiling face welcomed me.

"Hi! Welcome to Assembly," the greeter said as she held the door open. We shook hands as I passed and was ushered into the lobby. People scurried about, eager to visit with close companions. The sound of chatting and laughter wafted through the building. There were clusters of people gathered in the lobby, while other members bounced from group to group, saying hi and patting friends on the back. Ahead of me was the sanctuary, modern in appearance but cozy and inviting.

Luckily, I saw no sacrificial alter or line of young virgins.

Two greeters stood on each side of the entrance into the sanctuary, and they invited me in with smiles and outstretched hands. One reminded me of Mark Twain, with wild white hair jetting out and a large, protruding nose. His eyes squinted behind thick glasses and his head leaned forward, as if trying to focus on everything in front of him. He radiated, joy flowing out in a never-ending stream to any who came near. He shook my hand vigorously, welcoming me and placing a pamphlet in my hand. I sought out a chair in the back corner and scanned the sanctuary, trying to make snap judgments on the people and the church. A strong sense of community and connection enveloped me. It was a bigger group, yet there was no sense of burrowing into cliques like most churches. The people milled about, not hesitating to talk to the most gruff looking of characters.

A few oil-men stuck out as they sat in the sanctuary. They were men who would have looked more at home in a biker bar than a church. Yet, little church ladies with their nice Bibles and ironed Sunday best made no hesitation to start conversations with these bearded, tattooed characters. I sat, my spirit being pulled upwards by the sense that God was in this building. There was no hollow feeling, no dead air, no boundary separating God from his people.

The music started, and immediately people were clapping their hands, singing with might and raising their hands. It wasn't a feverish revival, but a joyous occasion. Instead of voices singing in unison with drudgery, spirits spoke out to God with thankfulness and tidings. Everything was just right. They were friendly and connective, but not overbearing. The music and sermon were full of life, but not extreme or exotic. The group was big, but not a sea where one could drown unnoticed. When I left service, it was obvious that I had found my church.

My heart broke before God, pouring out thanks and blessings. His love washed over me, showing that all of my former notions about who He was and what He was were complete hogwash. This was not a God who waited for me to do everything right before granting one wish. This was a God who wanted the best for me, and allowed me the opportunity to accept it. He was leading, and every time I said "yes" and stepped out in faith, I was rewarded with more of Him. This reward did not mean that struggles and failures weren't going to occur, but I could sense He was fashioning a new Christian out of an old, dilapidated human.

I felt a joy and fulfillment I had never experienced before. The need to fill the empty space was subsiding. Instead of seeking another high or another hit, I was seeking more answered prayer.

My passion was to become more obedient. Jesus was taking over every room in my heart, and He renovated every bit of ground won, from what had been dedicated to sin and was now dedicated for Him. Much like a statue is shaped from a block of marble, He was chipping away at the corners and dead parts, shaping beauty that would glorify His power and love.

Resistance to praying and reading still showed itself in desires to do mundane tasks. The television would beckon, asking me to get lost in a world of Xbox or movies. Shame from sin would push my heart away from God, saying, "He doesn't want to hear from me," or "I'm not good enough to go to Him with this." The more I fought those feelings that pulled me away from Christ, the more I was filled with the joy of living each day. It was not perfect, and He was not finished. For once though, I felt like I was on the right track in life.

Along with the amazing church experience, I became more intertwined with Massey's ministry. He invited me to join them for a show they were playing, and I was eager to say yes. There was a sense of a future with the ministry, and both Massey and I wondered if it was what God wanted.

I needed to ask for time off, so I sat down with Don one afternoon when it was just us.

"I was wondering if I could get Monday off," I started, anticipating the conversation wouldn't be an easy one.

"Of course," he said, always eager to oblige.

A little shock came from the ease of getting what I asked for. I was coming to love Don like a father or close grandpa because it seemed he always took care of me.

"I want to be upfront with you," I said. "You know I gave you my commitment for a year and a half to two years, and I aim to fulfill that. The only reason I would ever leave early is if God called me to go somewhere else. There's a ministry I'm visiting this weekend, and I've got no clue what's going to happen, but wanted you to know just in case God does call me. I don't want to pull any surprises on you or anything."

Don thought for a moment and nodded, "Well, just let me know what's going on. If that's where He wants you, then that's where you need to be. I would hate to lose you, but I understand. We have to do what we're called to do, and I would never get in the way of that."

I relaxed, happy the hard part was over. He and I had discussed faith before, breaking into conversation about Christ and what it meant to follow. He knew he was a sinner and had made a lot of mistakes, he understood Christ was the only way, and he knew there were changes to be made in his own life.

Don (a farm boy who didn't care about living) had been stabbed, shot, shot at, knocked out, beaten and many other methods of mayhem a wild boy could get into. But when we talked, I saw a man whose heart longed for something above. He desired rest, but didn't know how to get there.

I could tell he saw a chance to give back for the mercy God had shown him. There was an urge to go beyond what a boss needed to, and it was deeply appreciated.

CHAPTER 18

I drove hard while white lines split the pavement as they rocketed past. Eagerness pushed my foot to the pedal, driving the vehicle forward. I was on my way to meet Massey, the ministry's leader Brian and the rest of the crew, who were based eight hours away from Williston. I no longer had my Honda after selling it to one of the residents on the row. Stephen obliged me the use his truck, hesitantly handing over the keys. I thanked him profusely, knowing this was a kindness I needed to repay somehow.

The hours flew by and I prayed to the Lord, wondering if this was the path He had set up. I didn't want to leave Williston. It was satisfying to finally have planted feet. The church community wrapped itself around me, my job flowed, I made friends, my faith picked up, and Michelle and I talked often.

She and I discussed my working for the ministry. She pushed me to seek God on it. Her heart was for His will to be done, no matter the outcome. Our conversations covered faith, friends and family at length, wanting to consume every tidbit we could about the other person's life.

Michelle was coming to the end of her college education. After a fork in the road of her sophomore year, she chose to go with nursing. Her heart burst with enthusiasm to help the sick and hurting and she longed to give them the light of Christ. She wanted to become an oncology nurse, providing a special love to those struggling with cancer.

My goal was to become half that vital to others, and this ministry option appeared to be my ticket. The group was adamant about having strong knowledge of the Constitution, the Founding Fathers, faith and knowing the Bible front to back. It was as if ministry training had become boot camp.

Deep down, reservations poked and prodded. Did I really want to join them? Was this the right fit? Would God expect me to go some place I didn't really want to go?

If I was going to be a man of God, I would need the Word. The Bible would have to flow from me, useable at any time for any reason. The sword of the Word was to be sharp, always ready to defend, and Massey's sword was razor sharp. Scripture flowed forth from him, living and breathing historical facts as well. I was deeply impressed by the rigorous routine this ministry expected of its people.

I arrived at Massey's townhouse late in the night, ready for a little sleep before we were to pack up the bus. He greeted me with a hug, and ushered me in. I lay down on the couch, knowing we were going to be getting up soon. It was hard to sleep as the different scenarios played with my feelings and senses. I was happy to be with Massey, excited to travel with a world-renown band and wondered what God was planning.

The next morning we rose early and headed to the office. It was a small, non-descript building halfway down the main street. We were one of the first vehicles to arrive. We climbed out and pulled bags and child-care items from the trunk. Other people pulled up, and soon four or five small families were gathered inside the office, bustling to and fro in preparation for the trip.

The office was adorned with plaques of quotes from men like George Washington or Charles Spurgeon. Paintings of historic men responsible for making America looked down with solemn faces, watching those who chose to defend their creation.

I followed Massey, trying to stay busy and help in any way I could. He collected tracts and hand-outs, along with t-shirts and comic books. All of them seemed to revolve around Brian and his testimony.

"You should meet Brian," Massey said as he craned his neck around, looking for the man in charge. We headed through the attached garage to a sun-washed sidewalk in front of the office.

"Ahh, there he is."

Massey pointed to a large, looming figure standing near the street, pulling a few items out of the back of a car. He must have been 6'5", with long, rocker-style hair pulled through the back of a baseball cap. He was intimidating, towering over everyone while pointing and directing.

"Hey Brian, this is Christian," Massey said as we approached.

"Oh hey Christian, nice to meet you," he said, giving a firm handshake. He inspected the young man standing before him for a brief moment, then turned towards another errand. "Sorry, excuse me," and he walked off.

I shrugged it off, knowing everyone was in a state of excitement preparing for the trip. We loaded heavy amps and drum equipment onto the tour bus. Massey fired up the bus and pulled it out of the garage, stretching it across the slanted parking spaces opposite the office. I climbed the steps, noticing the clean tan carpet and the decorated walls. It had been a tour bus for a famous musician before being sold at a discounted rate to the ministry. I stood at the head of this beautiful bus, wishing I could help in some way. He turned the key, but the motor stayed silent. Without a sputter, the bus had died.

Others loaded baggage into the compartments underneath and paid no attention to Massey as he scrambled to find the issue. He leapt off the bus, dove into the storage compartment, and stared at the chargers and batteries, trying to locate the problem's cause. Behind us, I could hear Brian piping up, "If someone had checked this stuff, we wouldn't be waiting on this." He continued directing small comments towards Massey, who shrugged them off and put more pressure on himself to get the issue solved.

We tinkered with settings and connections, and the bus finally roared to life. Inside, children talked and cried while the group of families settled into their seats. Massey slumped into the driver seat, taking off his mechanic's hat and putting on the driver's cap. He fulfilled all the roles any one person could: bassist, singer, mechanic, driver, cheerleader, fundraiser and scapegoat.

Brian stood and asked for a moment of prayer. He bellowed with the oratory skill of a political candidate, reaching high for words and speaking with sentence structures that required a diagram. I focused, trying to ascertain exactly what he was praying about amidst the "Majesty"s and "Lord Father God"s. It was grandiose, taking on a level of prayer I didn't know existed.

Once he concluded the appeal to God, we pulled out onto the road. I sat in the front with Massey, watching the road disappear underneath while cars crawled by. We could look down onto their roofs, peering over them like a giant among ants. As Massey drove, the back of the bus filled with conversation and laughter. People stretched out to enjoy the seven hour bus ride.

"Are we going the right way?" a voice called out from the back.

Massey tried to get his bearings, "I think so," he responded. There was timidity in his voice, much like a dog with downcast eyes.

"You think so?" the voice retorted. Brian made more comments to the others in the back, and soon he was placing blame on Massey.

"You're supposed to know where you're going Massey," he laughed, passing off the chiding as a joke. "First the battery stuff, and now this? Come on man," he continued.

I looked at Massey, his face trying to wash the embarrassment away. Slight twitches of pain crossed his lips, showing chinks in his armor. And as soon as the chinks flashed, they were gone, masked by a toughened exterior.

He brushed the teasing off, "Yup, it was me. Sorry guys, I promise it won't happen again." A few more comments floated from the back to the front, and soon they were engrossed in their own discussions.

My sorrow deepened for Massey as I watched him struggle to put away the effects of the chiding. He did his best to push forward and smile. But as he spoke to me, I could see a shell that had been repeatedly cracked and repaired. Massey was a determined guy, and I held a greater respect for him the more acquainted we became. His heart just wanted to please his heavenly Father.

At moments, self-deprecating comments spurted out of Massey. He admonished himself for not going the right direction, not having foreseen the battery issue, and he took responsibility for any other problems that arose.

I contemplated the attitude on the bus, wondering if this was out of place behavior for a Christian group, or if they were so deeply connected that the pleasantries had stepped aside for truth. They were steeped in the Word of God, and I saw the flame of the Holy Spirit in Massey's eyes. He deeply respected Brian, and had a great love for the ministry. I couldn't argue with that. My little observation of their interaction couldn't see everything that was going on, and I didn't want to judge a trip by its first few miles, so I quietly watched with a desire to find the positive pieces of this group and understand why I rode on their bus.

The drive continued, and I made my way to one of the seats farther back. Brian took over the wheel, so I read a book on evidences for the Christian faith while Massey found solace with his family.

One of the other leaders, James, twisted his head sideways to read the spine of my book. I noticed his gaze and looked up.

"*Evidence Demands a Verdict* by Josh Mcdowell" I said. It was a 700+ page textbook, of sorts, that covered all the arguments against Christianity. Written by a man who set out to disprove Christianity once and for all, it soon became apparent to him that all his research and pouring over many different resources posited one distinct conclusion: Jesus Christ was real, and he really was God in the flesh. Josh Mcdowell became a believer and went on to publish that book as well as others, discussing the archeological, historical, philosophical and logical reasons behind the truth of the Gospels.

Brian overheard the name of the author, and commented, "Josh McDowell? He's kind of soft." I wasn't sure what he meant, but suddenly the book felt less prominent in my hands. I continued to explain the context to James, who listened intently.

"That's cool. I'm impressed you're reading the whole thing," he said, twirling the pen in his hand.

"Thanks, I really want to read all of it. I've been consumed with apologetics lately. I want to have a reason for my faith, and I want to be able to answer anybody who questions it. It gets hard to see people stumble and fall because someone claims they have evidence against God. I want to be able to help people understand that there is plenty of evidence for our faith, and faith isn't just blind."

He smiled and went back to scribbling on a notepad. A constant stream of business talk flowed from Brian to James, to Massey and back again. I sat back with my book, trying to blend in to the seat, so I could have time to reflect.

"Hey Christian, come up here."

I looked up from the thick cardboard and paper wall in my hands. Brian was glancing back in my direction. I set the book down and climbed into the front seat.

"Sorry about walking off on you earlier. I was in a rush, trying to get things situated," he said.

"No worries, I know how it goes. You guys were trying to get everything ready," I said. The trees blurred together in a stream of green, interrupted by fields and sporadic buildings.

"We don't usually bring visitors along on this kind of thing, but Massey spoke very highly of you, and said you might be interested in joining us."

"Yeah, I wanted to get to know you guys and see what it was all about. I want to do what the Lord wants, and I've got a desire to speak the truth like you guys do. I've never heard a ministry address whats going on like you do," I said.

"Most don't," he said. "We're here to battle what's going on in our schools and our media. Kids aren't getting the whole truth. They're getting one side of it. We want to give them the truth about the Founding Fathers, not what the liberal agenda wants them to know. Our kids are the next generation, and if we don't tell them this, we're going to lose them."

"Exactly. I see what's going on and it frustrates me. This country was founded on Judeo-Christian values, but those values are being lost. When Massey and I first met, I felt like he was saying everything I've been thinking," I said.

Brian kept focused on the road, tilting his head just enough to see me out of the corner of his eye.

"That's because we're determined to bring out the truth. We're willing to say what most churches don't want to say. We get persecuted for it, but the world needs to know. If we want to save this country, it has to get back to its roots. We have to stand up for God's morals, and not allow it to be dragged down by those who want to trample it," he said. "Our Founding Fathers knew what would happen if things turned into what they are today." He looked at me, "Is this a democracy or a republic?"

"A republic," I responded.

"That's right. We're not founded on the majority vote, but on a foundation of values, no matter what the society of the day thinks. People don't realize that this isn't supposed to be a democracy that goes with the flavor of the day. We're supposed to be standing on the Constitution and keeping to the morals God placed forth."

His words pushed forth with passion. His voice gained strength as he spoke and the speech grabbed flight like a jet off the runway.

"We can't sit by and let this happen to our country. I love this country and the men who have died to keep it free. Freedom does not mean doing whatever you want, but having the ability to do what you're supposed to do. We're spiraling down, and coming back to God is the only way this nation will be saved. We're battling the liberal agenda in the schools, where they're indoctrinating our children with feel-good stuff and immorality."

He continued preaching for the next hour. There were statistics about homosexuality, quotes from men like Thomas Jefferson and George Washington, and ways in which scripture had been forgotten by the church. We talked of the state of Christianity in America, and its role in the sliding of the nation. He dwarfed Massey with his seemingly endless knowledge, pouring like a mixed concrete into the spaces of my concerns. The cement was hardening, giving solidification with words I had never been able to speak. There was finally substance to back up how I felt.

The time passed, the conversation cooled and we finally arrived at the gymnasium where the show was to be held. We were in a small town, serene amongst the dipping sun and surrounding valleys. Clouds pulled themselves closer, threatening to hide the light before it found its way below the horizon. The casting shadows brought a chill to the air. As we unpacked gear, Massey caught me when no one else was around.

"I've never seen him pour into someone like that the first time he met them," he said. "You should feel honored, he must see something in you."

The compliment had me feeling like I passed some type of initiation. I wondered, "Perhaps this is a sign I'm where I'm supposed to be?"

The stage was set, and they began running sound check. I found a seat in the bleachers and scoped out my surroundings. Old, pull out bleachers sandwiched a worn-out basketball court that had been set up with rows of metal chairs. The rafters were dusty, showing years of minimum maintenance as they held the building together. The whole thing reminded me of the gyms I frolicked in as a child. A raised stage looked out onto the basketball court surrounded by walls tiled five feet high which, in turn, gave way to white-washed plaster.

The show wasn't going to be held at the high school, due to a last minute change of location. There were some complaints or issues among the townspeople as to whether or not it was okay to have such a presentation on public property. Instead of canceling or fighting to get their way, the sponsors arranged this plan B.

The man who had invited us was a football coach the community greatly respected. He was an older man, representing a former generation where football coaches were stoic and stone-faced, moral without question. People respected him, and therefore voted to give the group a chance. A few parents looked up the presentation online and read some bad reviews, and decided the group was just offensive and had no place in their community. Others felt the need for someone to stand up and speak the truth, wanting words to be put to what their hearts felt, much like me.

The show started and the band played, plowing through songs that sounded familiar from the MP3 player demo Massey had given me. The crowd clapped and some came closer to the stage. Overall, the older generation appeared to be on the edge. They were torn. The music was too hard for them, but they knew the message was what they wanted: morality, God, values.

The show ended and Massey, Brian and James grabbed microphones, starting the presentation.

For the next three hours, they spoke much like Brian did on the bus. They discussed the fallacies that were being taught to kids these days concerning our country's founding. They spoke at length on the "homosexual agenda", prompting several people to get up and leave. Brian spoke without apology, hitting on every controversial topic that brought a cringe from general society. He left no stone unturned, and was determined to not back down to any criticism of his words or his delivery.

Finally, the presentation came to a close. Brian was antsy, not wanting to stop, but due to time constraints, the sponsors needed to close down for the night. People filed out, while a few stuck around to look at the merchandise table set up in the corner, or to approach one of the speakers. We packed things up with another successful presentation underneath our belts. I felt like one of the crew.

Our bus pulled into the night, headlights flooding the road as we headed back home. We were all exhausted, quietly discussing different parts of the day. Brian and James talked over the particulars, while Massey and I sat together.

"Some people just don't understand us," he said. "It's hard, but we have to tell the truth. Loving people is giving them the truth."

I didn't say much. I was tired and wanted to let everything sink in. As a Lassie movie played on the television overhead, James noticed I was silent.

"You're pretty quiet Christian," he said.

"Yeah, I'm just tired and watching the movie. I think I'm more interested in it than the kids are," I laughed.

He shifted in his seat. Massey moved up next to Brian and poured over the show.

"I think I'm ready for something else," James said. We settled on a historical documentary and let the show wash over us.

A few hours into the trip, the group voted to stop for the night at a hotel. It was late and we were all exhausted, not wanting to arrive back at the office at seven or eight in the morning.

We each paid for our own rooms, and slathered on the good nights. I crashed onto the bed. I wanted to pour through everything, but was too exhausted to begin. I quickly fell asleep, welcoming the blanket of unconsciousness.

The next morning we all piled back onto the bus. Kids ran back and forth, energetic from a nights rest. The bus lumbered onto the highway, and we headed towards home.

At lunch time, we stopped at a McDonald's. The group piled out and bombarded the counter with orders and jokes. Two cashiers scrambled to handle us, hoping to get every order right. The meal was quick, with children stuffing french fries into their open mouths and denying the last chicken tender. Mom and Dad asked, begged and demanded the child take "just one more bite", while siblings played with a toy or stole fries off their brothers' plate. Once the kids were cleaned up and the trash thrown away, we clambered back onto the bus.

"I wanted to give a tract to the guy. I didn't mean for the girl to get one," I heard Brian say. "She was looking kind of weird. Not that I'm not happy she got it, but…" he trailed off. It didn't sit right. It didn't feel Christ-like.

But the group obviously had a love for God I couldn't deny. They were sacrificing their lives and dedicating every waking moment to spreading His Word and the values of our Founding Fathers to every child and school they could. Even if it didn't feel right, the desire to be sacrificing and noble was more powerful. Brian was rough around the edges, but Massey had told me several times about the prophetic gift Brian carried. Others backed up the story, saying that he could read their inner thoughts and had done it plenty of times during church service.

We arrived home and unpacked the bus. Each family piled into its cars and we all drove our separate ways.

"So, what'd you think?" Massey asked me.

I looked to the family that surrounded me. Two young children sat quietly with parents who looked worn-out. Their faces reflected years of sacrificial service and obedience.

"I thought the trip was fun. And I thought the presentation was pretty good." I was hesitant to bring up my concerns, wondering if I was out of line with my thoughts.

He watched the road as the car glided along carrying his family and a welcomed guest.

"It was. There's so much more we can do. We want to get to every school we can," he said.

"What about churches?" I asked. "I'd think they'd be a really good resource and connection."

"We tried that. Unfortunately, churches never seem to respond to us. Sometimes they say they want to do something with us, and then it falls apart. Other times they just reject us. I think we're too raw for them, and they're not ready to be attached to a message like ours. We're one of a kind, and I think we're the only ones willing to say what we say," he said. His eyes focused forward. "We want to spread the Word of God. We're loving people by telling them the whole truth."

The premise sounded legitimate. It seemed that most churches were attaching themselves to a watered-down message. Brian's approach of being raw with the truth had a certain appeal to me, which ironically produced pride in my heart.

God wanted me to pay attention, and He grabbed all of it the next day.

Every Sunday without fail, they got together for a church service. Brian would lead service and the families would listen. Brian began the sermon by talking about typical Biblical lessons, covering issues he felt needed to be addressed within the group. Soon, he was speaking prophetic messages to people in the room. Words flew fast to various seats. Heads nodded in agreement as mouths opened a little to the mysteries issuing forth. I watched as he focused on Massey, speaking at first small encouragements then quickly giving way to criticisms and commands. Then, he came to me.

"Christian, right now, you're wondering if you're on the right path. You're asking God if you're on the right track," he started.

I leaned forward in my seat. My prayers the past couple weeks had been on this exact issue, wondering if I was following God the right way, and if I was being led down a false road or seeing things in the wrong light. It wasn't just the path of where God was leading me, but was it the narrow path? I had prayed and wondered, "Am I doing this right? Am I following correctly on the narrow path that Christ said few would find?"

He continued, "If this was the path," he drew two lines on the whiteboard a few inches apart straight up and down, "you're like this," he drew a line that bounced lightly back and forth between the boundaries, never crossing over, but not straight down the middle. "You're kind of bouncing back and forth, but you're on the right track. The Lord wants you to know you're on the right path." He looked at me for a brief second and kept going, "Also, you've got spiritual gifts in the basement. They're going to come up. Don't worry, keep going and those will come up," he said, motioning with his hand from his waist up to his head.

I figured this guy really had a prophetic gift. He had no clue if I had gifts that were already grown. He had no clue whether I knew how to use them, or if I knew at all what they were. He could not have known my prayers or how I felt about my walk of faith. Some could say it was a shot in the dark, but coupled with the comments Massey had made, this was more than snake-oil sales.

We left service and I relayed my surprise to Massey.

"He hit it on the head with me," I said.

"Yeah, he's definitely got a gift," Massey said. "I don't know how many times he's read my thoughts and told me things nobody else could know."

The trip left me confused. I continued to have a sense something just wasn't right. It felt like they wanted to do the Lord's will, but was it being done their way or His? Was the leadership trustworthy?

As the miles passed in haste to return to Williston, the truck was filled with prayer and meditation.

"Lord, is this where you want me to be?" I called out, "I want to stay in North Dakota, but I know I could learn much by being taught in this group. I support their message, and I know it's a call to change this country around. Lord, I just don't know if this is what you want or not. Please lead me. Please guide me. I just want to do your will."

Peace came to me. He would put me where He needed me. If God wanted me there, they would confirm it by calling and seeking me out. There was no point in pressing until the door opened, and I felt a peace about the fresh conclusion. By the time I got home, I was ready to settle back into life in the oil patch.

After a few days of work, the battles sparked again. Confusion was rising, as doubts and questions disturbed my peace. I wondered what to do. I couldn't hide away those moments that felt "un-Christian", and I had observed some pride coming out of Brian that concerned me.

Ray's card found its way into my hands. He was a preacher, and a leader that spoke with wisdom during the BBQ with his family. I wondered if he knew how to handle men who were considered prophets.

"Ray, I was wondering if I could just ask you a couple questions. I know you're a really busy guy, but I have a dilemma and I'm not sure how to handle it."

"Sure, what's up?" he said, with hurried kindness.

"I'm debating joining a ministry, and just...I guess have some questions about the leader. He's definitely a prophet, but there's a, well, a pride or a hardness to him. I was wondering if you had any advice?"

He cleared his throat.

"Yeah. How old is he?"

"I don't know, maybe mid 40's?" I responded.

"He's coming right to that age. Prophets are usually hard-headed and stubborn. They tend to have to work a lot on their pride. At about his age, they come to a fork in the road. They either calm down and relax, or they get more stubborn." He spoke with a wistful reservation, as if it was more than just interaction that brought about his conclusion.

"I was a lot like that when I was younger. I'm still working on it, but we're kind of a different breed. It's hard not to be prideful when God has given you a gift like that," he said.

"Wait, you're one too?" I asked.

"Yeah. I was a lot like him, but I would say if he's not beginning to calm down and humble himself, then he may be hardening up."

The words sat heavy.

"So do you think I should not join?"

"Pray about it, and seek the Lord. He'll let you know what to do," he answered.

I thanked him for his time. There was a truth settling over the confusion. Doubts lingered, but confirmations of wisdom and a deeper, innate understanding chipped away at the blockage. It wasn't long before God made the next move.

I enjoyed my time at work, and I was getting to know my customers. They were men of different backgrounds and temperaments. I would drive onto site with huge pieces of equipment looming overhead and park next to the company man's truck. We would sit and discuss the weather or the oilfield as workers turned huge wrenches and slapped connectors onto pipe coming out of the ground. The diesel motor of the rig would fire up from idle as the blocks (a crane-like lift) would pull piping high into the air. I loved to watch the rig hands working, wishing I could be next to them, lifting 50 lb wrenches and turning pipe or catching rods.

But my job was to enjoy time with the customers, and to get them to enjoy me. There was one customer named Mike with whom I loved to meet and talk. He was in his mid 40's, but looked young for his age. He was laid-back, replying with easy-going responses and always willing to spend a few minutes talking. The first time we met, he and I spoke for 20-30 minutes before we both decided work was calling our names.

One day I met Mike in front of his office as he was about to leave. As we talked and discussed the usual topics, something was nagging and whispering inside me to ask, "Are you a Christian?"

I avoided the voice, nervous it could create an awkward scenario. A pad of paper sat atop his center console, adorned with a printed cross. I thought I could hear Christian music on the radio.

The words leaked out of my mouth. "Are you a Christian?"

"Yup, are you?" he asked.

"Yeah I am," I said, brightening at the discovery. How cool was this? Immediately I felt a new connection to Mike.

"I thought so," he said. "I wondered if you were, because I never hear you swear like all the other guys."

I took the observation and made a note. My language and actions really did reflect who I was to other people.

"Yeah, you seemed to be different too," I said.

"Well, you should come over some time," he offered. "I'm head of a church out of my house. And don't worry, it's not a cult or anything like that. I just felt called by God to start a church, so we have a small group that meets on Thursdays for coffee and Saturday nights for service. You should come out."

"I would love to. I've been praying for a community where I can connect with more Christians," I said.

He smiled and started his truck, "Then you should definitely come out. I have to get going, but I'll give you directions on how to get there."

I climbed into my truck and sat back. God had been working in a whirl-wind. Every day I saw God move in some way. Whether it was speaking to me through radio sermons, giving me exact verses, or bringing spiritual leaders into my life, He was there. My heart burst with joy for the foundation being laid.

Despite the nerves pulling at me to stay home, I chose to go to the Thursday night coffee and fellowship. Mike said it was a relaxed time where we could just talk and enjoy each other's company. I pulled up to the large white house at the corner of a four way stop. The house was a Victorian style, with white pillars and black iron. I walked to the door and gave a light knock. A woman answered the door.

"Hi, I'm Christian. Is Mike here?"

"Oh yeah, come on in," she said smiling. Her eyes lit up as she ushered me into the house.

"I'm Amy," she said. I was led into a large living room with a stair case lazily winding to the second floor. The carpet was a faded light blue, splotched with dirt stains and discoloring.

"Please excuse the carpet and the shape the house is in," she started, "We just bought the place and haven't had a chance to start renovating. The family before us owned this place for a long time and made some interesting choices." I laughed.

"It's a beautiful house though."

"Thank you, it'll be a lot better once we get a chance to work on it."

Changing subject, she pointed towards an elderly man sitting in the corner. He held his coffee cup with both hands close to his chest, warming himself and watching the room.

"This is Norm, Mike's Dad," she said, "Norm, this is Christian." She turned to me as if to double-check that she had gotten my name right. I smiled and nodded.

His own smile invited me farther in.

"How are you?" he asked with a soft, unassuming voice.

"I'm good, how about you?" I responded.

"I think I'm doing well," he laughed.

Norm was small and hunched, peering over his steaming coffee. His face glowed with kindness, yet a sober spirit hid behind his eyes. Amy motioned for me to follow her, giving a quick tour of the important parts of the house.

"There's the kitchen if you'd like some coffee or a snack. I think Mike is in there right now."

I followed and recognized Mike standing with his back to the sink, talking with another person. They both turned as we entered.

"Hey you made it," he said.

"Yup, I figured why not come and check it out," I said.

And we opened up, enjoying light conversation in sharing where we came from, where we had been, and what God was doing in our lives. They were a faithful family, passionate about God's work, yet relaxed in energy. I felt comfortable with a family that portrayed themselves as open, reasonable and loving folks. Mike spoke with a down-to-earth approach, able to rattle off reasons on why Michael Jordan was better than Kobe, or why the Chicago Bears would have a hard time this season. But he was filled with knowledge of the Word, and I recognized a standard in both Amy and Mike. They both wanted to follow the Lord.

It wasn't long before I found myself with Norm, speaking about my past.

"I spent a lot of time trying to find the answer in drugs and alcohol," I said. "The Lord has definitely brought me out of it, but I still have those moments where I struggle. Now, I'm learning more and trying to figure out what He wants for my life. I want to do His will, and there are a couple different options I have. I'm just not sure what one is the right one."

Norm opened his mouth as if to speak, and then thought better of it and allowed me to continue.

"I don't know what He wants me to do or where He wants me to go. I've got an opportunity to go full-time with a ministry, but I'm just not sure if that's really what He wants."

"The Lord leads us and will provide us what we need," he started. "If you look in Acts, there was a point when the Holy Spirit wouldn't allow the apostles to go to Asia, even though they wanted to. We should seek Him, and allow Him to work in our lives. He'll lead us where He wants us to go, and if He doesn't want us to be there, then I believe He'll direct us down a different path."

I kept pouring out to him, realizing God had given me an elder in the faith who could answer the questions I'd been battling for so long.

"I get torn about witnessing too. I want to witness to people, but should I be going out, telling everyone I know? I don't want to be wrong or disobey," I said.

Norm mulled the question. "Witnessing is allowing the Holy Spirit to open people up. The Lord will give us discernment on when to share, and when to stay quiet. God is the one who opens hearts. We can't do it on our own power. I find it's great to share God's blessings with other people. The more I share with people what God has been doing in my life and the more I give glory to Him, the more He amazes me. It's not about us, it's about Him. We're to focus on Christ."

I listened intently, soaking up all the advice and knowledge Norm had to offer. His words were washing over me with peace, calming my spirit and providing encouragement that God was there and would answer the questions I asked. I had to accept His timing to answer them, not mine.

"What was this ministry you might be joining?" Norm questioned.

I gave him the name, and his brow furrowed slightly, "I think I know which one you're talking about. They were in town not too long ago, right?" he asked.

A nervous twitter ran through me, wondering what he was going to say. His tone had not been in enthusiastic surprise. I wasn't ready to do battle over this ministry, yet I wanted to defend those that seemed to have the truth.

But I couldn't promise myself it was the truth in the right way either.

"Well, that was probably them. I approached the man at the table and wondered what they were all about. We didn't end up seeing eye to eye. I asked him a few questions about what they believed, and he didn't seem to have much patience. I'm not sure they understood the love and grace of Christ," he said.

I wasn't sure whether to come to their defense or to listen to Norm. He admitted he was a bit stubborn when it came to conversations like that, and I knew Massey's heart was in the right place, but I couldn't deny there was an apprehension in me bubbling up from below the surface.

"Pray to the Lord, and seek Him on it," Norm offered. "He'll guide you on what you should do. Just pay attention and be careful."

Warning signs were flashing, and I didn't want to be caught for a fool. I wanted to be a part of a ministry that represented God through love and mercy. Doubts lingered as to whether we as a society had misrepresented what God's love actually meant by leaving out the truth of his justice and might.

But as I watched Mike's family and spoke with Norm, I knew deep down God's love was open and merciful. The sins I committed and the life I lived deserved punishment. God could have easily turned His back on me. Instead, He was providing all kinds of resources in learning about Him. I may have struggled with questions for a few days, but the answers always came and provided a new light in my life. He was with me every step of the way, and would not let me falter.

I left the house at the end of the night with more questions, but plenty more answers than when I arrived. While I still wasn't fully sold on what God was trying to tell me about the ministry, my ears were opened wide.

CHAPTER 19

There were many different transitions happening in my life. My Father provided a church home as well as a family that wanted to wrap their arms around me. I debated what my role, if any, would be with Massey's ministry. Michelle and I were approaching the next stage in our relationship, making sure it was something the Lord wanted us to continue.

At one point, I felt anxious about marriage and relationships, and wondered if I'd have time for these things or if they were meant for me. Out of the blue, I received a text from an ex-girlfriend that had grown close to Jesus in the same time frame as me. She texted, "Do not be anxious about anything, but in every situation, by prayer and petition, with thanksgiving, present your requests to God. (Phillipians 4:6 NASB)" I was amazed. Out of nowhere God gave her a message to give to me. I responded, opening up about my struggles with the relationship choices. She continued, "God's got your answer. Remember you said you weren't sure if you were ready to give up singleness...maybe this is God's way of pushing you in the direction of a relationship."

A few minutes after that text exchange, a sermon came on the radio, delivered by a pastor who spoke phrases about how the Lord is our Father, and He has our picture on His fridge. He loves us as He loves his children, and is joyful to know us. He rejoices in us and sings over us, wanting to be closer with us and bless us abundantly. Peace and happiness washed over me, and I felt abundantly blessed to be alive.

Soon after, I found myself calling Mom.

"I wanted to call and see how you were doing," I started. She had been on my mind, and though we texted, she wasn't getting the attention she deserved. My mom was a patient, loving woman. She gave me space, periodically checking in to make sure I was doing okay, but otherwise allowed me to come to her.

"I'm doing alright," she responded. "Feeling a little tired, but I'm okay. How's everything going out there?" she asked.

"It's okay. I'm not sure what to do about this ministry thing," I said.

"Take your time and pray about it. We just want you to be very careful about making any decisions," she said.

"I know. I'm not sure I even really want to go. I don't want to leave Williston. But, I just want to do what the Lord wants me to do," I said.

"You'll figure it out," she said.

I toyed with the sheets on my bed. I'd been laying in my room, making a round of phone calls to all the friends and family I had been neglecting.

We continued our conversation with the usual pleasantries. Eventually, we said a round of "I love you's" and parted.

I lay back and tried to relax. There was so much going on. A strong feeling of wanting everything in order fought with my desire to trust the Lord. My goal was to find solace in my situations around me, yet He kept me in flux. If only my location, my relationships, my friendships, my career and my health had all been perfect–then I could've been content. Instead, He was allowing it all to flow, and I was battling against the rush of waves.

It was an interesting phase. Growth was happening in amazing spurts, but the situations themselves were anything but easy. The crash course in God 101 had me in a boat on the high seas, and He expected me to allow Him to steer. The battle came down to if my trust was found in Him, or in me being in control.

The more I tried, the more I failed.

But when I let Him plan things for me, I saw Him work. I just had to say yes.

The annoying buzz of a vibrating phone pulled me from church on Sunday. I walked out into the warm summer air, wondering why the Lord was allowing service to be interrupted. I always prayed that no phone calls would come during service. Especially at that moment. I didn't want to work or be on call. I just wanted to be comfortable. I sighed as the order came through. I had to set up some equipment and haul it out right away to a site an hour or two away. Dragging myself to the truck, I hopped in and began the day of work.

The equipment made it to site, and I turned around to return. I came into town, riding the highway and craving a nap. As I passed rows of shops and store fronts, I noticed a homeless man with a shopping cart. I had seen him before, but this time I felt a strong pull to bring him some food. I fought it, wanting to just go home. After a quarter of a mile, I gave in to the press of the Holy Spirit, and turned towards the nearest gas station.

The gas station had a few straggling customers as I picked out a couple sandwiches, waters and chips. I handed my money to the clerk and headed out the door. There in the parking lot, headed towards me, was the man.

He was bigger than I was, walking with a slow, meandering pace. An old winter coat and coveralls wrapped his bumbling frame. He appeared to be unaffected by the August heat, despite the several layers. I swallowed my pride and approached him, letting the first words that came to mind roll out.

"I saw you walking, and was wondering if you wanted some food." I held up the plastic bag. He looked at me and the bag, mulling over the offer.

"Sure," he said. He fumbled to clear a space in his cart and let me set the bag in the fresh spot. I watched him, noticing he spoke carefully. There was a childlike innocence in his voice, and I figured there must be some type of slight mental disability.

"Thank you very much," he said. He stuck out his left hand which was bare, while his right had tape and a cloth glove on it. "Don't shake that hand, shake this one."

I shook his hand, and going for broke, added in, "I felt like the Lord wanted to give you some food, so I wanted to give you that. Has anyone ever told you about Jesus Christ?"

He thought hard, searching back into his memory. "I don't know. I don't think so. I think maybe when I was a kid?"

"Would you like to hear about Him?" I said.

He thought for another moment, then responded, "Sure, I could do that."

I pulled down my tailgate, and hopped on. He meticulously placed his cart under my feet, making sure I was comfortable before climbing up. He was kind and humble, reminding me of a kid who only wanted to help someone anyway he could.

I tried to think of how to begin, and decided to start in John. I read about Jesus, and explained how Jesus had died, so we could have eternal life. I explained that God loved him very much, and if he would accept the gift that Jesus Christ had given, he could be saved.

He listened intently, pointing to certain parts I had read and asking me to read them again. While I did, he would stare off, as though unfocused eyes gave his ears an advantage to hear.

"That's right, that's right," he muttered, discovering some deep memories about what he was hearing. "I remember this. I remember hearing about this," he responded, excitement creeping in. "Wasn't there a part where he healed a blind guy?"

"Yup, there sure was. He healed a lot of people."

"I think I remember going with Mom to church or something. I think I remember this stuff," he offered.

We continued with accounts of Jesus and His interactions with people. The love He showed, the healings, and the teachings.

The man was getting choked up. A man named Elliott, who had been roaming the country for who knew how long, was touched. I could see tears welling up as we spoke. The words that he was loved and the action of someone caring for him affected more than I could have expected. His questions were simple, but full of wonderment at what he was being told.

"Would you like to accept Christ?" I asked.

"Yeah. I think so. I want to," he responded.

We prayed together, his words honest and raw.

"I'm going to call you Amazing Grace," he said after we finished. He followed it with, "Are you an Angel?"

I blushed and kept going, "No, but God loves you so much. I'm going to keep my eyes open for you, and I'm going to keep checking up on you."

I didn't know what else to do. I wanted to bring him home and give him a new life, but had no clue how to do it. I later found out he was doing a little work in exchange for a place to lie down at the car wash.

As we began our good-byes, he stopped me, grabbing onto my arm tightly.

"Wait, I want you to do something," he said.

I turned, wondering what I could do for this man whose heart had been wide open to a person taking five minutes out of his day. He fumbled through his pockets and stuck out twenty-two dollars.

"I want you to give this to the church for me," he said.

I hesitated. I didn't feel right taking the money. I began to deny it, starting to say the word "No…" before the thought flashed across my mind of the old woman who put her last two pennies in the collection for the synagogue. "And He said, 'Truly I say to you, this poor widow put in more than all of them; for they all out of their surplus put into the offering; but she out of her poverty put in all that she had to live on''" (Luke 21:3-4 NASB). I was not about to keep him from giving what his heart was telling him to offer. Reluctantly, I reached out my hand.

"Okay," I said. "Are you sure about this?"

"Yeah, I am. Just please, can you make sure that the church gets it?"

I put the money in my Bible, treasuring twenty-two dollars more than I ever had in my life.

"I definitely will. I promise you," I said.

I got into my 2012, commercial-grade work truck as he shuffled off with layers of winter clothes and a steel cart dragging behind. I offered him a ride, but he declined. I sat alone, ready to break into tears. My throat felt thick and my eyes fought the water works. I wondered, "Would I have been able to give up my last twenty-two dollars for the church?" I prayed over and over asking that he would be provided for.

"Lord, please just provide for him and keep him safe. Please Father, I want to meet him when I get to Heaven. Please Lord," I said trailing off. The words didn't materialize, but the emotion was left strong and definite. My soul cried out, groaning without words for Elliott. I was joyful that he had accepted Christ, but I was heartbroken at his homelessness, as if my own child had walked away. What's my responsibility for him now?

I had approached him hoping to make a difference and left more affected than I could ever imagine.

Chapter 20

Things were starting to fall apart on the farm property. Jason had decided Stephen and I would have to move back into our camper, saying he wanted to have a room for his son as well as his mother, in case she came for a visit. I wondered what had happened to the agreement we'd made. Anger flashed through, but a quick voice reminded me that I had the possibility of being content no matter where I was.

With reluctance, we set-up the camper to be liveable again. We parked it behind a fence next to the Quonset hut, which would shelter us from the snow drifts and winds that were going to come our way in a few months. I fought a bitter response, questioning God as to why His permissive will was allowing us to go back into the wretched camper. I pleaded with Him to provide some better housing. My emotions wavered as I tried to remember that living there was what was being asked, and I needed to be open and trust in the Lord.

However, when a person moves from a small camper with a bunk for a bed into a warm, clean and cozy house, a move back to the camper is fraught with drudgery and bitterness. We crammed our belongings back in, and tried to settle. It took a few days for the electricity to be properly wired from the Quonset to our camper. Finally, the air conditioner whirred to provide a relief from the summer heat.

Back at the house, friction was growing between Jason and the other roommates. He was losing grip with the comfort-zone he had tried to create and delicately balance. I could see a man who was slowly spiraling, with moods swinging and anxiety growing. They argued in the house, and we heard about it in our little space. One side would come to us filled with complaints, and then, as if aware of the complaining, the other side would come to confide in us with their part of the story.

Problems compounded as other people moved onto little patches of land spread throughout the farm in random buildings. One couple living on the other side of the Quonset became disgruntled with Jason. He discovered they were stealing things off the property, and had asked them to leave. He caught word they were planning a reunion with us, only bringing weapons and sour faces.

I received a phone call from him late one night, asking me to come to the garage. I walked in to find several guns sitting on the workbench.

"We need to be on guard," he said as he loaded rifles. "I found out they want to rob us, and they're the type to come in with weapons. They get off on that kind of thing," he said. "but we're going to be ready. I need someone to have my back, and I know I can trust you."

I examined the rifles and handguns. He was speaking, but I wasn't really listening. The guns had my attention. I wondered if this was what my life had become. A prior phase of drugs and threats had thrust itself upon me again. There was carnage in this world, and it came down to defend yourself or die.

In this town, there was little thought of the police or authority. Instead, some people thought about how to keep themselves and their friends safe. Robberies, guns and murder were regular news items in a small North Dakota town. We had heard about murders happening in man-camps and in front of bars. Dangerous brawls happened so often that several friends who grew up in town just quit going downtown. One man was shot in the face with a shotgun five feet outside the door of a strip club. A woman had been kidnapped while jogging in Sydney. The dark cloud of evil was hanging over a land flowing with black gold, and the sleepy farm towns had no infrastructure to handle it.

There were always rumors swirling of what was happening. Those who were in the know spoke of several different crime syndicates, sex trafficking, meth production and the like, which were all events common on tongues but absent from police official's microphones. Some people were there to make a living, while others were there to feed on it.

My fellow Christians and I always spoke of a darkness that permeated Williston. We could feel the evil swirling, and I recognized so many souls caught up in its clutches. The city itself, with amazing hearts leading the charge, was doing its best to clean up the problems and handle the flood of people,.

The worst of the problems was meth. I watched friends become gaunt and torn, hands fidgeting and minds racing from the effects. They spoke fast, they quickly moved. Then the crash would come, and they would disappear for a few days. Most of the time they would sleep, or just lock themselves in their room. It was a dance with the devil, and no matter how they tried, they couldn't get off the dance floor. And several friends had no interest in stopping.

I felt somber as Jason and I sat in a low-lit garage discussing emergency plans and positioning, calls for help and how to take proper shots. The adrenaline, pride-filled tough guy in me was wanting to become a guerrilla warfare expert. The peaceful Christian who had humbled himself before God wanted to live a life dedicated to so much more. Anyone could pull a trigger, but it would take more courage to stand in front of that gun and speak the truth of God to the soul behind the barrel.

After going over battle strategies, I slunk back to the camper with my guard up and collapsed onto my bed. I prayed, trying to find protection. My rifle slept next to me, ready to defend Stephen and myself if anyone came through that door.

No one did. The darkness lifted, and the sun rose in the sky. Later Jason said he'd struck an understanding, and had warned them we were all on guard. He knew the element of surprise was not in their favor, and without that advantage, they had changed course.

I have analyzed the situation many times after. My questions delved into whether it was a Christian thing to protect the ones I loved, or was I giving in to a human instinct of not trusting God? I wondered if protecting property was necessary with a gun and ammo. I wondered what God would think if I had shot someone in defense of my life and Stephen's. I knew better than to tread lightly with those questions.

The havoc of a wild life was taking its toll on Jason. He would disappear for a week or two, come back for a few days and leave again. Many times his excuse was that he just needed to get away. We knew the drugs were taking over, and his health was suffering. It is only so long a person can keep the power of drugs at bay, and sooner or later they consume the body and the soul. He already had heart problems, and the drugs were only exacerbating the issue.

He wasn't the only one with the heart issues either. One day I was driving for work in the late afternoon. My phone buzzed, and I saw Stephen's name.

"Hey man, what's up?" I asked.

"Oh, well…I've got a question for you," he said. He fought to stay calm, but the nervous flutters and breathing pushed through.

"What's up?" I asked.

"Let's just say, if someone happened to have a heart attack, is there anything besides the hospital that they can do?"

"Who the heck had a heart attack?" I asked, jamming the words hard into the phone.

"Manny," Stephen said.

"Is he okay?"

"Yeah, he's okay. I guess it was just a small one, but he doesn't want to go to the hospital, so I was wondering if there was something I can do. It's just him and me at the house right now," Stephen said.

"Well, I know heart attack victims are supposed to take Bayer aspirin, but he really should go to the hospital. If he's refusing to go, get him some aspirin and plenty of water. Make sure he sits down and tries to calm down," I said. "You sure he's okay?" I asked again.

"Yeah, he's just really weak. I guess he's had a couple already, and this one scared him."

"I can't imagine why," I responded, sarcastically. "I'll be home in a little bit, but see if you can get him to go to the hospital."

Manny didn't go to the hospital, but he seemed to be okay. We later spoke about it and he admitted he had survived several heart attacks.

"This one scared me," he said.

"We never know when we might go," I responded.

"That's true."

"Do you know the Lord?" I didn't want to mess around. Missing previous chances had put the onus on being up front.

"Oh yeah man. I definitely believe in God. He's the reason I'm still alive. I've been through a lot of stuff."

I relaxed a little bit, but the thoughts of his lifestyle and what effect God had really produced on his life troubled me. But, I knew better than to make my own conclusion of knowledge that was God's alone. After all, what could some say about the life I had been living while professing to being a Christian?

"You should start coming to church with me," I said.

He nodded, "Yeah I should. I need to get to church. I've been thinking more about God lately," he said. His eyes searched the room as his emotional walls started coming down. There was a deep sadness within, pushing to get out. He fought to keep back the tears, but I could see red rims around the bloodshot whites of his eyes.

"This last one really got me thinking. But I'm okay with dying. I just want a few more years at least," he said.

"If you ever want to talk, I'm here," I said. "I don't know all the answers, but I want to help any way I can." I searched for the right words, wanting to give him the truth of God and quote some scripture, but nothing came. I sat listening, sympathy rising.

"I been through a lot, and lived a long life. I know God's there; he's seen me through it all," Manny said.

He was in his mid 50's. A mumbling Texan who had come to work the oilfield, and had plenty of life experience to back him up. Much of his life had been spent with cars and drugs, but he was worn down now. Manny loved art and music, many times spending hours looking at art on his Ipad while sitting on the couch in the living room.

"Never know when we're going to go," he trailed off.

"Nope, we don't," I responded. I had no words, so we sat as I tried to radiate as much love as possible.

Manny and Jason's episodes were just the start of the health issues.

My mom let me know that she was going back to see the doctor and have tests done. She'd been dealing with exhaustion and some pain that wasn't adding up. Concerned that perhaps the cancer had come back, she and Dad went to get her checked out.

Our fears were realized when the tests came back positive. She had spots of cancer in her liver. The doctors said she would have to undergo radiation and chemotherapy, hopefully stamping out the cancer once and for all. As any victim of cancer will tell you, it's a life-long battle. Just because it was destroyed once, doesn't mean it wouldn't come back.

I wasn't sure how to handle it, but I felt comfortable with the situation. She told me, and I responded with confidence.

"Well, I guess we'll just have to beat it again," I said. She spoke with a similar confidence, but the exhaustion was creeping in.

"I know. I'm just tired. I don't know how I'm going to be able to do another round," she said. A tiny crack worked its way through my stronghold of confidence.

"You can do it Mom. You did it once, you'll do it again," I said, mustering up courageous speech I hoped would motivate both of us.

"Thank you dear," she said. "We'll see what happens. I don't know what I'm going to do with work. I don't think I can handle going through this again while trying to get all my work done."

"What about the others in the office?"

"I only have one full-time person now, and she's doing the best she can, but there are some things she just doesn't know how to do."

I hadn't heard Mom without a solution before. It occurred to me there wasn't just a physical wearing of the body, but these were the emotions of one who wasn't sure she had enough strength left. Her armor was cracking, and—

It hurt.

It scared me.

It brought questions I didn't want to ask.

"I'm praying for you Mom, and I know God has a plan," I said, trying to comfort myself as much as her.

"I know. I trust Him, and I know that He's with us," she responded.

There was a firmness in what she said as opposed to an acceptance of truth. It was a foundation being constructed upon. She was refusing to give up the high ground to fear and doubt. She refused to be pushed back by the realities of this world. Instead, she was setting her flag on the rock of her faith and salvation, no matter how she felt. She refused to allow the enemy his chance to pull her away.

"God loves us, no matter what," she said defiantly.

"I love you Mom. I love you a lot," I said.

"I love you too honey," she responded. I sat back, assuring myself she would be okay. This would be just another battle, and she would come out of it stronger.

I made her promise to give me updates, and we hung up. An unexplainable calm came over me. The Lord had her. While she would be fighting a vicious battle, it seemed just another step in her daily life. She would go get treatments, and then sleep and try to push back the nausea. Dad would keep my brother and me updated, she would text when she could, and I would continue to send both of them Bible passages. The routine was set, and the players were ready. Deep within each player, though, was an exhaustion that lingered. It was draining the first time around, and we all felt the dread of having to go through it again.

I relied on the faith that God was in charge, and refused to dig any farther. I sent my passages and called when I could. I asked Mom how she was doing and prayed for her every night. Beyond that, I tried not to talk about it. I asked for prayers from my small group, and let a few other people in on what was going on. For the most part though, I stayed quiet.

As the tough issues were springing up around me, one aspect of my life was turning out to be a wonderful blessing.

CHAPTER 21

Michelle and I concluded we needed to meet in person and decide if a relationship was realistic for us. We both knew there was only so much that could be said over a phone, and what was the point if we got together and didn't click? The agreement was made. I'd ride the train out to meet her, we'd spend a few days together and figure out what we were—just friends or more.

The days crawled. I'd look at my calendar, wondering how many more days God could insert into the wait. The time came, and Stephen drove me to the train station. I climbed aboard and settled into my seat, staring out the window at a darkening sky. The train strained to roll forward, and I watched out my window as we pulled past the lights of town. We glided beyond the large Halliburton industrial park and soon were swallowed by darkness.

Much like a dog taking off with a broken leash, I felt free. The tether had snapped, and I was running away, ready to play with other free spirits. I dreamt of the day I could board the train with a one-way ticket, leaving behind the dreary dust and industrial buildings for something with forests, rivers and lakes. My heart longed to head homeward, and the disconnect from the fields was invigorating. I added up the time. One year down, one to go. Could I make it another? The adventure had been exhausting, but my life brought more stories in a single year than most people do their entire lives. I wasn't sure what was going to come next, but the future was tugging.

It wasn't where I wanted to live the rest of my life, and the train ride confirmed that with every railroad tie crossed. The clack of the rails brought thoughts of those who had spent their lives hopping trains and bouncing from town to town. The itch was coming on again and it wasn't easily scratched. I calmed the thoughts back down, reminding the puppy inside me that there was still a year left of my commitment and a lot of life to live. God was producing my path and He was the one with wisdom. He had given me a wild ride so far, but I could honestly say my faith was leaps and bounds above what it had been just a year before.

The train carried us through the night and stopped periodically in Eastern North Dakota and on into Minnesota. Sleep evaded like a rabbit, darting away as soon as I thought I had it caught. I turned and curled in my seat, wishing I could lie down.

Soon the sun was peaking through thick trees, glancing off the small lakes we passed. Little cottages dotted the lake shores; like serene paintings caught out of time. The train window framed a picture of escape, beckoning me from the pumping units and iron derricks. I put my head against the glass and watched eagles swoop in to the surface of the water. They struck their claws, pulling up into the sky with a fresh catch squirming between sharpened talons.

I pushed away the lingering cobwebs of sleepiness, allowing my heart rate to quicken at the thought of meeting Michelle face to face for the first time. As the train crawled closer, the anticipation came to the forefront. The count down was happening and I was wishing it could skip a few numbers.

The call for Columbus, WI came over the speakers. Bodies staggered to grab baggage and gather belongings. I had jumped up a few minutes prior, packing my things in a rush to be ready. As soon as the train began its leisurely roll into the station, I was up and in line. Anticipation had replaced my nervous flutters. I felt calm, yet enthusiastic about finally meeting her. It all felt quite natural.

The line of passengers spilled onto the platform. It was a small brick station, fitting a tiny WI farming community perfectly. The fading red bricks below my feet interlocked, veins of cracks reaching outwards in every direction. I took the step and peered around the platform. Uniting loved ones paired off, giving warm embraces and kisses. Families packed luggage in cars, and others waved to people getting on the train. I scoped around, not seeing the long curly brown hair or bright blue eyes that had adorned the pictures sent.

I fought depressive thoughts, believing there must be a good reason.

Maybe she was stuck in traffic. Or perhaps we had confused the arrival time. I walked around the train station, my bag in one hand with the other stuffed into my jacket. The train idled at the stop. A few stragglers were standing around, eking out the remnants of nubby cigarettes. A gazebo sat in front of the station on a small section of grass. I put my bag on the picnic bench and slumped down. My eyes scanned the people for familiar features.

The train started crawling eastward. I craned my neck to watch the engine as it worked to leave me behind. After the train cleared the station, I turned my head back to look again. I saw a cascade of curly hair. I grabbed my bag and jumped up.

The woman disappeared, and I picked up my pace, hoping to catch another glimpse. As I rounded the corner, the back of a girl who appeared to be in her early 20's stood motionless. She scanned the vacant platform, her back still towards me. I walked closer, hoping I'd finally found my missing person.

She turned and instantly lit up. I dropped my bag and stepped quickly, throwing my arms around her. We hugged tightly, warming each other and not wanting to let go. I picked her up, squeezing and swaying back and forth. We stepped back to gaze at each other. She was even more beautiful in person than her picture was. I sank into her eyes, not wanting to look anywhere but at her.

"I wondered where you were," I said. Joy filled me, happiness moved with each word.

She laughed, "I was on the wrong side of the tracks. I went to the coffee shop and had to wait till the train left."

"Wait, coffee shop?" I asked.

"Yup, would you like some?" she asked, smirking. I grabbed her hand and started towards the shop. A little burst of caffeine sounded like the perfect medicine. A seventeen hour train ride was tough on a person, especially considering the lack of sleep.

We climbed into her car after scoring a cup of coffee and began the trip back to her abode. I talked at a furious rate, not quite listening to what was coming out of my mouth. She rode the verbal surf, allowing me to expel the waves of language and expend some of the steam that had built up.

"I'm sorry. I'm not normally this talkative," I said. "I guess this is what happens when you're cooped up on a train for seventeen hours with no one to really talk to."

"It's fine," she smiled. "It's funny."

"Well, I'm glad I can be amusing to you at least," I laughed.

We drove into Madison with the sun hovering low in the sky. I peered up at the tall buildings and compact houses. Large letters perched atop mini skyscrapers, spelling out the name of the firm or bank that occupied the space. Modern grocery stores lined the roads while shops clustered together in strip malls. It felt good to be in a bigger city. People milled about on the sidewalks as mopeds chaotically flew in every direction.

She turned the car onto a residential block and cut the engine. We walked towards a large house, set on a street of similar two-story houses.

We headed in and were greeted by several of her roommates. The house was home to seven college aged girls. My mind exploded at the thought. I wasn't sure if there were seven college aged girls total in Williston.

We said our hellos, and they asked their standard questions. How was the train ride? What's it like in North Dakota? Whose your favorite backstreet boy?

"What would you like to do tonight?" she asked.

I nestled my bag into a corner next to the couch where I'd be sleeping. The girls deserved credit, trusting some guy from a Christian dating site to live with them for the next few days.

"I was thinking we could go out for a nice dinner," I said.

"I've got an idea of what we can do before that," she responded. Curiosity hooked me, and I gladly agreed to follow.

We left the house, turned the corner and walked a short journey towards the lake. Madison is on an isthmus, located between two small lakes. Michelle decided I might enjoy getting to see some trees and water, after she'd been told many times how much I missed the lake back home. Our conversation was jovial during the walk, as our fresh faces enjoyed the autumn air. The leaves were turning bright yellows, reds and browns before lazily floating to the earth's surface. We came to a dirt trail, following it as it led deeper into the woods. Bits of blue peeked through the trees, as the trail eventually led to a large lake. On the right side of the lake was Madison's skyline, while across from us were homes sporadically placed among the trees. We sat down on old sandy stones and gazed peacefully at the water. The waves lapped the wooded shore and a chill in the air brought our bodies closer.

We took turns scratching each others' back, silent against the serene backdrop. She knew me well. I was happy, content to be sitting next to a wonderful girl who was dedicated to providing health, wellness and joy to others.

That night we chose to go downtown. The capitol building and various government structures poured light onto the night scene, posing as the center focus of the city. After checking out a few restaurants, we found one that had a waiting time under an hour. They took my cell phone number to call when the table was ready, and we headed back into the night. Soon, we found ourselves in front of the water again, huddled together from the cold blowing off the lake.

While we still had a lot to learn about each other, there was definitely a spark. Our conversation had been smooth the entire night. Nothing felt forced or awkward. Jokes were cracked about various sights and happenings. The conversation wound around and delved into God's plans for our lives. I was happy that we had spent so much time communicating from miles away. There had been no pressure to be physical, and the boundaries had given me time to get used to God's desire for abstinence outside of marriage. It was refreshing to leave that complication behind and to bask in the most wonderful aspects of getting to know a kindred spirit.

Soon we ventured back towards the restaurant, deciding that a wait inside would be better than shivering outside. My phone vibrated as we stood at the entrance, and with a broad smile, I held it in view of the hostess. We sat down, pulling out the menus.

"So do you enjoy living here?" I asked.

"Yeah, for the most part," she said as she scanned the room. "I'm a country girl at heart, so hopefully some day I can move back to the country."

I couldn't help but smile and bob my head, "Me too. I don't mind the city, but it's definitely not some place I want to live for the rest of my life. I like the idea of being completely self-sufficient and living off the land. I'd love to raise some animals and grow my own food." I paused. "But whatever the Lord wants me to do, I'll do," I said as an afterthought.

"Same here. I just want to go where He wants me, but I hope it's to a farm," she laughed.

The waitress appeared out of nowhere, interrupting the flow of conversation. We gave our orders and waited till she had everything she needed. As the waitress walked away, I continued, "So have you had much of a chance to disciple with your roommates lately?"

"A little bit, but, a couple of them are dating guys they say they wouldn't marry. I'm not really sure what to do. I'm not sure whether to say something, or to just love them."

I leaned onto the table. The low lighting danced shadows across her face, accenting the soft, delicate features that mesmerized my concentration.

"Isn't it loving them to point it out? Especially if they've already said these aren't the type of guys they want to marry?"

"I suppose. They say how they want to marry Christian guys, but a couple of them are with guys that aren't really followers or don't care about it. I guess it's just sad because I see my friends giving in to stuff that they normally wouldn't." She looked towards her water. Concern weighed on her heart, bringing the corners of her lips downward.

I couldn't help but relate to the issue. I had lived the double life. I had gone the route of trying to be a Christian in name, yet living a life of my own standards.

"I don't want to be judgmental," Michelle continued. "I was really judgmental when I first got saved, and I don't want to be that way again. I used to see that kind of stuff with my roommates and called them out on it."

"That's not necessarily a bad thing," I responded.

"The way I did it was," she laughed. "I want to speak truth, but I want to do it in love. I want to say it with grace and mercy."

The comment stood strong. The balance between truth and love rested on an even plane in the statement.

I poked at my food, wishing I'd ordered what Michelle had.

"I'm sure you can do that. You just have to come to them humbly," I said. I hesitated, then added, "although sometimes a stern rebuke is necessary."

"That's true, I just wish I was better at it."

We continued sharing our past struggles, already knowing most of it from emails and phone conversations. We had spent hours on the phone, not sleeping till two or three in the morning.

I felt like I knew her inside and out, making our dinner communion smooth and enjoyable. Instead of boring introductions and shallow discussions, we were able to delve into the struggles of our daily lives.

"I can't deny that I'm a little worried about my mom," I said. A look of concern came across her face.

"Are the treatments not going well?" she asked.

"They're going okay, but they're wearing her out. I know God is with her, and she knows it too, but it's just hard to watch. It's hard to not be there for her."

"We could go to MI for a day if you wanted," she offered.

I hesitated at the thought. I wasn't sure why, but I didn't feel ready to go see my parents yet.

"No, that's fine," I said, settling on a halfhearted conclusion. "I'll do that next time. I'd rather just focus on getting to know you right now." It didn't sit right. I was assuming another trip could be made.

"I pray for her a lot. It's just hard to see her going through this. It was hard enough the last time," I said.

"I'm sure it is. How is your dad doing?" she asked.

"He's okay. He's doing his best to take care of her and be there. I think maybe this situation has woken him up a little bit to what's important in life. So I do praise God for that," I said.

Her hands remained still in her lap, but her shoulders leaned forward.

"They have the house up north and all," I said. "She has wanted him to retire for the past few years, so they could spend time together, and I feel like now maybe he's seeing the point."

"Hopefully they can go up there again some time soon," she offered.

"I sure hope so," I said. My mind wandered to memories of relaxing with Mom. We would watch movies or hockey games with pizza on our plates. Her puzzles sat like trophies on the floor upstairs, each one fastened together during every stay at the house up north. I missed home.

Michelle's eyes sparkled and a smile grew on her face. I snapped back, basking in the glow. Her countenance was comforting as it dispelled the turmoil beneath the surface of my heart.

Leaving was hard. We were falling for each other fast, and it was difficult to embrace knowing we'd soon be separated. I saw tears swimming in her eyes, and my arms longed to pull her onto the train. I wished the backside of the train could roll west while our hands held fast, knowing we could spend the rest of our days together. I climbed the steps, then waved from the window of my seat with a drooping hand. A smile was forced as the train shuddered forward.

A chain had been tightened around my neck. The train was pulling, forcing me to become an oil salesman again. A vacation on the sandy shores of a new relationship was fading with the reality of semis and the smell of grease. I settled in for the long ride and tried to do some writing. When the writing fell flat, I began to read. When the reading went stagnant, I listened to music. Nothing was satisfying the loss of this exciting new phase in my life.

So I prayed, thanking God over and over for the beautiful gift He had provided.

"Lord, thank you so much for Michelle," I thought. "She is an amazing woman that you've blessed with a heart of gold. I'm not sure if she's the one you want me to be with, but if she is, I will do my absolute best to take care of her. She is above and beyond what I could imagine. I thank you so much for the opportunity to get to know her and to at least have this chance at meeting her. I don't know how you have it planned, or how it all works, but I do know that if you want us to be together, that we'll be together. Please just guide us. Show us your way. Not our will, but your will be done."

I sat back as a smile crept across my face. God had introduced me to one of His special creations.

CHAPTER 22

"Do you have a few minutes?" Edward asked.

"Of course, what's up?" I responded. His face was solemn and searching. We sat in my truck, fresh from a full meal at the same place I had met Ray and Mark. The food jostled for position in my stomach.

Edward had come from the ministry Massey worked for. A few months prior, he had called, wondering about work in Williston. He had said it was his time to leave, and he wasn't happy with what was going on. He was hired as an electrician, and he took over a friends rental lease who was moving.

Jealousy teased me when we moved his furniture into the apartment. It was a great place for a wonderful deal. I had been in town longer. The situation at the farm was not getting any better and I had been praying constantly for a new place to live. Yet God blessed him with the apartment. I did my best to squelch the uprising within. I asked Him for forgiveness, and determined to have faith that I was in the correct spot.

After all, Edward had spent twelve years of his life trying to serve Jesus to the best of his ability. Years were spent on the road, as he traveled thousands of miles to stand in front of supermarkets and gas stations. He had given the gospel to thousands of people and spoken with thousands more. His life had been sacrificed for the purpose of serving a ministry. He had been worked to the bone and was now ready to get out of debt. He wanted a place to live. He wanted a life. I swallowed the self-centered emotions and renewed a sense of support, giving all I could while he was settled into town.

Now he was helping me.

"So, I don't want to steer you away from the ministry," he began, "but I feel like I have to warn you to really think about it before you join."

After what I'd witnessed, I wasn't ready to join. I hadn't received a phone call yet, which helped the process. I had concluded to wait on the Lord, feeling He wanted me to be patient.

"Why's that?" I asked.

"Just some of the stuff that happened to me and some of the things that happened to other people like Massey," he said. "Brian used his gift to control people. There was one girl he decided I should marry. It was crazy because I told him I didn't want to marry her, but he kept telling me that it was the Lord's will. He would yell at me in front of everyone, saying that we weren't following the Lord's will. I was really embarrassed, and so was she."

My jaw sank lower as he continued.

"He made me take on the rent of a house I had no ability to pay for," he said, letting all that had been pent up flow out. "I didn't have the money since I spent it all for a trip he wanted us to take. I paid for the gas. I paid for the hotel rooms. And when we came back and he wanted me to rent a house for 900 bucks a month. And when I got it, he decided it was supposed to be a ministry house. Yet, he had always told us that guys and girls weren't supposed to live together." Edward was burning. The fuel of bitterness and memories were shooting the flames higher as he let loose of everything that had been held in.

"But that didn't matter. He told me God wanted me to get the house, and if I rejected it I was rejecting God."

"Wow," was all I could muster.

"And you should have seen how Massey got treated," he said.

"I noticed a little bit of it on the trip. It kind of seemed like he was a scapegoat." I said.

"It's terrible. Everything was put on Massey, and when something went wrong, then it was Massey's fault."

Edward fumed for another twenty minutes, telling of the treatment other people had received from Brian as well. Marriages had been split and people were made to feel they had lost out on salvation for leaving. Edward himself had been told he wasn't in God's will for leaving and that he was just chasing worldly possessions.

I was convinced God didn't want me to be a part of such a situation, and I was thankful He had allowed me to be so hesitant about whether to join or not. I was happy He had made me wait, and even more thankful He had put it on Edward's heart to warn me.

When Massey found out, there wasn't as much thanks.

"I just want to say I don't appreciate that Edward went to you instead of coming to us about all of this," Massey began. I wondered how he had found out about our conversation.

"I know it wasn't your fault, but it's just that Edward has one side of the story. He never came to Brian about all this. And honestly, when someone comes against the ministry, I feel like they're coming against me."

I listened, not quite sure what to say. Massey was defensive, subconsciously aware of what it meant for his name by association. He was dedicated to Brian, and desired to think the best, but in personal conversations, Massey had shown a glimmer of understanding. As quick as the concerns started to come to the surface though, he buried them deeper. I saw his pride with a shovel full of dirt, standing over a hole that held truth that was tearing Edward up.

Over several more conversations, Edward continued to share his heart. It was hard because I truly loved Massey, but it was a struggle to support the work he was doing. His heart was to do God's work, so I did my best to support him with hope our Father would take care of him. I'd sit on the phone late into the night, conversing with Massey over the struggles he faced in the ministry.

"I'll do anything the Lord wants me to do," he'd say. "And He knows that. I'll do anything for Him."

"And He sees that," I would respond. "He will bless that. Your heart is in the right place."

I questioned: What do I say to him about how I really feel? What do I not say? I prayed each night that God would release him from the ministry. I called out with exasperation in my voice, praying the ministry would stop hurting people and be brought in to non-existence. I wanted Massey out of it, and I wanted a humble turn around for Brian.

It wasn't that I wanted to see them destroyed. I desired to see them all renewed and to truly experience the love of Christ as they ministered it to other people. The line between Christ's love of grace, humility, and mercy, and speaking the truth without apology couldn't be under a guise of love, but needed to be real. As I saw it, there was a drastic differences between how the people in the ministry were treated and the love my church families spread. I did my best to preach these things to Massey.

"Christ loves us, and He died for all of us." I said. "He had grace and mercy for us, and we need to grow relationships with people. It's through those relationships that we can show His love. It's forgiveness and support that speaks volumes. People hear truth all the time."

"I know, you're right." he said. "And I'm doing that. That's what I focus on is relationships. When I call people, I want to know how they're doing. I want to know what's going on in their lives. I would do anything for them, and anything for you."

"I know you would," I said. "I know you love me, and I love ya too."

"I definitely do. It's hard. People aren't donating. I'm behind several thousand, and I don't know what to do. I don't know if I can do this. I don't have money for rent. I don't have money for bills right now."

"You need to have faith," I responded. As cliché as it sounded, faith was what he needed to hear. "The Lord is faithful, and He will provide everything you need. Just you wait and see. He'll give you what you need," I said.

Massey was quiet on the phone for a second. "He's always provided. He's always given me what I need, even if it's at the last possible moment. I'm just so sick of this roller coaster! I get so tired of living under this pressure and this stress. I just want to have a quiet life." He paused, then finished with, "Like you."

"I know." I decided to take advantage of the opening, "Have you ever thought about leaving? You don't have to be in one ministry all your life to be doing the Lord's will. There are other things to do in His great creation."

"I've thought about it. I guess if He wants me out, He'll provide the door."

He was right. God's timing was His timing, and I wasn't about to force it.

My Father's timing became clear in my own life not long after. Conditions deteriorated rapidly at the farm. Jason disappeared without telling anybody where he was going, Stephen hadn't worked for a month or two and was struggling to get back on the employment train, and I was going insane living in the camper. The electric company came on a Thursday to shut off the power. We found out Jason hadn't been paying the electric bill, and the farm owed over 800 dollars. Manny convinced the electric company representative to come back in a few days, so we could figure something out.

I was bitter, sick of all the problems and confusion that had continued on property. Jason would change the rules depending on the day, then become upset when people weren't falling in line with his thought process. There was a chaotic undercurrent flowing through everyone. People were tense and anxious, finding no rest on the island above the oil-sea. I tried to call Jason, hoping to find a solution, but got no response. I was sick of the mess, so I went to the group of campers down the hill and called a meeting. I explained the situation and asked if we could all pool some money together to at least get the electric bill paid in order to make sure the power stayed on.

One of the other renters called Jason and let him know what was going on. He texted me, telling me to deposit the money in his bank account so he could straighten out the mess.

"Screw that," I said to Stephen as we sat in the camper. Dark skies draped over us in our well-lit tube as the cold fought to find its way in. "There's no way I'm forking over more money when the deal was that we paid rent, and he took care of the bills. It's not my fault he doesn't have the money to pay it. I have an idea where that money went, but of course it's our job to pick up his mess."

Stephen was quiet. My anger was fresh and flowing, bursting from the wounds of a volatile living situation. The edge I walked was painful, and I wanted out of the mess. I craved solace.

On Friday morning I slumped with a huff into my chair at work.

"How's it going?" Darryl asked.

"Not so well."

Darryl and Don turned to look at me, acknowledging that this was not a normal response for me to give.

"What's up?" Don asked.

"Well, if either of you happen to hear of an apartment or anything—please let me know. I'm so sick of what's going on out at Jason's. We had the electric company come out yesterday wanting to shut the power off because we're 800 dollars in the hole." I said, venting fumes. "I'm sick of it. I'm done."

"Sorry to hear that. I don't know of anything, but I'll certainly let you know if I hear of something." Don said.

Darryl nodded.

Saturday morning Darryl called.

"So have you found anything yet?" he asked.

I wasn't in the mood to talk about it, but felt the conviction to amuse him.

"No, not yet. Still looking right now."

"Well, my wife and I talked last night, and we want to offer you our apartment," he said.

They were living in a nice house they had owned for over a decade. Where was this supposed apartment?

"My wife manages an apartment complex and we had one set aside in case we sold our house before we moved. We talked it over and want to offer it to you," he said.

I couldn't believe my ears.

"It's a two-bedroom, one bath apartment. It's 700 dollars a month and you cover electricity and heat," he said. "Is that something you might be interested in?"

"Of course! I would love to. I'll have to talk it over with Stephen, but as of right now, yes, we want it."

I rushed in to the house to tell Stephen. His face showed no excitement, no joy at the prospect of moving off the property.

"I don't know, I mean it's more expensive. We're only paying 250 dollars each here," he said.

"But this is an apartment," I pleaded. "We'd have a bathroom, laundry, a kitchen that we could cook in. Besides, I think there's still a propane leak in there."

"I don't know, I don't think there's a leak," he said, trying to divert the subject.

"I know there is because I almost died from it."

My temper was rising and the eagerness was being extinguished by frustration. I wanted to leave the property for the comfort of a sanctuary. Thirty minutes later, God ended the argument for me.

Manny summoned us to the house, saying Jason's mom wanted to meet with everyone. We gathered in the living room, not sure what it was all about.

"My husband and I have been talking, and we've decided that we want everyone off the property. We know what's going on here, and we don't like it. We know there are drugs and partying going on, and honestly we've decided we just want everybody to leave."

She broke the news with kindness, understanding it wasn't all of us who were involved, but it was apparent the easiest step was to clean house.

"We know Jason's involved in all of it too," she continued, "so we're hoping we can get him some help."

We were somber at the news. Our time of camaraderie and enjoyment was coming to an end. The house had been a home, and in that time we had all had our fun, but I was celebrating inside. God had provided an apartment only thirty minutes before eviction.

"When do we have to be out?" I asked.

"Not today, but we'd like everyone out by Monday if possible," she responded.

Not much was said. The guilty parties knew who they were. The indulgences were catching up with the culprits, although I wasn't above anyone else. I had spent my time and made my mistakes. There was joy in the knowledge that Stephen and I could be free from the temptation that sat around us.

I called Darryl, excited to take hold of the offer presented.

"When can we move in?" I asked.

"As soon as you want," he responded. "You guys just have to come down and sign the lease and it's yours."

"Thank you so much Darryl. You don't know what this means. I had been praying for an apartment and you called thirty minutes before they kicked everyone off the property. God definitely provides," I said.

"Yes, He does," Darryl said. "Glad we could help you guys out."

There were too many times in my life where the thing I wanted was not the door God opened. His timing never lined up with mine, but His plan was never faulty. Even though I had been through so many hard situations, He had grown my faith exponentially.

Sermons had set the foundation.

I was learning fire and passion from Massey.

I was learning love and mercy from Norm.

I was learning how to be studious and balanced from Mike.

Patience was being taught through my living situations.

Faith was being grown by the upheaval on my path.

Christ was growing my prayer life.

Christ was giving me enough to keep going when I needed it.

I was being stretched, strained, pressed, pushed, compacted, forced and torn, but I looked to the Lord, and He was by my side.

I was learning the hard way, that faith required a person to battle doubts. It wasn't easy living on faith. The truth was, I had to bear down and accept, that even though I didn't like a situation, God knew what was going on and was taking care of me. I didn't like the camper, but it offered shelter. I didn't like the living situation, but I was, for the most part, safe. I had almost been pulled into a damaging ministry, but I held onto the faith that if God wanted me there, He would show it. There had been deaths, guns, drugs, violence and threats of job loss, and through it all, my faith and reliance on God had only grown. The fires had sparked and raged, then died with His solutions.

My questions about the ministry and about where I was living washed away, leaving behind the glowing embers of smaller struggles left to be solved. But as that blaze disintegrated, a spark was preparing to burn my whole forest down.

Chapter 23

The road curved to the left and I followed. A row of pine trees stood squat and solemn to the right of the bending highway. I was just north of Stanley, coming back from dropping off equipment. Sunlight washed over the fields of harvested land. I looked to the clouds sitting in the sky, wondering what it would be like to float along in wisps of white.

My phone rang. I glanced at the screen and dread wrapped around my heart.

"Hey Dad," I said.

"Hi Christian." His voice lowered. "Um…I talked to the doctor today, and he said that you should probably come home."

I had feared the phone call would come. I wanted to deny it would ever happen. Mom hadn't been responding to the treatments like we hoped. Instead, they left her exhausted and in worsening condition.

"We took your mother to the hospital last night. Her heart rate is really high, her blood pressure is down. There's swelling in her legs and she's running a fever. They're not sure why, and they can't seem to get it under control."

I listened as the sea was beginning to pour over my little row boat that I thought had weathered all the storms. Dad was struggling to keep going, but I was proud of his composure.

"So you should probably go ahead and come home. When do you think you can?" he asked.

"I can be home tomorrow night. I'll book a flight tonight." I said.

We exchanged reserved "I love you's".

Immediately I called Stephen's mom. My Dad had kept his family up to date, and she had texted me with the offer to help if I needed it.

"Would you possibly be able to find me a flight to come home?" I asked.

"Oh honey, I'm so sorry. I will look right now. When would you be flying home?"

"As soon as possible," I said. "I was thinking tomorrow morning."

"I'll get right on it and let you know," she said.

A few hours later she called while I was on site. I had been called out to a work site that night to help solve an equipment situation. As soon as I finished, I called her back.

"I found a flight," she said.

"Okay. I have to ask a big favor," I said. "Would you possibly be able to book it and I'll pay you back?"

"I already did," she said with a fragrant sweetness. "I had to call the airline because it was the last seat, and she did everything she could to get you on the flight."

"Okay. How much do I owe you?"

"It was 800. But we want to pay it for you," she said, aware I was going to argue.

"No. That's not necessary. That's too much."

"No, we want to. Please, we want to do this for you. This is the least we can do."

There was no fight in me left. I allowed her to book it, and began to plan on how to get to the airport in Minot, which was two hours away. I called Stephen as soon as I hung up with his mom.

"I need to ask a big favor," I said.

"My parents told me what's going on," he responded. "I'm really sorry. What can I do?"

"I need a ride to the airport. My flight leaves at 5:30am."

"No problem," he said.

We agreed to stay up and leave around 1:30am. I got home, quickly packed a bag and waited anxiously. We made the trip to Minot, and soon I was in the air flying over grand expanses of green, brown and blue. The little plane landed in Minneapolis and I followed the stream of people pouring into the terminal. With a few hours to spend before my connecting flight carried me home, I found a seat to relax. It was a thick, comfy chair. I sank in.

Throngs of people moved about in the terminal. They were walking each direction, living out their daily lives. They glanced at their watches as they rushed to prospective gates. They ate their burgers at terminal restaurants. They lived their little lives in their little spheres. And here I sat with a dying mom back home. I was 26, and about to lose my mom to cancer. She was only 56.

An immediate pang of bitterness pulsed quickly through my body. These people milled about living their lovely little lives while I sat here enduring blow after blow. I saw wide smiles and heard laughing voices. They're so lucky.

The thought struck me, "How many people do I see each day who have this type of trauma in their life? Plenty of people lose a loved one too soon. How many of them do I pass without realizing they're going through what I'm dealing with now?"

The truth softened the hard edge. The bitterness gave way to sadness. It was sinking in that I was one person out of 7 billion, and many of them had suffered tragedy. We were all going through some type of personal pain in a world that had given itself over to sin. Our fathers had chosen Satan over God again and again and again. We scorned when we should have forgiven. We murdered when we should have fed. And now I was having to deal with an imperfect world. I was about to lose the woman who had brought me into this world and loved me more than any other person had on the globe.

I fought the choking sensation. I wasn't ready to let her go. I saw in myself an inherent flaw, but wasn't about to accept it as a weakness. But, the tenderness that was cleansing my heart dried out. Quickly, my attitude hardened again. Even though we all had our issues, my need to wrap up in a blanket of self-pity was more important. So others had seen family members die and gasp for air. They had walked in on jilted lovers sharing intimate times with strangers. They had been fired, beaten and maligned. So what? At that moment and at that time—I was the center of my universe. My pain trumped all others.

God understood my pain, and He didn't dismiss it. He had watched His innocent son beaten and brutalized by the same people He was trying to save. Despite knowing those atrocities, it was hard to leave my grief behind. Wallowing in self-pity was addictive, expressing itself in a masochistic sense that I couldn't let go. Deeper than the self-pity lingered a calm and acceptance that felt perverse to entertain.

The hospital walls smelled clean and sanitized. It was a beautiful building with lobby sections furnished with modern furniture cast in light browns amidst tan carpet. There were little sculptures, and even a waterfall ran down the wall in one section. I noticed the waterfall slid down the tile wall, and continued through all the floors. I watched it dropping, into the unknown, but with the present knowledge that it didn't end where I stood.

Dad escorted me, showing the twists and turns necessary to arrive at Mom's room. We came to a room like all the others, except for a different number plate on the wall. I took a deep breath and peeked in. She was lightly sleeping and looked peaceful. Her hair was stringy and thin, her face gaunt. She had lost a lot of weight since I had last seen her. She took a shallow, noisy breath in, then exhaled quickly. I sat down next to the bed and put her thinning fingers in my hand. I massaged the back of her hand, gazing down at a face with still of recognizable features, mixed with proportions that were unfamiliar.

Her eyes fought to open, and she turned her head just enough to see who held her hand.

"Hey Mom," I said quietly.

She gained a little strength, showing miniscule glimpses of the bright woman who had had enough energy to put up with a kid who never stopped talking, a kid whose imagination jumped from wars in the forest to spaceships in the living room.

"Hi Honey," she said, a smile pulling into view.

I kissed her and then moved to kiss her forehead.

"I love you so much," I said.

"I love you too." And as though her frail body had decided to fight me, her strength gave way.

"I'm sorry, I'm just really tired," she said, eyelids moving to close.

"No, it's fine Mom. Get some rest."

After a few minutes, Dad and I stepped out with the doctor. The doctor was kind, but professional. I could sense her heart was soft, while knowing a certain level of business had to be maintained.

"Where are we at?" Dad asked. He was respectful and quiet.

"Unfortunately, her body is reacting to the chemo and radiation, and that's why she's having all of the symptoms we're seeing. After doing more tests, we've found the cancer has spread throughout her body, and since we can't stabilize her…we can't give her more chemo or radiation." I was surprised at how well Dad was taking the news. She continued, "We can make arrangements for you with hospice if you'd like."

"How long do you think it'll be?" Dad asked.

"A few days, maybe a week or two," the doctor offered.

We thanked the doctor for her help and waited until she started walking the other way. Dad pulled me in for a hug. I clung tightly for dear life. My dad's eyes were watering, and his face was fighting to remain stoic.

"I love you Dad."

"I love you too."

Soon we were united with my mother's cousin Jane and my brother. Jane and Mom had been best of friends. They loved each other deeply, and we had given up just calling her Jane for as long as I can remember. She had always been "Aunt Jane" to us. I was thankful for the family that surrounded me. My dad, Aunt Jane, my brother Shane. It suddenly felt like we were fighting the elements as a close-knit team. All the dross of previous battles or disagreements had been burned away, leaving one unified group. There was unity in misery.

I called Michelle that night to give her an update.

"How are you doing?" she asked. Her voice was overflowing with compassion.

"I'm alright."

"How is she?"

I grimaced at the question as my desire to emotionally seclude myself raged.

"The doctor said she has a few days to maybe a few weeks. I guess it's the chemo and radiation that's causing the fast heartbeat, low blood pressure and all that stuff, but because the cancer has spread throughout her body....she's in a catch-22."

Michelle whispered, "I'm so sorry."

"It's okay. God is with her, and honestly, I don't want to see her suffer. Heaven is just an upgrade. It's us who are less fortunate."

And I believed that. It wasn't just a statement that sounded true on the surface. I didn't throw it into my repertoire and repeat the mantra until I intellectually agreed with it. Instead, the truth welled deep within my heart. I couldn't explain it, but there was a peace residing. The tears hadn't flown yet. There were moments where it hit and I felt grief, but I wasn't distraught. Most of my emotions were settled in the goodness of God. I could feel Him close. And I was just thankful I would have a chance to say good-bye.

"Do you want me to be there?" Michelle asked. "I want to come be with you for this."

"Normally, I would fight you and tell you no, but honestly; I just don't have the energy," I said. "I think I need you here."

"I'll be there," she answered with a thick sweetness. "When would you like me to come?"

"Whenever works for you. We're moving her to hospice tomorrow morning."

Michelle arrived, and we immediately went to see Mom. They moved her into hospice, and we settled in along side.

The room was quaint, with wood floors and off-white walls. The decorations were homey, welcoming visitors to find a slice of solace in the middle of the emotional turbulence.

Dad hadn't left Mom's side. He occupied the chair next to her bed for hours, holding her hand and gazing at her resting figure. Aunt Jane would come to sit with Dad or get him to take a five minute break. When Michelle and I arrived, almost everyone was there. Shane and his girlfriend Ella, Aunt Jane and Dad. Mom's brother and his wife were on their way.

I saw a glimmer of activity in Mom when we came in. Her eyes fought to open, and she turned to see us.

"Mom, I want you to meet Michelle," I said grasping her fragile, long fingers. They trembled in my palm.

She struggled to speak, but could only muster the strength to mouth the words "It's nice to meet you." I kissed her on the forehead, repeating the words "I love you." I determined to speak them as often as she might hear.

Drooping eyes stared towards the ceiling as she mouthed "I love you too. Very much." Soon Mom was asleep again, succumbing to the enemy that was tearing her apart inside.

Dad walked in and immediately tapped Michelle on the shoulder and led her out of the room. I looked to Ella with shock. What was he going to say to her? My dad had been known to be brutally honest, especially in times of stress. Not knowing Dad's demeanor, I worried for Michelle.

"What is he going to say to her?" I asked Ella.

"I don't know," she said, her own eyes wide.

A few moments after they had left the room, Shane entered.

"Did you see Michelle and Dad out there?" I asked.

"Yeah, they were talking. Why's that?" He settled in next to Ella on the couch facing me.

"Do you know what he was saying to her?"

Shane looked confused.

"No, why?"

"Dad pulled her out, and we're wondering what he's saying to her," I said. Ella nodded.

"I don't know, but they were smiling."

A sigh of relief escaped. Michelle worried about being a burden. I wanted her to be a part of the family, and to know she was supposed to be there. This was her first time meeting my family, and the circumstances were unfortunate, but to me that made the difference. If she was willing to be there in my time of need and to not shrink at the situation despite not knowing anybody—then she was the caring and considerate girl I wanted to have.

They came back into the room. Michelle came next to me and put her arm around my waist. Her eyes fell upon Mom with sadness. Her caring instincts were kicking in full force.

The next time we were alone, I asked what happened with Dad.

"So what did he say to you?" She looked surprised at the question. "He just said that he was thankful I came to support you like this, and that I was always welcome. He said I was part of the family and if I needed anything, to just ask."

It caught me off guard. My dad had never approached a girlfriend of mine like this, let alone during a family crisis. I was also amazed at the timing. After a struggle with whether it was appropriate for her to be here during a personal family crisis, Dad swooped in and made it his priority to make her feel welcome. God had worked through him, opening his heart and his arms to assure both of us she was right where she was supposed to be.

Soon my uncle arrived to round out the group. We took turns holding Mom's hand and spending our last quiet moments with her earthly presence. Dad continued to mill about the hospice center without much sleep. He would take cat-naps in the chair next to her bed and eat in the cozy kitchen down the hall. We had to argue with him to take a few hours and go home. He finally succumbed, deciding he would go home, take a shower, try to sleep and come back. It wasn't long before he was back by her side, feeling guilty for having left.

The dynamic of our family was changing before my eyes. While Mom was still on earth, I could sense that her last mission was to unite the family under a single banner. For so long, my relationship with both my dad and brother had been distant. We were chaotic electrons, flying every direction at their own independent speed, but the crisis of losing our nucleus was sobering. She had held the men of her family close by her love and compassion. These were three men who were all fragile in their own way, strengthened by the unique love she lavished on us indiscriminately.

For the first time, we were learning how to strengthen each other. My dad would sit me in the study a few rooms down, speaking openly about how he was doing. Dad had always given the expected answer to questions, but when I asked how he was doing, he responded, "I don't know. Not real well." It was raw, and drew me closer. I could feel my own grief, but had no idea how to relate to a man who was losing his best friend—perhaps his only true friend. They had been married 35 years, and she was the only one he had opened up to. His single source of true emotional release was dimming, and for the first time my father was letting me in to his world.

I didn't have many words to give, but I offered my ears and my love.

It was similar with Shane. We had always had a tenuous relationship. It was brotherhood built more on what we didn't have in common than what we did. A distant communication kept us up to speed on the other's life. We loved each other, but only in a way brothers could. Now we were connecting and sharing the same vulnerable, open emotions that I was finding with my dad.

And in the midst of it all was Mom. She had no clue that she was the sole reason for the nourishment of these relationships. Aunt Jane and Dad connected. Aunt Jane and I grew deeper. Uncle Chris became integral, offering both hope and outlet. I could see on Uncle Chris' face the pain in losing his sister. It wasn't just losing his sister, but I could read on his face the tiny regrets that lined my own father's face. Regrets of communication loss. Regrets of time not spent. Pain of misrepresentation and credit not given. Our chairs circled her bed. At times there was laughing and joking, while other moments no one spoke. For those few days, our world fit into that room.

Saturday night we were all there. Gospel music played quietly on a little stereo while we all sat silent. I was staring into space towards Mom, watching her chest heave with labor and reflecting on my own regrets. I thought about how careless I had been with my time. My mother had invested so much patience and time into me, yet how often did I take her phone calls for granted? Often my friends would comment on my tone, asking why I "sounded so down and sad" when I talked to her. To be honest, it was just the way I was. I loved her deeply, but felt myself take her presence for granted.

Thoughts of not visiting enough bombarded me. I had only been 45 minutes away for several years, yet I made a trip once a month or so to see them both. Each time I carried home a bag full of laundry, they would comment, "Came home to do some laundry and get a free meal?"

I would laugh it off saying, "Well, and maybe to see you guys too." It was all in good fun, but now the regrets were pressing. I could have spent more time at home. I could have invested so much more time with her.

As the regrets prodded, the thoughts about a post-Mom future came forward. I wondered what it would be like for us as a family. The biggest worry was Dad. My fear was he would become a hermit and give up on life. They had never been the social types, instead looking to each other for connection. I wondered if Dad might just shrivel up without her.

Her chest heaved up and down, gasps for breath emanating from her slack jaw. Dad was asleep in the chair near the window while my brother held her hand, his head bowed and his mind deep in thought.

I watched her.

I love you Mom.

Her chest sank. I waited.

CHAPTER 24

"Shane," I said. He stared into space. "Shane." He looked up. I nodded toward Mom, and he looked. He got up and shook Dad.

"Dad, wake up."

There was no movement in Mom's chest. I had watched the last vestige of air escape her body, releasing a bound soul to Christ.

Dad jumped up, pushing his way to her hand. By this time we were all awake, focused on the bed. We watched in silence, allowing Dad to be alone with her in the moment. He kissed her, his head to hers. I watched him tear up, not wanting to let go. He pressed harder in and then released. We each took our moment with her empty body and said good-bye. In succession, we each held a lifeless hand and kissed a relaxed forehead. Dad stepped back, saying to himself "It's not her anymore".

I walked around the bed to Dad and Shane. They were hugging while tears flowed. Their arms opened up and welcomed me into the middle. I buried myself in between them and cried. I was surrounded and safe, finally allowed to let the emotions break. After a few moments, I regained my composure and stepped back. I wiped the tears from my cheeks and accepted that our time on earth with her was over.

We stepped out of the room while the nurses situated her body. A light wave of relief washed over us. There was sadness, but it was tempered by knowing she was no longer feeling pain.

After saying our last good-byes, our family—minus one—walked into the cool November night. It was past 2:00am. I looked up to the sky and the stars were clear. They twinkled and sparkled as the moon watched from its position above. I took a moment to take in the beauty of God's creation. Michelle stood by my side, locked arm in arm. My eyes dropped back to the parking lot where everyone was giving hugs and getting into their cars. There was an oddity in just leaving, but I knew this was the natural order of it all. After a person dies, the living keep moving.

A day or two later, I met with Aaron. Every once in a while we would come together while I was in town. Something prodded me to call him. I needed a good solid discussion with the man who had seen me through my high school years. We connected in a town near by at a little coffee shop beside the highway. The chairs were big and inviting, much like the airport in Minneapolis. Instead of observing travelers, I examined myself.

"I know it's kind of a dumb question, but how are you doing?" Aaron asked.

"Confused," I said.

"How so?"

"To be honest, I feel like I should be more torn up. It's weird, but I don't feel the grief that I think I should. Then I get frustrated, wondering if I'm callous or selfish because I feel this way," I said.

"You feel peace about it?" he asked.

"Yeah, I guess you could call it the peace that transcends all understanding. It's just that, am I allowed to feel that way? I cried for about ten seconds or so with my dad and brother. That was it. I don't know…I'm torn."

"You're allowed to feel that way. As Christians, we know that when a believer dies, they're getting something better…"

"An upgrade," I added.

"Exactly. So don't get down on yourself because you're not torn up like you think you should be. Everyone is different in how they react, and there is no right way or wrong way to grieve. Don't doubt your love for your mom," he said.

"Thanks. You hit it on the head. I guess I felt like I was doubting that I loved her like I should," I said.

"Don't. I know you loved her. She was a wonderful woman, and you should be very proud. And I know you are," he said. "Just let God's peace reign in your heart. You'll have those times of grief along with the times of feeling fine about it."

"I do miss her. I miss her a lot. I keep wanting to text her and tell her this or tell her that. Then I have to remind myself 'Oh yeah…'"

"How's your dad doing?" he asked. That was the million dollar question.

"I don't know," I said. "I've been surprised at his honesty. Usually, he doesn't say much and doesn't really tell me what he's thinking, but he's been upfront, which I'm thankful for. I was afraid he'd just push it all down. When I've asked how he's doing, he tells me that he doesn't know, or that he's not doing well with it."

"That's good," Aaron said.

"Yeah. I'm worried about him after the funeral when everyone leaves. I'm worried he'll curl up in his shell and give up on things. He and Mom didn't have a whole lot of friends, but at least we have some family close by," I said.

"He may surprise you," Aaron said. "And if he's got family around him, he'll be okay."

We continued the conversation, jumping from topics like *The Lord of the Rings* to where we both had been in the past few years. It was a refreshing couple of hours, something I needed to encourage the weaknesses. The time at home had been a barrage of emotional peaks and valleys, culminating in a defining moment of my life.

Aaron made random appearances in my journey, sliding up next to me at just the right moment. He would give advice, encouragement, scripture or ears to hear when I needed them most.

"I want you to know that you set the foundation for my life," I said. "I know I was all over the place when we were meeting while I was in high school, and I was all over the place in college, but you were a huge influence, and I credit you with providing that foundation I was able to go back to. I just want you to know how much you meant to me, just being there and caring. It means the world, and I love you."

Tears were piling up as his eyes reddened.

"You don't know how much it means to hear that," he said. "I love you too, and am so proud of you. You've grown into such an exceptional guy, and I'm always interested to hear what's going on in your life. I just…I'm honored. I'm thankful the Lord put you in my life," he said.

"I'm so thankful He put you in my life too," I responded.

Our meeting ended too soon, and I knew the next hurdle to face was the funeral itself.

I was asked if I'd like to give a eulogy. I debated. Did I desire to stand up during the funeral of my mother and speak about a woman for whom words could never be adequate? Or was it more honorable to take my last chance to speak? I decided to give a eulogy and so did Shane.

The suit I bought for her funeral was snug but looked nice. I kept thinking, "She would have liked to see me in this." I was pestered by an urge to text Mom about the funeral, my suit or Michelle. I had to remind myself that no one would pick up at that number anymore.

Services were held at the same church where I had met Aaron. Mom and I had attended the church in hopes of finding a new family. Little did I know I would be ending my time spent there without her. The funeral began and a friend of the family was the officiating pastor. He was kind and personal in his description of Mom, relating to the full sanctuary of her love for everyone. Everybody spoke of the unconditional love she held for all with whom she came in contact. I was satisfied with the turn-out, glad to know that she had made an impact on that many people.

My brother spoke his eulogy, connecting the importance of a life spent here on earth and what Mom meant to him. He beautifully intertwined threads of philosophy, faith, real-life anecdotes and truth.

After he finished, I got up to speak. My eulogy was as follows:

"As some of us stood around Mom's bed, acting as the well-wishers to a soul bound for Christ's presence, I recognized her final contribution to the ones she loves. Through this whole process, we've gained new family members, reconnected with old ones, initiated others and strengthened the bonds of all. And I know she would have had it no other way.

Many people have said to me how they looked up to her, what a role model she was to them and what inspiration she provided. To me, all of this was a given. Mom raised me in a home filled with love, understanding, strength, care and faith. But to be a witness to the fruits of her beauty with all whom she met will never escape me. I hold a new love and respect for her, realizing now just how deep and wide the roots of her impact really have grown.

The shell she has left behind is merely a reminder of the grace and mercy a lifetime of love and faith can create.

I will miss her deeply, and everyday I will do my best to carry on in the ways she taught me and expected of me. Now, I know she expects me to grow with those left behind. To provide compassion to all, to look for common ground among us, and to follow in Christ's footsteps as closely as possible."

I sat down, keeping the tears at bay. Dad squeezed my knee. Many people approached after the funeral to give their condolences.

I greeted them with hugs and thank yous. Their thoughts and reminiscing of how she affected them brought warm smiles.

One friend approached me and commented, "I've been to a lot of funerals, but this one was by far the best. I want you to know it really touched me." It put joy in my heart, fulfilling the hope that there had been someone who was touched. My prayers had been that the Lord would use her death to save someone. Even if it was just one life, it would be worth it. I continued to pray from the day she died that I might get to know at least one reason she wasn't healed.

God was faithful in that request.

I returned to Williston hoping to just blend back in. My plan failed, as people immediately rallied around me. My small group at church was amazing, as well as a few other families that opened their homes. I received several invites to be adopted for Christmas day. Various families showed me what church was truly about. It wasn't about sitting in the pew on a Sunday listening to a preacher speak (my pastor was fantastic—a man of integrity and passion). Church was about the family. I was learning that when I served the church family, I received ten times what I gave. We as a flock were to help shepherd each other, not look to the pastor to do all of the shepherding for us. Our pastor demonstrated this in his leadership, allowing the Spirit to freely flow in a gentle and respectable manner.

Life was returning to normal…until right before Christmas.

I pulled into the church parking lot on a cold night. A light snow was topping the few inches that had already come down. I wanted to park in back, where the lot was larger. Light poles on top of concrete bases that were three-feet tall cut the pavement spread in half. I carved a wide turn, lining up the nose of my truck to drive into a spot. As I made the arc, a car cut in front of me. I looked to see where he had come from, and I was think—

Wham!

My ears rang. A thick dust hung in the cabin of the truck from the deployed airbag. It took a few moments for my senses to return before realizing there was a large light pole sitting atop a concrete base a foot closer to my windshield than it should have been.

Curse words flew out. I looked around the truck, assessing the damage. Ego: hurt. Pride: broken. Fear: rising.

Oh, and the truck was in rough shape too. A windshield that had been prepped by stones and chips was now full of spider-web cracks. The front end was caved in, pushing the radiator up into the engine block. I was amazed at the damage done by the 15 mph impact.

I pulled the truck over to the side of the church, hoping no one saw the ridiculous mistake I had just made. A tremor ran through my hands as I dialed my boss.

"Don?" I asked.

"Yeah Christian, how's it going?" he asked. He sounded chipper.

"Um, not real well." I wondered how I was going to explain this. "I was pulling into the parking lot at church, and hit a light pole."

"Okay. How much damage did you do?" he calmly asked.

"It's pretty bad."

"Is it drivable?"

I tried to turn the key.

"I don't think so, It won't start back up."

He sighed, "Alright. You're going to have to call the police and file a report, then call a towing service. Put it in the back and we'll figure it out tomorrow." His calm approach felt like a caring father saying, "it'll be okay".

I called the police to file a report. The police officer was professional yet understanding. He filed the report, issued no ticket, and helped me find a towing service. The tow truck driver was kind as well, providing a sliver of comfort by saying "this type of thing happens" and by keeping the mood light.

We parked the truck in a row of other company trucks, facing away from the yard so that no one could see the damage.

When the CEO Chris found out, I was immediately called into his office. I hoped to wait to discuss the matter with management when Don was there, but Don was out sick, and our division's secretary called Chris to tell him I had crashed a company truck. He walked me into his office and shut the door behind him. I sat, somber and humble.

"What in the heck were you thinking?" he started. I knew from previous matters he didn't have a strong love for me, and frankly I wasn't thrilled with him either. I could tell by the raising voice that this would not be a conversation like the one I had with Don.

"I was making a wide turn in the church parking lot. There was a car that came across my front, and I was looking to see where he was coming from and hit a light pole on a cement base," I said. My eyes shifted from him to the desk beneath his hands.

"And why didn't you tell anybody?" he asked, anger building.

"I did. I called Don, and I filed a police report," I said.

"He's not here," he continued, "and you parked it so that no one would see? When were you going to tell someone?"

I didn't have much I could say. Even though it had only happened the night before, he was right, and I knew it.

"You must have been going 30 or 40mph!"

"No, I wasn't," I said. I deserved the chewing out for what had happened, but I wasn't about to let the facts be changed.

"I was going maybe 10 or 15 mph."

"There's no way the airbag would deploy going that slow," he said, shaking his head.

"I swear to you, it did because I hit perfectly square! I promise, I was only going 10 or 15mph."

"And you expect me to believe that when your windshield looks like that?" he argued. The shaking head and heavy sighs frustrated my pride, when I already felt horrible.

"It had a ton of cracks in it already," I responded. He shook his head again, muttering to himself.

"If you would quit being an idiot and just slow down," he grumbled.

My voice rose up with confidence, "Not looking? Yes, that I admit. It was a terrible mistake made because I wasn't looking, but I was not going too fast for the parking lot. How am I supposed to go 30-40mph in that parking lot with a wide arc?" I wasn't about to be made a bigger fool.

"Well, we're going to have to talk to corporate. I don't know what to do with you. I should just fire you, but we'll see what they say. Until then," he paused, "You're on leave."

He motioned for me to get out of his office.

"I'm really sorry, I really am," I said as I got up.

There was no response.

I got a ride to get drug tested and walked home. It was -10°F out, but I didn't care. It was time to think. My Christmas break was going to be spent wondering whether I still had a job or not.

The tension of not knowing my fate beat at me. I doubted myself and my surroundings. I felt that for the past year I had been brutalized by a life in North Dakota. So much for an adventure. I had wanted one and had gotten much more than I bargained for. My excitement wasn't a shoot-out at the OK-Corral or a search for buried treasure. This adventure hurt.

I wrote in my journal the day after: "I may be losing my job. Last night I totaled my truck in the church parking lot. I'm on leave till after Christmas. Lord, I'm lost. I praise you and worship you, but I swear I've been getting hit non-stop. Lord, I trust you. I know you will provide. It's just hard to have joy when I feel so much shame and embarrassment. Honestly Lord, I trust your plan and will, but I'd almost rather be done with the company. But your will be done. You are a great and magnificent God, I'm just a lowly stupid soul. Father, please help me. Please take care of me. Please have mercy on me. This one hurts. I'm beginning to feel like Job. I've crashed my truck, lost my mom, had been stuck on the farm and have had many faith struggles. But, Lord, I will do what you ask. If it's to stay with the company, I will. If it's to work another job, I will. If it's to move, I will. If it's to stay, I will. I will follow You and I love You. Just please Lord, don't let go of me. You've seen how incompetent I am. I don't take care of myself. I pray you would give me your heart, your joy, and your wisdom. Lead me. In Jesus' name, amen."

I began praying about ministry opportunities. A nagging hadn't ceased with the demise of my connection with Massey's ministry. Instead, Michelle and I wondered if maybe this was God's way of freeing me up to go into seminary. I prayed, asking for God to show the direction He had in mind. We wondered aloud together whether I would move if I lost my job or try to find another in Williston. We concluded that if I did indeed lose my job, then I would go to a seminary or Bible college in Wisconsin. Websites of various schools adorned my browser, and a few had made the top of my list.

Both of us were praying. Both of us were seeking. Most of all, both of us were doing our best to be patient. The waiting game was unbearable though. I would lie on the couch, staring at the ceiling for long periods of time, drifting in and out. My thoughts would follow rabbit trails past Wonderland and back again. Doubt and fear crept in, seeking to unhinge me and force me to try and solve the problem alone. Then faith would reemerge with the words of Scripture, pushing me back into trusting the Lord. I wanted to trust Him with all my might, yet the little dark voice was working overtime.

"He's not going to take care of you on this one," it said.

"Abraham had to wait and was patient. Look how he was rewarded," I said.

"What if you get to Wisconsin and that wasn't His plan?" it said.

"Lord, please don't leave me on this. I'm so sorry. Please have mercy and lead me where you want me," I pleaded.

"What if you get fired and can't get another job out here?" it said.

"Job lost everything, yet gained twice as much after," I said.

"Maybe you should just try and get on a rig. Then you'll finally make some real money," it said.

"God provided me this job and this blessing. I will not turn my back on that," I said.

The voice retreated, waiting for another opening to make an attack.

Christmas came and went. One family invited me over for Christmas dinner. They provided food and warmth, love and care. Afterward, the gentle husband offered his spare pick-up until I found out what the decision was.

"Drive it as long as you need it," he said. He was a quiet man, peering through thin glasses atop a stubby nose.

"Thank you so much. I appreciate it beyond words," I said.

I loved the family, and my heart was filled with joy that I had such caring people in my life. God shone through them, providing the little joys that made me feel wanted.

They weren't a family who went on treks to the middle of Africa in order to build orphanages for blind children. They didn't house twenty poor people a month or heal the deaf. God ministered through them in their quiet, humble, daily gestures. I was blown away by their love and giving, as nothing of theirs was off-limits if needed and their home was always open. I prayed the Lord would bless them like they had blessed me.

CHAPTER 25

The chairs were a stiff, cheap plastic. The kind of chair you might see in an elementary school, only sized for grown-ups. I shifted, coming to rest my chin on my hand as my elbow propped me up on the table. Norm was hunched over his hamburger patty with whole wheat bread. He ate cautiously, savoring each bite.

I found comfort being around him. He was a self-confessed rambler, and that was fine by me. He would talk and talk, suddenly checking the time and realizing he was late. Then he would talk a little bit more.

But he pointed everything back to Christ. I would watch him search his Bible high and low for the right scripture to give. When he was opened up by the Holy Spirit, the words would become more defined as he spoke. They would grow and strengthen, like a flower opening to the spring rain. His eyes would brighten while his hands directed the symphony of words. I found counsel in our talks and love in his heart.

"How are you doing?" he asked.

"Eh, not so well," I responded. He waited. "I'm just having a tough time right now. I feel like everything is piling on at once. There's just been one thing after another, and now, right after my mom dies, I crash my company truck. I feel so embarrassed."

"Mistakes happen," he said.

"I know. I just can't believe I was that stupid. I guess it's hard because I'm doubting what the Lord has for me, and wondering where I'm supposed to go and what I'm supposed to do."

"When my wife died of cancer four years ago, I really had no clue what to do," he said. "I battled about why it happened, and, of course was attacked by the enemy over it, but God was with me. He would remind me in scripture of that fact, or messages from other people. When I was feeling defeated, He would speak through someone to raise my spirits. The Lord was never far."

"And now," he continued. "It's a testimony. I don't know how many times I've been able to connect with others who have lost a loved one, or been able to share what the Lord has done in my life because of it."

He pulled out his Bible, sliding pages with nimble fingers to find a passage. He came to rest on 2 Peter 1:12-13 (NASB), "Therefore, I will always be ready to remind you of these things, even though you already know them, and have been established in the truth which is present with you. I consider it right, as long as I am in this earthly dwelling to stir you up by way of reminder."

His hands folded over the Bible, "I read this back to myself, because sometimes Satan attacks me, and I think 'Oh, they don't want to hear this again.' or 'This won't matter to them', but then I read this, and I remember that it's good to remind people so that when I'm gone, the testimony of what God did in my life is still there," he said.

I took in all he was telling me with hope that it would give rest to my soul. I felt a little better, knowing he was right. Norm had gone from alcoholism and deteriorating relationships to a man full of the Holy Spirit. Sometimes his zeal tweaked some people's nerves, but he didn't mind. He kept his eyes forward and gave as much love as he could to everyone he met.

"Thank you very much," I said.

He had listened carefully while I vented, allowing me to let it out. His words lifted me back up, renewing my strength and pushing me to keep going. He had a way with helping people discover what God was trying to say.

The running joke amongst Mike and his family was that if you went out with Norm, you needed to budget extra time. Norm would invariably run into someone he knew every five minutes. And, I found this phenomenon to be true. No matter where we went, there was someone who would perk up and call out his name. His demeanor never changed. He was always kind, hugging his Bible or his notepad much like he had his cup of coffee the first night we met.

Norm wasn't just giving God to people in coffee shops either. He had begun a daunting project, which started as a vision God gave him to make a "home for the hurting". It would be a center that was open day or night, offering counsel as well as community services to all who walked in. It would be Christ-centered, but not church run. The center was to include helping the homeless, but not limited to that effort.

Through the providence of God, an old building sandwiched between a photography shop and a jewelry store had been donated. The building was crumbling and torn. The second floor was see-through to the first floor in places, while rain dripped through the ceiling. And much like Nehemiah who rebuilt Jerusalem, Norm had his detractors. The neighbors were less than thrilled with the idea of Norm's project, never missing an opportunity to say why it couldn't or shouldn't be done.

He introduced me to the plan, and asked if I would be willing to come on board to help. As he took me on a tour through the building, I wondered at the extent of the project, but I knew God was bigger than both of us. The crumbling brick didn't matter. The torn up boards were no problem. The leaking roof could be fixed. If God had given him this vision and brought about the confirmations both of us had experienced—then it would be done on God's timing.

Norm was determined to do it on His time instead of our own. Often I would have to speak truth to Norm when Satan would rain doubt upon the project's feasibility. We had nothing to worry about since this was Christ's future home for the hurting. One confirmation that stood out was a story Norm often told. One night he was sitting in the front of the center at a fold-out table looking out onto the street. He was reading his Bible when a man entered. The man looked up towards the ceiling and around the vast space, eyes sparkling. He questioned, "Is this a homeless shelter?"

Norm recalled the look on his face, "He looked as though he wasn't seeing the building as it was. He was amazed at how nice the place looked. He just glowed with joy at the place as if he were seeing the finished product. I truly believe God opened his eyes to see the finish product so I could be encouraged." I held onto that story, using it to lift us up when the doubt attacked in full force. There were moments when I would text verses to him or call with some words.

"Thank you for that," he would respond. "You don't know how much I needed that. I was just being attacked with doubt, and then God comes through you to remind me that he's with us."

I learned not to wait for a booming voice, but to act upon a whisper from within. It was apparent that if a verse came to mind along with a thought of Norm, then sending it was probably the best course of action. Often I would get a response back saying, "That was exactly what I needed to hear." or "I just read that too."

After the first of the year, I received a phone call from Don.

"They're going to let you come back to work." I breathed a sigh of relief, despite a small part of me wishing I could be on my way to Wisconsin.

"I take it corporate decided they weren't going to fire me?" I asked.

"No, they're fine. What are you doing right now?"

"Not much."

"Ok. Let's meet for some breakfast," he said.

We met over breakfast and coffee. Don asked what happened, and I gave him the time-line of events.

"Well, you probably should have reported it right away."

"Yeah, I was waiting for you, but that was the wrong move."

"It's alright. What's done is done. We all make mistakes," he said.

I was thankful for him. No matter what happened, he was even-keeled. He saw through the issues of each day and understood that one event did not necessarily shape a lifetime.

"Everyone makes mistakes. I've made all kinds of them," he said.

"I've definitely made my fair share. I just really hope I don't make any more like this," I said.

"Well, if you do, we'll deal with it when we come to it," he offered with a laugh.

I wasn't sure I could survive my commitment of two years to the company, but with Don's open and humble face showing me support, I knew could keep going.

"How are you doing with everything?" he asked, shifting gears.

"I'm alright. Living life a day at a time," I said.

"That's all you can ask for," he said. "Well, we should probably head back to work. You ready?"

I pulled up from the booth and threw on my jacket. I wasn't ready to head back to work, but it was time. My mission was to fly under the radar and just finish out my term. The truck accident had worn my pride down to that of a humble servant. I had approached the job with an over-confidence in what I could do, but within a few moments, was reduced to a man who wanted nothing more than to leave each day without making a mistake.

We left the diner in Don's truck and crept up to speed. Semi-trucks with oversized tank batteries and pipe pulled through gears as we passed on their left-side. I gazed out the window at all the traffic. It was thick as sludge, pouring down the highway with clouds of exhaust drifting towards the sky.

"How's your dad doing?" Don asked.

"He's surprising me," I said as I continued peering out the window at the big tires that rolled viciously over the highway next to us. "I guess he's been going out to dinner every week with my uncle and aunt, and he's been making sure to get out of the house and do stuff. I'm really proud of him."

"That's definitely good," Don said.

"Yeah. I wasn't sure how he was going to do with all of it, but I've been impressed."

Don pulled his truck into the parking lot and sat for a moment before turning the key.

"You'll have to drive Darryl's pick-up until we figure out what to do with yours. They might just total it," he said.

"Really? Man…" I said. I was still embarrassed to show my face, and a little more shame would pile itself on if the truck was totaled.

I grabbed the keys to Darryl's truck and fired it up, waiting for the motor to blow some heat to the cabin. Darryl and his wife had decided to move to Florida, leaving at the beginning of the year. He had been itching to trade in the company and North Dakota for the capital of baseball spring training. Despite starting out as his replacement, we became friends. The company never got rid of him; instead they put me into a vacant hole sadly left by Wes when he passed away suddenly. I never told Darryl the truth of why I had been hired. I didn't see the need, so I settled on just getting to know him.

He was kind and helpful, opening his heart to me when we talked about God. There were things I prayed that our conversations had some effect. I knew a change of location to Florida might provide enjoyment for a little while, but it couldn't provide inner contentment. My prayers were that he would come to understand the contentment that comes with an active relationship with Christ.

Once the truck situation died down, I turned my attention to the next whirlwind of tension on my horizon. The storm had been building far off in the distance, and as I tried to repair things on the homestead, it built speed and proceeded to tear apart my own dwelling.

Tension between Stephen and me had been mounting in the past couple of months. We were not seeing the even balance on several issues, and there were underlying currents that prevented a return to normal. The issues of distrust between us were painful and sore, hurting when they were brought forward.

Many nights I drove home from work, praying out loud.

"Lord, I don't know how much longer I can handle this. I'm trying to love him and trying to be supportive. But what can I do? Is this one of those situations where I turn the other cheek? What do you want me to do Lord? I'm going nuts and I just want to move on. I want to have a quiet life for a little while."

But a voice whispered, "Wait. Be patient."

I fought that voice, but continued to take a deep breath, and renew my love for him. There were times after an argument, he would offer to make dinner and be quite the conversationalist. I appreciated those times and was as pleasant as I could muster. My hope was positive reinforcement, but soon, the happy moods gave way to shut doors and days without talking. I was watching him spiral, not quite sure what to do or where to go.

"Is Stephen okay? We haven't heard from him in a couple of days," his mom texted me.

"Yeah, he's okay. I haven't heard much from him either. Next time I see him, I'll tell him to call or text you," I responded.

The conversations with his parents revealed the extent to which his shell and resistance were expanding, separating him from the world. My patience had worn thin through the past year, creating a dichotomy between two men who wanted solidarity, yet were pressed together in one apartment. We both knew our collision was inevitable, but lied to ourselves that the fireworks would happen.

My nerves were shot with my living situation, so I spent my time away as much as possible. When I wasn't in the weight-room, I was helping with the youth group at Assembly or going to Mike's church. Norm and I were meeting regularly and I was spending a weekend every so often with Michelle.

The rest of life was good, but it always felt like there was one thing separating me from perfection. I prayed and begged for Stephen and me to find a commonality, so I could rest from the whirlwinds. The strange part was that most of the issues happening in a radical life in a Boomtown, wasn't from being covered in oil or burning on a exploding rig. The fires being set in most lives was from the temptations money and freedom brought. I watched this happen in my own life as well as those all around me.

In the midst of it, I made sure I was at church every Sunday. One Sunday I sat down in my normal row, and noticed a young man a row behind me who was about my age. He looked kind enough, and the Spirit encouraged me to speak to him. We'd shaken hands and smiled during the greeting, but that only strengthened the pressing on my soul. The pressure remained throughout the service. I tried to fight it, but concluded I would act at the end of the service, considering saying yes to God was a lot better than saying no. The words of the pastor blurred between my ears, making no significant impact as my mind churned with questions about this young man.

Immediately after service, I shuffled with the rest of the people filing out and happened to line up next to him.

He stuck out his hand, "Hey, I'm Reece."

"Hey Reece, I'm Christian."

"Are you new here?" I asked.

"Yeah, I just moved up not too long ago," he said.

"Oh? Where are you from?" I asked.

"Texas, but I've been up here for about a month or so."

He had a close buzz cut and a thick frame. There was kindness in his demeanor, as well as a noticeable humility, but there was also an air of experiential confidence that only living life out on your own can bring. He was mature for his age, relating easily to me as we conversed in the lobby.

Reece had started working for a new company, in an effort to leave the trucking business for new experience.

We met occasionally for dinner and a chat. He was living far out of town in a small trailer that had no stove and little room for him and his roommate. We spent several hours together, and enjoyed the company of someone who thought similarly. We talked of the end-times, politics and society. He was conservative, recognizing the currents flowing beneath society and how they related to the Bible. I could tell he was seeking the Lord, and was eager to gain a deeper understanding of who God is.

One night we were leaving the church, and he turned to me.

"So, I could use your opinion on something," he said.

"Sure, go for it."

"There's this guy at work who offered me a room to stay in. The thing is, there's eight or nine people living in the house, and he wants $800 a month. I'm tempted to take it, but I'm not sure what the Lord wants me to do."

I mulled it over. It was tricky to give advice about what God's will was for people.

"Have you prayed about it?"

"Yeah, but I still don't know. I really want to get out of where I'm living now, and this would be a step up, but I'm just not sure I feel right about it," he said.

"Well, wait on the Lord and pray. He'll start showing you one way or another. If it's what He wants for you, then doors will start opening. Otherwise, the whole thing will start breaking down," I said.

"Sounds good. I have a feeling that it's not where I'm supposed to be, so I'll wait and see what happens."

I wondered what our Father was doing in Reece's life, but I had my own questions that needed answers.

Stephen's temperament had become more volatile day after day. I watched a person who had met me in the Wal-Mart parking lot with vigor become reduced to a moving shadow. The struggle had reached a height of explosion within, and I recognized the need for something to change. After a discussion of his future in Williston, he allowed me to call his dad. We agreed that he should go back home, at least for a little while. I returned to a beaten Stephen, sitting on his bed, shoulders slumped and head down. He looked empty.

"Your dad is coming to pick you up. Your parents want you to call them, and he wants you to know that they love you. They love you a lot," I spoke softly.

His eyes didn't move; he just nodded his head.

That Wednesday, Stephen's dad came to pick him up. Stephen looked refreshed, moving about with a speed I hadn't seen in a long time. There was hope in his voice, and an enthusiasm with his movements. I couldn't help but feel a sense of relief at the sight of him getting some type of help. It had been painful to watch him struggle with each crashing wave of depression and confusion. The lies had built up a prison around him, keeping him from seeing the beauty of the outside world. I was glad to see the chance for a new start.

I had tried to explain the release telling the truth gives, and the freedom of living a life with Christ. I did my best to be a friend and to relate to the pain of a depressed life. There had been plenty of mistakes in my attempts to open his eyes, but I also was firmly aware that it was up to him to make the necessary decisions. His pride fought the need for help or admitting a wrong choice, but at least now he had accepted the grasp of a familiar, loving hand.

God's timing was perfect. I was sad to see Stephen leaving town, but at the same time, hopeful that he could get the help he needed. He had given me my start in Williston, and had helped when I needed a lift. I was ever thankful to him for that, and hoped he would understand it meant the world to me.

With the departure of Stephen came the need for a new roommate. After several conversations with Stephen's dad, I had concluded that Stephen wouldn't be returning. I also shared that I would need to look for a new roommate, and began the search. Reece's name came immediately to mind.

"Are you still looking for a place to live?" I texted.

"No, I just got on with a new company and they offered company housing," he replied.

I was bummed, wondering why the Lord had put him on my heart with such strength. Every interaction with Reece had impressed me, and there was an eagerness to get to know him better.

Within fifteen minutes, another text came through.

"Is that room still open?"

"Yeah, you want it?"

"Yeah, I'll take it," he said.

Later he told me that immediately after he had turned down the offer I had made, he had realized the mistake. He was trading living with a fellow believer in a great apartment for company apartments with people he didn't know. The Lord had clearly shown him he was making the wrong choice. A day later his bags were on the apartment floor, and we were cleaning up what Stephen had left behind.

A few days after Stephen had moved back home, I received a phone call from his brother.

"I wanted to tell you something I think you should know." I perked up, wondering what had brought about the phone call.

"I want you to know that…well, that your mom's funeral changed my life. I had made some really bad choices, and my life was going down the wrong path, and it was her funeral that woke me up. I just felt you had to know that, her funeral saved my life," he said.

After six months, I had received that one reason I had been looking for. God had answered my prayer just when I needed it.

"You don't know how much that means to hear," I said. "I've been praying for God to give me a reason for her death. And I always said that even if it was just one life saved, it was worth it. Thank you so much for telling me that."

"I was on a trajectory that I shouldn't be on, and it saved my life, so thank you," he said. His voice shook as the tears welled up.

I thanked God over and over, so grateful that my prayer had been answered. It was a blessing, considering how often people didn't get an answer to the "why" question. I knew that my mom would have given up her life to save one person, and she would be pleased that it was Stephen's brother.

CHAPTER 26

The weeks passed and my focus changed from the past deluge of destruction to the immediate happenings. I had a roommate who was eagerly seeking Jesus. I had a girlfriend in Madison to whom I was becoming more attracted with each visit and phone call. My boss at work was a complex man who wanted to get closer to Christ, but was held back by his former lifestyle. My dad was grasping for a new life without Mom, and my close friends in Doug and Sarah had moved back to Idaho on a wing and a prayer. Continual change was the one constant in my life.

Likewise, with Doug and Sarah. They left with 300 dollars, and arrived with no money, a broken truck, and no idea how to get started. Doug and I talked occasionally on the phone, and they had had even more struggles to deal with. Each time things settled down, they were hounded by another obstacle or issue. My heart broke for them, watching them ride the crests of a storm-churned sea just like I was.

Massey was fighting against the burden of ministry work placed squarely on him. While other people were quitting, he was taking on more responsibilities and attempting to raise more funds. A few months before, we had talked about his struggles to raise $2,000 dollars a month. With the growing of his reliance on God, he was raising over $20,000 dollars a month.

"I can't do it, I just can't do it. I'm $4,000 in the hole right now, and I need it in two days," he told me as I consoled him during what had become a common conversation.

"Have faith in the Lord. Has He steered you wrong yet?" I asked.

"No. Every time He's come through. I'm just sick of having to struggle. I just want to feel at ease for a little while. I want some of the calm, normal life for once. I'm not sure how much longer I can do this," he said.

"I'm praying for you, and I know He'll take care of you," I responded.

And without fail, two days later Massey had his support funds and was able to be paid his wages. It never made sense to me that his wages were determined upon whether he raised enough money or not. I trusted the Lord, and constantly prayed that Massey's eyes would be opened, and he would be released from the ministry to live a life that truly understood God's love. I took every chance I could to tell him about how much God loved him, even if I was still trying to figure out what that really meant. He understood that the Lord loved and had mercy, and Massey was sure to always be gracious and kind to others, but I saw him struggle to see how it all fit together. He wasn't being treated with grace and mercy by his elders, which made it more difficult for him to flourish. I had begun praying God would make it clear to me what His love truly meant and how I could fully understand it, so that I could help show it to Massey.

He hadn't talked with Edward since I had learned the truth of how destructive the ministry was to those who were involved. The stand-off saddened me because Massey needed Edward more than ever. They had been best friends for twelve years, supporting each other through thick and thin. Now that Edward had left and made a donor aware of the issues, the ministry had completely black-balled him, and Massey was caught in the cross-fire. He loved Edward, and Edward loved him.

Edward was happy though. He was thriving working as an electrician, and was getting engaged to the girl he met right after leaving the ministry. His faith was struggling to find solid ground, and I could see similar issues in Massey's own faith. They had to understand they could not earn the gift of salvation, and God was looking for repentance, not handing out condemnation.

Edward's bitterness was deep, and I couldn't blame him. But there was still a soft spot for Massey. Despite my pleas with both to contact the other, the chasm remained. Edward refused to give up on the Lord, but the struggles with forgiveness permeated in our conversations. His passion would rise, speaking against the injustices with anger. I certainly agreed, but feared encouraging the path of bitterness. The separation between Massey and Edward brought more frustration in me, since it was obvious they could help each other gain new insight. The silence remained, and I loved them both. All I could do was pray and love.

The fresh calm in my life gave an opportunity to turn to other people's problems. I had done my best to focus on them during my own issues, but it was hard to not be consumed by personal problems. This was a chance to take what I had learned through all of the valleys, and to walk on that faith. As I proceeded to work my job, teach youth group, attend small group and lift weights, the faith response was taking effect.

No longer did the issues of the day sway my faith in who God was, and if He was good or not. Instead, I found a new strength I had never understood before. I had always heard people say, "you need to rely on the strength of the Lord", but I could never understand what they meant. I tried to give up in hopes the Lord would take over, but giving up on trying provided no inspiration or comfort. I tried to plow through problems and call it the Lord's strength, but that didn't work either.

What I was finding out was that God's strength was having the faith that He would see me through. It might not have been the outcomes I wanted, but I always grew, and I always learned. It was those moments when I could either put faith in my own efforts, or trust that the Lord had not forgotten about me. That strength was found in standing firm on the Lord's provision, no matter who said what.

Circumstances gave me the experience to provide words of wisdom to others who were struggling—even those who were my elders.

Norm's center for the hurting was moving slowly. We had named it "The Refuge". He was determined to allow Christ to bring things to fruition, and wanted to do each and every thing God's way. We had seen small miracles happen during the waiting. Norm had come upon people who offered him huge commercial kitchen counters and sinks for a great price. Pristine shelves and storage units had been donated, along with plenty of mattresses and other items. The Lord had brought skilled tradesmen to help with issues in the structure; in addition an architecture firm wanted to donate its time. Pretty soon the roof was fixed with a fresh covering, the windows given tight seams, the electricity was being rewired, and those who inspected gave us encouragement by saying, "Shouldn't be a problem."

But Satan harassed Norm any chance he could. Doubt would creep in, making Norm wonder if things would ever get finished.

"The Lord has gotten you this far, and while you can't exactly see what He's doing…we know He's been working," I said. Norm listened, taking care to be silent and allow the Holy Spirit to speak to his soul. "We rely on the Lord, and if this is His vision, then it will be completed. He's confirmed it plenty of times, and He keeps providing things. It'll be on His time though," I said.

The truth was deep within Norm, but it needed to be prodded to the surface. The struggle was in standing tall on the truth when the whole world was tipping sideways.

"Stand firm. I know people are going to come against you, but they also came against Nehemiah. Keep going, and don't worry about the naysayers," I said.

I had been sitting with one of the naysayers just before our conversation. I had felt the need to remind Norm that these people were thinking with the logic of men, and the Father's reasoning doesn't always line up with ours.

"I definitely needed that," he said. "Thank you for letting the Lord speak through you."

"That's what I'm here for," I said. "I felt like I had to let you know, and to tell you to keep going. Don't give up, and don't let them talk you out of what you know to be true."

Feeling renewed, Norm chose to change the subject.

"How's Michelle doing?" he asked. It was a joy to hear the question come from my friends and family. People were asking me how we were doing, and I was able to give an honest, open, joyful response.

"She's doing well. She's been working hard and keeping busy," I said.

"How are you two doing?" he asked, prodding below the surface.

"We're doing great. She's such an amazing girl," I said. "I'm very thankful God put her in my life. She has a heart of gold and is so caring and compassionate about everyone. She's one of a kind."

"She's a keeper. Hold onto her," he said. I could hear the joy in his voice.

"Do you think she'll move out here and work at the hospital?" he asked.

"I'm not sure. We're praying about it right now, trying to figure out what the Lord wants her to do. She's been offered a great opportunity in Madison working in the field she wants, so we're praying."

It had been a difficult process. We were at the point where a decision needed to be made. We wanted to be together, and felt the Lord had a plan for our lives, but we were unsure about where He would put us. She had tried to apply to a hospital in the area but was met with little interest despite the dire need for staff. She had also shown interest in several other hospitals, but each time we both felt the pull of the Madison offer. When we prayed about it, that opportunity floated to the surface.

"Keep seeking the Lord on it, and He'll show you guys where you should be," he said. "I would love for it to be here, but you need to go where the Lord wants you."

"Thanks Norm," I said. "It would be hard to leave. I'd be leaving family and friends out here. People have been so great to me, and God has done so much."

"And He's not done. He'll use you wherever you go," he said.

It was true, but I didn't know what that might look like. The roads in my life were being built to make a difference there, and it was fascinating to see. The different projects I was involved in were having a real-life effect on people, and I could see how God was growing them and training them. I could see it when a person sought God for a decision, or when they talked about something He did in his life. That was the real joy: to hear them give God praise for something great He had done. It was wonderful to hear them rest on Him in the times of trouble, and say that they know He's got them in His hands.

Reece was learning these things first hand, as he searched for God's guidance on whether to stay in a relationship or not. As the relationship progressed, he saw the difference between them becoming more apparent. He wanted a communion that sought God while she wanted a relationship that sought each other. After several weeks of tension and hurt feelings, they both agreed it was best to end it.

Reece swayed with the hit, but quickly regained himself. He accepted it and understood that God hadn't left. Growing his relationship with the King of existence was more important. However, at the same time, Reece wanted the best for her. He loved her and wished she could see the joy in following Christ, but his ship couldn't steer in two directions. We had discussed at length the importance of putting God first in life. He accepted the notion that when God was the top focus, then everything else lined up. It was a scary proposition to support. But Reece wouldn't let go of God for an earthly pleasure, and understood that God wasn't out to make him give up everything in life. Instead, God wanted to provide much more than he could have ever found on his own. He wanted to reshape and remake Reece to bear His image.

We used each other as sounding boards as we talked openly about our issues. Late at night after making dinner, we would sit at the little round table in the kitchen. Full from our chicken and veggies or Hamburger Helper, conversation would flow to questions we had been facing.

I was resting on my elbow, staring off into space.

"You okay?" he asked.

I looked up to come back to reality.

"Ever feel like you're not doing enough?" I asked.

"All the time. I feel like there's so much more I could be doing," he said.

I shifted to my other elbow and stretched across the table.

"Me too. There are all these people who have done amazing things," I said. "I heard a story about Margaret Thatcher where the guy who was doing a biography on her was talking to one of the guards that stood outside her residence. The guard said her light didn't turn off before 2:00am, and it was on before 6:00am. I feel like the people who do great things are so driven."

"I feel like that too. People like our Founding Fathers. Those guys were a lot smarter than we are today. They were learning things in their teens that we still haven't grasped." He thought for a moment and added, "Did they ever sleep?"

"I don't think so. And I know I'll never be like them," I offered. "I like my sleep too much."

"Yeah, we're pretty lazy," he laughed. "So what do you wish you did more?"

"I don't know. I wish I had more passion. There's such a separation between my ambition and my drive."

"I know what you mean."

"But I feel like you've done a lot with your life already," I countered. "You have a house, you've lived in different parts of the country, you've worked on a crab-fishing boat and even got out of being homeless," I said.

"True, but there's a lot more I could be doing."

I couldn't argue. I had a hard time not looking at my life and wondering what had been left undone. The biggest difference I saw between me as a 27 year old oilfield sales rep and the leaders of multi-million dollar organizations wasn't necessarily talent or genius. I saw drive in them.

"Same here. I should be taking my ideas and working on them. Instead I sleep in on the weekends," I laughed. "I wonder if I'm producing or consuming? There was an article I read online about habits of successful people, and one point it made is that successful people produce more than consume. Think about it: when we're watching television, reading things, eating food, whatever it is—we're consuming. There are people out there who are producing all of these things," I said. "I think about these people who are all part of the production. There are people who have to write the tv shows. There are people who act it out. People who edit and direct. They're all doing the work to make a creation other people can enjoy and consume," I said.

My mind flared with passion at the idea of being a producer. It seemed to all boil down to those two options.

"I want to be one of those who can point to something and say, 'I did that'."

"So what stops us from doing what we want to do?" he asked.

"Laziness?" I responded.

"Probably," he said as he sat back and tapped his fingers on the table. "But, we're where the Lord wants us to be. We just have to do what we can with what we've been given."

The story of the servants and the talents came to mind. The master provided his servants with a number of talents (a measurement of money, but many have spoken of the talent's symbolism as a variety of things given to each person) before leaving on a journey. He asked them to do what they could with their allotment, and he would check back with them after his travels. Two of the servants doubled their talents, while one dug a hole and hid his. The master was happy with the two who worked with what they had, but was angry with the lazy and foolish servant. I feared being that servant. God had provided me with talents and gifts, but I wondered how I was really using them for the Kingdom. Christianity is not a consumer relationship. It is a producing faith, in which we're called to do what we can for the growth and health of the Kingdom.

"I need to do better," I said.

I looked at my phone for the time, noticing it was already a half an hour past our bedtime. Yet, neither of us were tired.

"How do you think you could?" he asked.

"I feel like I could be sharing my faith more. I could be using my talents to do something for God. I could have more drive to do His work," I responded.

"There's always more we could be doing. I'm sure you'll find something," he said.

"You're probably right. I want to be able to help people understand who God is, and what it looks like to have Him in your everyday life. I want to feel like I'm doing all I can and making accomplishing something," I said.

CHAPTER 27

As summer flowers burst in bombastic displays of color, the heat of the day was seeping farther and farther into the evening. The sunshine was supplying light hours after the work day, dimming only after bedtime. Daylight was stretching to 10:00 or 11:00 at night, and the full flavor of summer tasted refreshing. There was a newness of life I hadn't felt in a long time. I was on a fresh wave of faith, and the joy of the summer season was the perfect compliment.

Since things had settled down, I decided mid-summer would be a perfect time to go see Michelle. We had traded visits, sharing in the burden of travel. She witnessed the enigma that was Williston, and had brought stories back to her own friends and family. Deciding to visit the beauty of Madison, I bought a round trip train ticket and caught a ride with Reece down to the station.

When life becomes calm and the excitement of your faith life has settled down, the temptation comes to be praying for something different. One should take care when asking the Lord to stretch, to grow faith or test oneself. That request is likely to be granted.

Standing on the brick platform, I prayed in my head. I asked to be stretched. I asked to be tested.

The train rolled in from Montana as the sun was avoiding its obligation to dip below the horizon. It was nice to be standing in the summer North Dakota heat, instead of the below zero temperatures that blasted us all winter. My feet found the familiar steps of the train and climbed to the sitting section. I strolled along, looking for an open seat. I found one and sat next to the aisle.

I pulled out my journal and began writing with the hope of doing some productive activity. I had started the practice the previous summer, and had enjoyed recording all God had done or all the struggles I was facing. Not long after, a woman who appeared to be in her mid 40's politely interrupted my thought process.

"Excuse me," she said as she pointed to the seat next to me. I noticed a bag and jacket sitting in the space.

I pulled my stuff near as she scooted past my knees and settled in. She smiled and eyed my journal.

"Writing?" she asked.

"Yeah, kind of. It's actually a faith journal," I said. The familiar press of the Holy Spirit was lightly nudging me to continue.

"I like to write down what's going on in my life, things I'm struggling with or things God does in my life."

"Really? You're a believer?" she asked.

"Yup, are you?" I responded.

"Yes I am."

She watched me continue to write, looking as though she were pondering what to say next. Eventually, she spoke up. "May I ask you a question?"

"Sure," I said.

"Who do you think Jesus Christ is?"

"Well, He's my Lord and Savior. He was God in the flesh that led a perfect life, and He died on the cross so as to pay for our sins, a debt we could not pay for ourselves." I responded.

I saw her brow furrow slightly.

"Would you be able to show me where you would find it says He's God?" she asked.

The question caught me off-guard. This was not the normal line a believer would say to another. I pulled out my Bible and quickly prayed in my head, "Lord, please show me what I can give her." I came to John 1:1-2 (NASB). It read, "In the beginning was the Word, and the Word was with God, and the Word was God. He was with God in the beginning." The thought "case-closed" came to mind.

"Do you mind if I read you mine?" she asked. I nodded, and she pulled out her Bible. It read, "In the beginning was the Word, and the Word was with God, and the Word was **a** God. He was with God in the beginning."

I was astounded by her translation. I had never heard of a Bible diminishing Christ in that sense.

"Christ called himself Son of God many different times," I said.

"But He wasn't God," she replied.

Then it hit me. She was a Jehovah's Witness. Touché Lord.

She pulled out a manual. Each passage I referenced, she flipped in her little booklet to find the right commentary. I peered over her hands to see a list of different passages, and sections of commentary underneath. Many of them postulated that the translations of the NIV, King James, NASB, ESV and others were wrong. It was only their version—which she happened to carry—that was truly correct.

I pointed out that Christ said He was the "I am".

She commented that He was making the statement "I am the one who was sent".

"That's not the correct translation," I argued. "It was because He said 'I am' that they wanted to stone him. They knew what it meant for Him to say that. They knew He was saying He was the same entity that spoke to Moses in the bush, who also claimed himself to be Yaweh."

She flipped through her little book, trying to find a response. I stopped her.

"Please, look at me, just for a second." I said.

She looked up, her eyes blank above a distant smile.

"Just because they tell you that their translation is the only right one, doesn't mean it is. Please, put down the book they've given you to answer all the arguments, and listen. You don't have to believe what they're telling you," I said.

She smiled and looked back to her book to find another passage she could use.

The little book was doing its best to discredit the other translations at all points. In the commentary, it stated that the KJV made the same change as her version. I texted Norm, wondering what his King James Bible said in relation to John 1:1. Sure enough, it said "…the Word was God" as opposed to "…the Word was a God".

She didn't buy it.

"Look right here," she said. "It gives the verse and everything."

As we went back and forth, I began to feel myself wondering if maybe she had a point. The little crack was being whittled. I prayed for God to help, feeling overwhelmed in this battle of theology.

A few minutes later, a young man was walking past and noticed our Bibles out.

"Are you guys having a Bible study?" he asked.

"Kind of," I laughed. "Care to join?"

"Sure, I'll be back in a few minutes," he said.

I sighed a breath of relief. I was going to get some support. Not only did the Lord send some support, he sent one who would understand the importance of this question better than anyone else.

The young man was a Messianic Jew, or a Jew who believes that Christ was the Messiah sent, and the one to whom prophets were pointing, as opposed to mainline Jews who deny Christ was the Messiah and are still waiting for the fulfillment of the prophecies.

For the next few hours, the three of us debated back and forth the importance of who Christ really was. She was adamant that

He was a created being, while we both pointed to scripture after scripture that left no option other than Christ being one in the same as God. Eventually the arguing died down, and I prayed for her silently.

When the theological discussion ended, we talked of our lives, our upbringing and why we were on the train. She spoke of her work with the mentally handicapped. Passion sparked in her eyes, and at one point tears began welling up. Her heart was in the people for whom she worked, and I could tell it was central in her life. Whether she knew Christ was God or not, she wanted to show His love to those people any way she could.

We conversed gently, and the words "Love her with the love of Christ" kept coming to mind. It was important to see her as a human who felt emotions, harbored insecurities and hoped in dreams. Without seeing her as real, I would merely see her as a wayward person who needed to be beaten with the truth. As we said good-byes, I watched her walk down the aisle, wondering what life had in store for her. I prayed again, begging the Lord to start opening her eyes.

The reflection of those hours continued for the next several days. I had to first assure myself that all the translations and scholars were right. After that, I began reviewing how I had reacted, what I had said, and what I was looking for. There were times during the debate when I became angry and impatient. Towards the end, I had allowed my young Jewish friend to take over. I silenced my mouth, fearing the rude responses that might fly from it in anger.

The conclusion was I needed more patience. Added to that was the rational question of: when did it become pointless to continue? Should I have ended it ten minutes in? Isn't there a righteous anger in seeing a heretical stance being supported?

Some of those questions have not yet been answered, but my prayer was answered. I had been stretched. My faith in what I knew and why I knew it had been tested by God. He sat me next to a person who would put my interest in theological debate through the fire. He also pointed out my issue with impatience and anger. I could see it had showed in small glimmers of these weaknesses throughout the past couple of years, and I was uncovering just how deep the impatience was imbedded.

My friend the Messianic Jew and I continued talking late into the night and shared phone numbers. We talked of music and life, and wondered what the Lord had in store for both of us.

"My grandma is dying, and she refuses to open her eyes to who Christ is," he said. "She won't even let His name be spoken in her house. I'm barely allowed in the house because I accepted Christ." He struggled with the next thoughts.

"And it's hard to imagine my family members going to Hell since they won't accept Christ," he said.

"I'll be praying for them," I responded. There wasn't much a Christian from the conservative suburbs could say to this young man. He was living the life that the Bible has predicted for those jews who accepted Christ. Rejection, condemnation, anger and bitterness against those who had 'blasphemed' God by saying Jesus was His son, His flesh, His bodily extension.

By comparison, what had I known of persecution for my beliefs? I had been laughed at, criticized a little and called some names. He wasn't welcome in his grandmother's home.

"It's hard, but I know Christ is the one," he affirmed.

"Keep with Him, and He'll see you through," I encouraged.

I continued to pray for the young man after he came to his stop. To have a faith that separated a person from his family was the call to sacrifice. He was setting himself completely apart, and was the physical embodiment of Christ's statement in Luke 12:51-53 (NASB), "Do you think that I have come to give peace on earth? No, I tell you, but rather division. For from now on in one house there will be five divided, three against two and two against three. They will be divided, father against son and son against father, mother against daughter and daughter against mother, mother-in-law against her daughter-in-law and daughter-in-law against mother-in-law."

This young man was my first time experiencing a Messianic Jew and his struggles. My heart went out to a brother, and wanted to support anyway I could. We stayed in contact for a few days afterward, but soon both fell into our own lives.

My trip to visit Michelle felt short, but well worth the time. We spent our moments together taking walks and enjoying the natural landscape around Madison. We would walk the city neighborhoods, pointing out interesting architecture or little houses that embodied what we might like to have, all while strolling down the sidewalk hand in hand. Our nights were spent in her new apartment, where she lived with two friends. Each evening, the fight would commence over who was going to sleep on the couch, and she would win, delegating me to the bed.

The end of school had brought her to the start of a career in nursing and a new living situation. After much prayer, we concluded she was being called to stay in Madison. With the path laid before us, I debated what to do. I told her, "I can do sales anywhere. You get your career going where God wants you to be."

With her career decision settled, I began calculating when I might be able to move to Madison, and if that was what God wanted me to do. The prayers began along with thanks for having the opportunity to get to know her. I felt the door was open, but didn't want to push it.

"If you do move, when do you think you would?" she asked.

"I'd probably move at the end of the two years. It feels like that's the right time to do it, and would make sense since I made my commitment to Don for one and a half to two years," I said.

"Couldn't you leave at a year and half?" she asked. Her eyes opened wide, pouring fawn-like hope into the already difficult situation.

"I've thought about it, but that doesn't seem right. I'd rather finish up my two years, have the time to save some money and then move." It was difficult not to lose my train ticket and stay. Much like a sailor on leave, I was having a hard time reasoning why I should go back. Commitment and honor kept me from making any rash decisions. The fierce tension between dedication to the job that God had provided and the woman He had put before me was pulling hard. All I knew was I wanted to be with her. If He wanted it to happen, it would. Not my will Lord, but yours be done.

So in similar fashion to the past, I said my good-byes and boarded the train. As soon as I was onboard, dread magnified. I didn't want to be heading west. Staying with her was the only favorable option. But the train started, and the chain slowly pulled me back. I nestled into my seat, pulled out a book and tried to put off the thoughts of having to return to work.

As the train came closer and the landscape looked more familiar, I sank lower in my seat. I was a prisoner of rails and it was hard to get my feet to move when the stop came. The reminder came flooding through, "Remember all the people you have here, and how much you're getting involved with."

I settled on that thought. Even though the clouds gathered close to the earth and threatened to release their stores of rain drops, a new hope was building. There was plenty to be done here, and God was the one who was going to do it. There were things to do and people to care for. I was God's vessel, a doorway through which He could help those who needed it. If He gave me words, I was supposed to speak up. If He gave me actions, I was supposed to move.

The next few months were spent doing just that. My time was focused on doing whatever I could to help those around me. Whether it was giving rides to strangers, handing food to those on the corner, or giving encouraging words to friends. The action of being a Christian didn't need to be selling every single item I had and moving to a country in the middle of Africa. I wasn't being called to that. The burden in my heart was for the welfare of my friends and loved ones.

Chapter 28

The summer drew to a close.

Days were turning into nights with an uptempo beat. Darkness overpowered the light at 7:00 as opposed to 10:00 or 11:00. The wind began to bring a slight chill through my bones, forcing me to shove my hands a little bit deeper into my pockets. The world around me was preparing for the next winter in subtle ways. People started moving a tad bit slower and outer layers grew thicker. Talk centered around predicting and expecting the coming winter to be one of the worst yet. The oil field was tapering off as companies blew through the rest of their budgets.

The blast of growth in my faith was beginning to wane as well. I reminded myself often of the adage that there are seasons for faith. There are times of growth and times of pruning.

There had been temptations of sin that had caused me to stumble and reboot, and other situations where my reactions were not as Christ-like as I would have liked them to be. But I was learning to trust.

I wasn't the only one learning how to trust. Doug and Sarah were barely making it in Idaho. He held several jobs, then was again looking for work. I got a call one night that took me by surprise.

"We're thinking of moving back to North Dakota," he said.

"You are?"

"Yup. We've been trying to make it here and just can't. As much as we would rather stay, I know can get a good job in North Dakota," he said.

"What's the plan then?" I asked.

"We'll be moving back in a month or two. We started looking at jobs and places for rent. I think I found a place I can work that pays pretty well. They've promised me plenty of hours, so we'll see…" he said.

"I'm sorry you have to come back, but I can't wait to see you," I said. It had been too long since we last spent time together. It was on the day they left town. Doug and I had spent several hours replacing a starter in his truck. The truck made it to Idaho, but barely.

"We'll have to get together as soon as we get back into town," he said. "What about you? What are your plans?"

I sighed at the question. The decision process had been long and arduous. Doug had an idea of the tussle I was having.

"I'm thinking of leaving at the beginning of October. Michelle and I talked it all out and I think I'm going to be moving there," I said.

"That's awesome. We're really happy for you. It's too bad we won't be able to see you much after you leave, but you better know we're coming to your wedding," he said.

"Well of course! Even though I didn't get to come to yours," I said. It was true I hadn't been able to attend their wedding, but that was okay. They married in quick fashion to avoid costs and settle into God's plan. Doug had a moment of clarity while meeting with a men's group at their church. They asked him why he hadn't asked Sarah to marry him, and he couldn't give a good answer. The best he could do was, "they didn't need a piece of paper to tell them they were in love. They knew they loved each other, and that was good enough."

The men responded that a wedding ceremony wasn't necessarily for them, but to make a public statement before God.

Their marriage was a chance to show themselves and God this was for real. It was something God set forth for the betterment of society and the family. Doug realized he and Sarah were taking the sacred combining of two people too lightly.

They married without much pomp and began life as husband and wife. When he told me, I was thrilled for the newlyweds. I never knew how to say the words he needed to hear, but was thankful the Lord had spoken through wiser men.

"Are you for sure moving at the beginning of October?" he asked.

"I'm not sure. I think so, but I've been praying. I know I'm ready to leave town and get the next chapter started. But, I also have to finish out my two year commitment," I said.

"Good for you. Well, when we get into town, you'll have to come visit," he said.

"For sure. You better be ready for me."

"Oh we will be," he responded.

I had mixed feelings on Doug and Sarah coming back to Williston. It was sad they were having such a rough time in Idaho, but I was excited to see them again. Doug had changed so much since we first met. He still had some rough edges showing, but he had mellowed in stunning fashion since Sarah had entered his life. His patience with other people was growing, and there was a softer side coming forward that I hadn't seen before. I could tell he was tired of putting energy into keeping everyone away. She had deconstructed some of the walls and was bringing about a different man. Along with the change of moods came the growing faith in God's good plan. They struggled financially, however never lost faith that God would see them through, and He did. They always had enough for food and bills, even if they had to scrape by.

Their news of moving back was the major story of my life towards the close of summer. It was good to have life settle down. I was no longer sitting in campers with drugs in me and on the table. I wasn't near bars where people pulled guns or knives. My companions were church-goers and lovers of God. Some might say the excitement of life was gone.

But a different excitement was sprouting. I was becoming a man who saw God do amazing things. Whether it was friends who had been healed, or amazing provisions—God had given me stories I could share. I wasn't struggling with life on the row anymore and seeking him out. Now He had me making friends with fellow believers in the weight-room. One of those brothers had begun teaching Reece and me Indonesian Kung-Fu for free. I had presented Christ to several people. Some of those conversations had resulted in great connection, others in interesting debate. I was provided for through church members and friends, and had seen a wealth of "Glory to God" moments.

My life was not perfect, but it was of much higher quality and value. My work had improved, and I felt more driven to give my best effort. I was making close connections with customers and even privileged to share in some of their God moments.

One customer shared the story of God's pronounced effect on his wife. While sitting in our trucks, driver's window to driver's window as we always did, I could see another level of energy emanating from him. His face beamed and the thick Louisiana draw sloped up and down with the twinkle of his eyes.

"I thought you might appreciate this, and I'll tell you because I know you're one of the only people out here who'll really believe it," he said. "Well, my wife was diagnosed with dementia a while ago, and we've been dealin' with the treatments for it. There was a medicine they were going to try that was goin' to cost a lot of money, and they didn't even know if it was goin' to work. Her doctor told us she'd be lucky to know her grandchildren within two years. It took a toll, but we figured it was in God's hands."

I listened, already beginning to smile. With God stories like this, there was always an interesting outcome.

"One night she and her women's Bible study were prayin', and she felt the need to pray about her dementia. So they spent time prayin'. The next day, she had to go to the doctors to get some more tests. She got the scans done, and we waited for the results. She just called a little bit ago to say the doctor couldn't find any trace of the dementia. She was completely healed," he said. His face was wide with a smile, excitement popping from his voice.

"Really? Praise God," I said. "What did the doctor say?"

"He was amazed. Said he's never seen anythin' like it. I guess she told him it was God, and he just said 'could be'."

"It's amazing to me how doctors see awesome things like this, and many still don't believe in God or miracles," I said.

"Yeah, one wonders," he responded.

I thanked him for telling me the story, and was happy for his family. His wife had received a brand new chance at life, and the dread of slipping into dementia wasn't pressing down on her anymore. Best of all, he was giving God the glory and sharing the good news. I told him he should tell more people and spread the word.

"I would, but I think you're the only one up here who would believe it."

I could see his point, but encouraged him to share anyway. I had run into more Christians who had a vivid faith here than at home. Out on the edge of society, where the darkest of clouds hung, was the brightest of lights. God was working powerfully through people, and I was getting a front row seat.

The darker thoughts of "Why couldn't Mom be healed?" poked through the joy of the moment. I fought not to think about why one person could be saved and another allowed to perish before her time. I reminded myself that at least one life had been saved from her death, and that was worth it. The truth that our lives are sacrifices for God's glory was shining in the darkness, and the promise of just reward pushed the sad, angry emotions away.

Another story of joy included Massey. My communication with him had waned because of friction with the ministry. We had become closer brothers and had shared open, vulnerable moments. Yet, the weight of the ministry still sat heavily on both of us. I had quit donating after Edward opened himself up to me on the issues within, and it was difficult to offer advice outside of "maybe it's time to leave".

I gave Massey the open opportunity, saying, "It's not wrong to think about leaving. All ministries have a time and a place. You need to do what God wants you to do."

"I know. I guess to be truthful, I'm not sure how I would even leave," he said in a moment of complete honesty.

"Let God show you," I said.

And the Lord did. A group of former members came together to write letters to the board, cluing them in on what was happening. They spoke of mistreatment, verbal abuse and being black-listed. Edward was included in their ranks, sharing his insights about how destructive it had been for him, as well as commonality between the ministry's actions and those of cults.

Massey read the letters, and his eyes were opened. Soon after, he tendered his resignation and left. Immediately after leaving, the Lord opened up an opportunity for him to continue his career in welding. I had never heard so much joy and freedom in his voice.

"I'm so thankful for the Lord providing me this job. It pays great, I can get as many hours as I want, and it sounds like I'm really making an impression. I've already gotten two raises," he said. I congratulated him over and over. I couldn't hide my joy at the news.

"I have a lot of pain and bitterness to work through," he said becoming somber. "I had my heart into this thing, and I can't believe I didn't see it. I don't know if I couldn't or didn't want to, but it breaks my heart that we hurt those people. That's what hurts the most. I was a part of that, and I didn't see it. How many people did I harm because I wasn't paying attention?"

"Massey, you can't hold it against yourself. You cared about people and about doing whatever the Lord asked. I don't know how many times you told me that you would do anything He asked, even if it killed you. And you did. Your heart was in the right place in this whole thing. I can't say I know how you feel or can truly give you guidance on how to get through it, but just know that you never came to me putting the money before the friendship. I always felt your heart was to serve God, and God recognized that," I said.

"Thank you man, you don't know how much it means to hear that. You're not the first one to say it either, which must mean it's got some truth to it. I want people to come to God, not drive them away," he said.

"And you do bring them to God. I love you, and I can't tell you how happy I am that you have a new life ahead of you. Use this time to be with your family and to love them. It's time to get your house in order and be there for your kid's childhood."

"I feel like I missed so much of them growing up," he said.

And he had. He had been on the road non-stop, fundraising and seeking out new connections. There were no vacations or breaks. Ministry came first, and family was expected to be a part of the sacrifice.

"You've missed some of it, but the Lord has blessed you with a chance to make up time. They're still young," I said.

"They're so happy. I come home from work and they come running to me. I get to spend time with them on the weekend and enjoy my family. Man, I just can't get over it," he said.

"You don't know how happy I am for you. This makes me so excited and overjoyed," I responded. "And God isn't done with you. He's going to use your experiences and the struggles you went through for the good of others. He will turn this curse into a blessing, and He'll provide guidance to those who were in a similar situation."

I was filled with love for him, finding a new gear in connecting to a man I had called my brother since we first met. And we had been brothers the whole time, but I couldn't deny the strain the ministry had put on us. I had been supportive of him in any way I could, and I knew he loved me deeply, but our phone calls had become sparse and rough before he resigned, and a new level of enthusiasm came flooding through after that.

Soon after Massey left, the ministry folded. A few members followed Brian, while others eyes were open to how much damage had been done. I praised the Lord that he was bringing the ministry to an end and leading people out of it. My prayers continued for Brian, that he would understand what Christ's love truly meant.

Chapter 29

"There's this guy I know whose looking for a place to crash," Reece said.

We were eating dinner late on a Monday night, relaxing while our cat sat in the third chair as if she was one of the crowd.

"Okay, when was he thinking?" I asked. I was hesitant, and not sure why.

"This weekend. I don't know, what do you think?" Reece asked, a resistance creeping into his voice as well.

"Well, that's fine. You should tell him we're going to be having Bible study on Friday," I said. We had talked about having one, and figured if there were going to be others in the house anyway, now was the perfect time.

"I'll let him know. We'll see what he says," Reece said.

His co-worker commented that he wasn't into that sort of thing, but it was fine, and he'd stay out of the way. We both wondered if he'd actually show. We agreed on Friday to be the inaugural Bible study and set to work. I texted friends and people I had met, setting the stage for Friday night's gathering. Now we just had to find other people to invite.

Througout my time in Williston, I had continued my side passion of powerlifting. My consistency had grown, and I was toying around with the idea of competing again. Eager to get into the weight-room, Reece started joining me. We would don our athletic shorts or old-man sweatpants and trudge into the aged rec center, ready to clang some iron.

The weight-room itself looked like a throw back from the 70's. It was just how I wanted it. Cinder blocks washed in gray paint housed old, smoothed out bars and cumbersome iron plates. The pads on the benches were torn, the squat rack creaky. Only a few souls occupied the place at a time, letting me lose touch with the world for an hour or two a day.

The employees came to know me well, beginning to call out "Old Faithful" as I walked in. They would scan my card and double-check the radio to make sure some type of rock music was playing. I felt comfortable, as if I were walking into my own basement.

Reece and I strode in, ready to do some training and see how buff we could get. As our muscles warmed and the plates gathered on the bar, I noticed a young man fervently pushing himself. I had never seen him before, but noticed him look our way once or twice. He was in his mid 20's, short and small.

Halfway through our workout, he approached.

"Hey, I was just wondering, do you guys play racquetball at all?"

"Eh, not really. I played it a long time ago, but don't anymore. Thanks for the offer though," I said.

"That's alright." He examined us for a moment, and extended his hand. "I'm Patrick."

"Good to meet you. I'm Christian and this is Reece," I responded.

We shook hands and made small talk. His family was originally from the Williston area, but he'd been raised in Arizona. He was back, working in disaster clean-up, as opposed to the oilfield like everyone else. After a few minutes of chatting, he returned to his workout and we returned to ours.

Our bodies grew sore and weary from the beating, and we eventually relented. We were hungry and ready for relaxation. I had my bag packed and was approaching the door when I felt the urge to speak to Patrick.

"Hey, do you want to come to a Bible study on Friday?" I asked.

He thought for a moment then said, "Yeah, maybe I will. I'll have to see what I have going, but I might."

"Sounds good, let me get your phone number, and I'll text you my address," I said. We traded information and gave a pleasant good-bye. Reece and I stepped out to a dropping sun and walked the sidewalk towards my truck.

"I just felt the need to invite him to the Bible study," I said. I had almost resisted the little voice telling me to, but I put one foot in front of the other and rejected my fear and excuses.

"I did too. I wasn't sure why, but I was going to do it if you hadn't," Reece responded.

"Well, we'll see if he shows"

Friday came; Patrick showed. He arrived with Bible in hand and toe shoes on his feet. Other people including Edward arrived, and we began the first ever Bible study in our apartment. Several of them were people I had met in the weight room, while a couple were friends or co-workers. Reece's co-worker never showed, opting to stay at another apartment instead.

The night's conversation was warm, touching on different areas as we delved into our lives. The group members were casual with each other, and talked with a vulnerable openness I hadn't expected. Our fellowship as Christian brothers took priority over our vast differences of age, race, or background.

The night drew to a close, finding a natural end when several comments of "I should probably get to bed soon," were heard from heads gazing at watches. We prayed the night out and several guys left. Soon, it was Patrick, Reece and I.

"Ya know, I really felt like I had to ask you guys if you wanted to play racquetball," he said. "I've never done that before: just walked up to someone to ask if they played racquetball."

"We both felt the need to ask you to Bible study," I said. "Reece said he would have if I hadn't."

"Sounds like the Lord wanted us to meet," he said.

Patrick left after talking a little while longer, and Reece and I reclined, satisfied. The first Bible study had been a success, and we all agreed to meet again the following week.

I was intrigued by Patrick. He spoke with a confidence in biblical knowledge that I had rarely encountered, as if the lessons had been learned over a long history. He was our age, yet I could tell he had lived a faith which led to a deep experiential knowledge.

Come to find out, God had led him back to Williston. He mentioned he was on a three-part journey the Lord had given to him through dreams, prophetic messages and confirmations. This was the second part of the journey, and he wasn't sure how long he would call Williston home.

A bit of me was intimidated by his faith and knowledge. So often I had met people with a similar confidence who were following their own path, speaking half-truths and thoughts conceived away from scripture. But everything he spoke matched with what scripture stated.

And, there was a reason. Patrick had lived an interesting life. He had been raised in a family that knew of God, but couldn't quite grasp the every-day of a relationship with Christ. His mom had admitted she went to church more for the community than for God.

He had lived a life searching for answers in himself and knowledge, before the Holy Spirit woke him up. Realizing he needed to get a strong grasp of God, he threw himself in head first. He spent days in the desert, walking and trying to hear the voice of God. At some points he became lost, thinking he had heard the Lord tell him right or sensing He wanted him to turn left.

"I figured out that the Lord wasn't necessarily interested in which step I took when I was just walking," he said to me one night as we were having a long discussion about hearing God.

"I learned it the hard way when I was in Amsterdam too," he said. "I arrived in Amsterdam and had no clue where my hotel was. I prayed and God led me, corner by corner to my hotel. It was a pretty amazing thing. I would stop at a corner, pray, and it was as if an arrow was pointing me the way to go. The next day when I had to get to another place across town, I figured I'd just leave my map. I didn't need help. I had God. I was lost for two hours, having absolutely no clue where I was. I finally asked someone for directions. Come to find out, I was on the other side of town in the wrong district."

"Huh, you were genuinely lost the first time. The second time you were testing Him, weren't you?" I said.

"Yeah. It was one of those things where I didn't use what I had been provided. The first day I really was lost and needed His help. The second time I was testing Him and trying to make Him do what I wanted Him to."

Patrick had learned many of these lessons over the course of his seven year faith-walk. Whether it was speaking a word to someone that fell flat on its face, or learning what the true path was and wasn't, he was seeking God in everything. He had almost become a Mormon at one point, falling into their methodical witnessing tools that brought a person step by step to their faith.

"Before I knew it, I was almost baptized. The Lord woke me up, and I wondered, 'What the heck am I doing?" he said.

He backed off and found a new drive to believe in the Bible and to use it as the Word of God, measuring anything a person taught against scripture. He wanted to follow the Word, teach only what God wanted taught, and not bring people to an errant understanding of who God was and what it meant to be a Christian. Not only did he want his words to be obedient to God, but he was eager to live his life completely in service to Him.

On several occasions, Patrick sold all he had. It wasn't out of an attempt to be poor and holy, but because God was preparing him for changes in his life. One of the times, the Lord told him to sell all his belongings so that he wouldn't be tied down for his first journey. This journey took him on the road with a backpack and a smile, with our Father providing for his needs every step of the way. His obedience had brought him to a homeless shelter, to Kansas City and to Williston. His passion had been to follow Christ at all costs, and he had done his best to keep true to the path.

With Patrick's stories fresh in my mind, God presented me my own moment to make a choice, showing what can happen when you agree to follow the Lord's call.

The highway flows through Williston from the north, and at the head of town, curves west and continues towards Montana. I followed the familiar highway, about to end another workday. As I headed west to make one final stop, I passed a man on the side of the busy highway with several large bags of luggage. He stood calm, thumb out, head turning with the cars.

I continued on my way, denying the deep urge that was burning throughout my body. After a quarter of a mile, I relented, turned the truck, and looped around to pick the man up. As he set his luggage in the back of the pick-up, I nervously eyed the traffic, looking for other company vehicles. Something was telling me the effects of the choice wouldn't be short and simple.

The man climbed in and shut the door bringing a whoosh of chilly air.

"Thank you so much for the ride," he offered. He shook my hand with a weathered, fragile grip. His hair was wild and white, while his eyes were set deep behind wrinkled cheeks. Age had made its mark on him, yet he carried a gentle glow.

We began on our way, and immediately I understood why I needed to pick him up.

"I was praying that the Lord would give me a ride, and here you show up," he said.

I chuckled to myself, amazed at how God puts things together.

"Yeah, I could tell He wanted me to pick you up. I actually drove past, then came around because He wasn't letting go of me."

"I thank you for the gesture. It's been a rough week for me," he said, eyes scanning the distant plains.

"Why's that?"

"Well, I was in town to take care of my mother-in-law, and just the other day I got in a bad accident."

I turned to him, concern on my face.

"I'm alright though, the Lord kept me safe with that one," he said, with a slight wave of the hand. "But I have no vehicle, and I've got to get back to Canada. So thanks for the lift. I just need to get to Culbertson, and I can get a ride from there."

The request sounded simple enough, and I leaned back and made myself comfortable.

"So how long have you been a follower of Christ?" I asked.

"Oh, a long time. I was in a cult-type thing at the beginning, but realized something wasn't right."

I cringed at the statement, wondering if perhaps I had made a mistake.

"But, now I follow Christ and only Him, and I'm part of a nice little church back home." He turned to me, asking, "How about you?"

"I go to a church here in Williston, as well as a home church. I've been really following Christ for about two years now, although I was raised in a Christian home. I guess you could say I was born-again two years ago."

A kind, gentle smile opened up as his eyes continued to twinkle. I felt a strong peace next to the man. We pulled into Culbertson, and I stopped at a small diner. The traffic flowing past the corner was light, and I wondered how he was going to find a ride to the border.

"Are you sure you'll be alright here?" I asked, wondering if I needed to head north with him.

"Oh yeah, I'll be fine. I'm just thankful you picked me up and brought me here. I'll be good from here."

We got out and grabbed his luggage. I saw a farmer's strength in his arms come out as he lifted the heavy bags, betraying his weak and frail exterior appearance.

"Well God bless young man, and thank you much," he said, waving as I got back in the pick-up. I turned the truck around and headed back east, a cloud on my mind. I couldn't shake the feeling that someone from my company had seen me pick the guy up. As the road pulled me closer to Williston, I calmed myself, saying, "I'm sure I'm fine. And if not, oh well. It was something for the Lord."

The next day, I discovered my worries were not unfounded.

"Kyle wants to talk to you," the secretary said. The look on her face told me that she already knew what was going on, and her expression danced between bewilderment and sympathy.

"It's not safe to do that type of thing," she offered.

I shrugged the comment off, "I know. But honestly, I wouldn't have done it if God hadn't told me to. It's okay, if I'm in trouble, so be it. I'll go talk to Kyle and see what he says."

I made my way over to his office, trying to calm the nerves. I didn't want to be in trouble again. My only hope had been to lay low and avoid any more problems, but if the Lord had called me to it, and I were to be fired for doing His work—then I figured that could be slated as a blessing.

Kyle hunched over his keyboard, staring at the droning computer screen. He looked beaten, ready to give up on it all. The tall leather chair I had sat in as a young man without a job still stood in the same corner. I settled in and spoke a little prayer in my head.

"So what happened?" he asked. He was kind with his words as always. I never felt threatened or battered from Kyle. Even in the midst of some of my biggest mistakes or issues, he was calm as ever, always ending our conversations with, "Thanks for the hard work Christian."

I drew a breath and began, "Well, I figure you probably already know the gist of it. I picked up a guy who needed a ride and brought him to Culbertson. But to be honest Kyle, I wouldn't have done it unless God had told me to. I know it may sound crazy, but when the Lord guides me to do something, I do it."

He put his hand up, "It's okay. I'm a believer too, so I understand what you're saying. It's just that it's a dangerous thing to do, and it's with company property. We don't want you getting hurt or something worse by doing something like that."

"I totally understand, and I agree with you. I promise, I won't do it again, unless He guides me to. And that's rare. But I completely respect the company, and I don't want anything to happen to your property or me."

His body relaxed. "That's fine, and that works, but I do understand. There's been times where I've had God telling me to do something. I remember that day I came to ask you about the sales job. I'm not sure why I did it. I just felt like I needed to go talk to you about it. Normally, I wouldn't have given it a second-thought."

"That's the Holy Spirit," I laughed, a smile breaking across my face.

"I suppose," he responded.

We talked more about what was going on in his life, and I urged him to go back to church and to seek Christ on the problems he was facing. They were tough issues that brought a lasting pain into each day. I longed to see him happy, to hear enthusiasm come from his voice, but I knew the decision was up to him.

"As far as the incident, I'll consider it handled. I don't think we need to go to Chris or corporate with it. I confronted you on it, and it's settled," he said.

"How exactly did you find out?" I wondered.

"Somebody saw you do it and called me. I don't understand why someone is so concerned with what other people are doing. They should be minding their own business, doing their own job."

I weighed the information. Go figure, I could feel someone watching me as I picked the man up, but the Lord brought me to a merciful judge, allowing the incident to be put to rest without much fanfare or trial.

I thanked Kyle, and took one last look as I left. He appeared worn-out, running on fumes in every aspect of his life. He had a tough job and a tougher home life. I prayed for him, hoping God could bring some refreshment to his sully and barren world.

CHAPTER 30

Patrick lived down the hill from us, a five minute walk from door-step to door-step. I found it interesting that God had brought him to that apartment, and us to ours.

One night while we were sitting in the car chatting over anything that had to do with faith, he made a request.

"I was wondering if you might be willing to help me with a couple of things God has called me to do," he said.

"I'd love to. We'll have to pray about it to make sure it's what the Lord wants, but I'm game," I said. I was eager to get more involved with doing God's work. I wanted to have the thrill of doing things most people didn't, and I knew the only way to get to know Him more was to step out in faith.

"There's a task I keep hearing that I need to complete. I need to go into one of the bars and sit. I've been avoiding it because I don't want to, but I can tell time is running out."

"Are you supposed to meet someone or witness?" I asked.

"I'm not sure. I just know I'm supposed to go there and wait. I was wondering if you'd be willing to help me out," he said.

"Yeah, I'd love to."

We prayed and found no blockages to my help. Patrick told me he'd let me know when it was time, and I nodded.

"Just give me a call," I said.

The call came a few days later, and we piled into my truck and drove toward the bar. We sat with the brick walls of the bar to our backs and spiritually prepared.

"Would you mind if you sat in the car and prayed while I went in?" he asked.

"Of course." That was fine by me. The thought had been on my mind, and his saying it brought the confirmation I needed.

He climbed out, and I started praying out loud. I wasn't sure what to say or where to go with my words, so I asked the Lord for His protection and that He would show Patrick what was needed.

A half an hour passed and Patrick pulled himself back into the car.

"So?" I asked.

"Not much happened. No one showed up that the Lord pointed me to. I sat in the corner and waited and prayed," he said. He was nonchalant in his answer, shrugging it off.

"I don't know if I should have done it sooner, or if the other person didn't follow through," he said.

"Well, we did our best," I said.

This wasn't the first time things hadn't lined up like he expected. He told me of an instance where God instructed him to go to a place and wait. He waited, but no one ever showed. The next day, he chanced upon the guy and asked him what the deal was.

"The Lord told me to go meet you yesterday and I didn't see you."

"I'm so sorry man. The Lord was telling me to go and I just plain didn't go. I'm not sure why, but I'm sorry. I was supposed to be there."

I took note of the story and filed it away. It clicked that there were two sides to many requests the heavenly Father made. It opened my understanding to the fact that we are vessels for His work, and our free will is in whether we say 'yes' or 'no'.

Disappointed that nothing happened, I started the car and pulled out of the parking lot. I was happy at the same time. I had said yes to helping someone fulfill the Spirit's direction. I had done my part and was honored to have been asked.

This wasn't the only request Patrick had either.

"I had a dream that I need to fulfill, and the other night the Lord was telling me time was running out. I was wondering if you would be willing to help, since I can't do it on my own," he said.

I was eager to start another fulfillment of God's request.

"In the dream my hands were bound and I was blind folded. I was led into the Mormon church. Then I got up and preached to them, speaking on what the Lord has put on me to speak."

I shifted in my seat. Perhaps I had been a little hasty?

"Alright, I'll help," came out of my mouth. "Are you sure it's okay that I help you with this?" I asked.

"Yeah, it's fine," he said. "Reece can help too if he wants."

I asked Reece later that night, spelling out the dream.

"Sure, I'll help," he said. There was an eager approach to his answer. I could see the desire in his eyes to help in God's work.

The dream didn't make much sense. I had never heard of a prophet being bound by the hands and blindfolded (although one was asked to bind himself to a bed), but I was learning a valuable lesson: some things only happened once in the Bible. An axehead only floated once. Oil was spread from jar to jar one time. A prophet bound himself to a bed once. I accepted that the Lord worked in mysterious ways, and made up my mind to join in the task.

The three of us agreed to fast for the week leading up to the fulfillment of the dream. We drank only water, spending our cravings on prayer and reading scripture. The times I felt healthiest and most energetic were the hours I spent reading and in prayer. Nourishment poured from God each verse I read, and the addictive craving of food pushed me back to Him. As we neared the chosen Sunday, I was getting antsy. My thoughts danced from what it would be like, to what people would think, and what the outcome might be. I kept reminding myself that none of that mattered. I was to do what the Lord asked, and pay no attention to what anybody else thought.

The Sunday arrived and the three of us went to church, worshiping and praying with all we had. The whole service, the Mormon church next door was on my mind. What was God's reason in this? What if they didn't even let us in? I placated the thoughts with the knowledge that the Lord would get His will done His way. We were merely vessels.

The sermon ended and I took a deep breath. It was time.

We met Patrick outside and sat in the grass facing the Mormon church. We prayed, asking for strength and for God to open the doors He wanted us to use. We laid hands on him, praying God would provide strength and guidance. Feeling satisfied with our prayer, we took duct tape and wound it around his hands in front of his waist. We placed the makeshift blind-fold over his face and put him on his feet. Reece and I walked on either side, leading him in the grass towards the building. Nerves were sharp, but a sense of being separated from the rest of the world was also flooding in. A light flow of adrenaline began replacing nervous angst with confidence.

A couple held the door open for us as they curiously commented under their breath. Reece and I smiled and tried to look as kind as possible. We entered into the sanctuary and sat towards the back. Most people acted casual, not giving too much thought to the kid in blind-fold and duct tape, or to his two odd looking companions. I bowed my head, praying for light and strength through the moment. I prayed that their ears would be open to hearing what he had to say.

The bishop stepped up and started speaking to the congregation. I saw a glance our way, but he did nothing to draw attention to us. The words flowed, and the people settled in. I looked around at the congregation and gauged the members. They were normal people. There were families with little children who squirmed against their parents arms. There were younger people and older people, skinny and wider. They looked like a next door neighbor or a co-worker. I had noticed several work trucks in the parking lot on the way in. It proved to me that there were even Mormons in the oilfield. I wasn't awestruck by the normalcy of the congregation, but it set into my mind that they were people just like me. They were searching for the right way to God, and wanted to be connected to Him. Wasn't that what all religions were doing?

The little girl sitting next to me poked my arm. I looked down to see a children's book written in Spanish. She started reading and pointing, guiding me along as she spoke in Spanish. I smiled and listened, having no clue what she was saying. Her mother corralled her, and I turned my attention back to the service.

The service was nearing the end and Patrick leaned towards me.

"Is it almost over?" he whispered.

"Yeah, I think we have one more song to sing and then it's done," I said.

"Lead me up front during the last stanza of that song," he said.

I took a deep breath. As the song neared the end, I looked to Reece and gave a quick smile. We decided he would stay back, and watch things from there. I put my hand on Patrick's elbow and began leading him forward. Eyes turned toward us row by row, following as we made our way to the front. We reached the front row and turned towards the entrance to the platform. Immediately bodies jumped up and hands grabbed us. They quickly ushered us out the nearest side door, attempting to stop short the commotion.

"Let him speak," I said, incredulous at being stopped.

"He's not speaking," one man said, his hands still on us.

"You're preventing a message from the Lord," I shot back.

"What's that message?" the man argued, a group of them surrounding us.

"He's trying to fulfill a vision from the Lord. Don't stand in the way of the Lord's will," I said. I was adamant and flush with heat.

The bishop stepped in, arguing that Patrick would not get to speak to his congregation and pressing as to why we thought he would.

"Can we go somewhere and talk?" Patrick said calmly among the ruckus. We all paused, realizing he made perfect sense. I immediately calmed down, feeling embarrassed at my excitement when a cooler head could have prevailed.

Patrick leaned towards me, "alright, you can probably take off the blind-fold."

I pulled the blind-fold off and unwrapped his hands. The man I had been arguing with was next to me as we walked down the hall.

"I'm sorry for getting riled up," I said.

"It's okay, I'm sorry for grabbing you guys like I did," he responded. His face was humble and kind, and I smiled.

We shook hands with the men and sat down in the bishop's office. He introduced himself and we each introduced ourselves. Reece had joined in the sidehall commotion and followed to the office. I felt the sensation of three disturbers in the principal's office.

"So what is this message you have for us, Patrick?" the bishop asked. He was kind, but focused, zeroing in on why we were here and why the get-up.

"Well, God gave me a vision that I had to go to the Mormon church blind-folded and hands bound. In the vision I was to get up and speak," he said.

"And what did He want you to speak about?" The bishop asked.

"Usually when I speak, I have five points that I speak about: Love, Freedom, Righteousness, Grace and Holiness. I just know the Lord wanted me to speak to the congregation on these things."

I leaned back in my seat, allowing Patrick to take control. The bishop listened closely, nodding his head at intervals to Patrick's points.

"I understand, but I have to be protective of my congregation. I hope you understand why I can't just let you get up and speak," he said.

"We're sorry for causing a scene. That honestly was not our intention," I said.

"That's fine, and I hope you guys understand we just have to be careful. I don't think I can let you speak though," he responded.

A silence hung in the air. The three of us looked to him as he analyzed us. My hope was deflating, but I told myself it was in God's hands.

"What do you think Christian?" the bishop said, turning to me.

"I guess my whole thing is that if the Lord has given him this message, it would be wise to let him speak. And I know the Lord gave him this, but we don't want to cause trouble for your church. We really are sorry for the commotion we caused; it wasn't our intention. We were just trying to fulfill what God had asked," I said.

"I commend you guys for doing that, and for you two helping him. What church do you guys go to?" he asked.

"We go to Life Church, but we promise they were not a part of this. They had no clue about it," we spoke up.

"I know them well; they're a very good church," he smiled. "How about this. I'll get your email address and think it over, and if I decide to let you speak, I'll send you an email, and we can go from there."

"That works for me," Patrick said.

We exchanged pleasantries with the bishop and then with the other leaders that had gathered together outside the office door. We shook hands and gave kind farewells.

The three of us exited the church into a drizzling rain, relieved to have finished the task. We weren't sure why it hadn't happened like it was supposed to, but were calm in knowing we had tried our best. We agreed to meet back at our apartment, eager to end the fast that had turned grueling in the last days.

The table was loaded with the fixings for nachos, our first meal in a week. Velveeta cheese mixed with taco seasoned beef simmered on the stove while dishes full of tortilla chips sat on three plates. Grapes and other snacks waited for our fingers to pick and pull. Our hands revved at the starting line. We prayed over our food and dug in, three men ready to feel splitting bellies. An hour later, Reece and I lay on our respective couches, bellies full and eyes heavy. A movie played while we recounted the day.

I was confused by the failure to get Patrick's message across. I had a hard time not thinking that we were 0-2 on tasks, but I didn't know what else we could have done. I couldn't forget the prophets who had messages which weren't always well received. Sometimes it was the visual message that the Lord wanted to get across. I was also embarrassed at not being calm and collected. I had felt a rush of what I thought was righteous anger, and had been protective over Patrick and God's message. As soon as Patrick spoke though, I felt reactionary and ill-prepared. I had spoken on my own behalf, not on the Holy Spirit's.

The lessons from it all stuck. Sometimes I may have to put myself in the ringer to do the Lord's tasks, and they may not always make sense. Patrick never heard from the bishop, and never went back to the Mormon church. I was sad he wasn't given a chance to speak, but thankful the three of us had been through a refining moment, and we each had taken away our own lessons.

I learned many things from Patrick, and as we grew closer, my humility grew while my pride shrank. The intimidation gave way to curiosity, as I wished to learn everything from him that I could. If he asked something, I was willing. This obedience grew me tremendously, giving experiential understanding at which my 27 years had only hinted. We prayed out loud together, discussed the debate of tongues, sought out visions and dreams, and witnessed.

I loved him more each day. I knew God had introduced us for many reasons, and I praised God with thankfulness and blessing.

The Lord used him in a mighty way, in order to answer a prayer I had been asking for the past several months. My hope was to truly understand what God's love meant. We heard so often about His love, and how much He loved each and every person, but I couldn't sense it. The tangible nature of that love was just out of grasp, like cookies just a hand's height out of reach.

Patrick had a couple of movies that he insisted I watch. They were documentaries of a man who went on his own spiritual journey in order to find what a real-life relationship with Christ looked like. What he found changed his life forever, and impacted me beyond words.

The director who made the movies started with a single man who healed people on the streets. The healer would go to strangers, being led by the Holy Spirit, and ask if they wish to be healed. This man pointed the film director to another healer, who in turn sent him to a prophet and so on.

I watched video footage of people who had given up the comforts of life and dove head first into a life of following Jesus. I watched healings, prophetic words and changed lives. By the end of the first movie, tears were collecting, threatening to pour down my cheeks. The love of this God was not in His rules and condemnation, but in His pouring out to heal and encourage people. I saw hearts break at the mention of life time struggles and how the Lord wished to heal them.

I watched a man named Todd White heal a Muslim in Jerusalem. The man was limping along, and Todd quickly stopped him. After setting him on a bench, Todd prayed, a leg that had been shorter than the other from birth was evened out. Todd continued on, being discovered by a Christian whose father needed to be healed from a heart condition. After healing the father, Todd was asked if there was anything he wanted.

"Is there any possible way to get into the Dome on the Rock?" he asked.

The Christian fellow looked concerned, knowing that non-Muslims were forbidden. His eyes brightened, and he asked Mr. White to follow him.

They walked through the narrow streets of Jerusalem, winding and turning into dense, hidden sections. They came out to a balcony where a man in a yellow shirt stood. His eyes widened and his face lit up, arms reaching to pull in the healer. This was the same Muslim who had been healed a few hours earlier on the street by Todd. It turned out the Muslim man worked at the Dome, and if anybody could get the healer in, it was he.

He happily obliged, moving them in and gaining access to a place forbidden to Christ's people.

I was awe-struck at the accounts and happenings in the movies. My heart broke open, recognizing I had a God who could move all creation in order to show His love for His people. I sat quiet realizing the truth that most of the world had no clue who God was. They had ascribed all these evil traits to our Lord, yet when I watched people who were dedicated totally to Him, love and healing poured out in every direction. They could be hit or beaten, but it never stopped them. They wanted to forgive their attackers and continue to tell the gospel. These people were unbreakable, filled with a force of love that couldn't be hindered.

CHAPTER 31

"You should think about waiting until the end of the year," Don said as he committed his patented lean-back in the old, rickety desk chair.

"Why's that?" I asked.

He was one of the few people who knew I was planning to leave and was supportive of the choice. I had told him of my plans to move to Madison to be with Michelle, and he wanted nothing less for me.

"Because then you'll get your Christmas bonus. It might be nice to have a little extra money before you leave. After all, you deserve that money. I'd hate to see you leave a month or two early and not get it."

I was ready to leave, but something inside was warning me that work wasn't going to be waiting in Madison for several months.

"You might be on to something. I may do that," I said.

"Think about it, and just let me know," he responded.

I called Michelle later that night to get her thoughts.

"I know it's not what you want, but it might be wise for me to stay till the end of the year so I can get that bonus. I'd really like to have a little extra money saved," I said.

"It makes sense, but I'm having a hard time already. I trust you, and I want you do to what you think is right," she offered. Her response was soft, reflecting on what we had become. We loved each other deeply and wanted to be together. However, our hearts wanted to follow our King, requiring a patience to let the situation work itself out.

"I think I'm going to do it. It's not what either of us really want, but I can't turn down that money," I said.

The agreement was difficult. I didn't want to make any rash decisions, and a deeper desire within me was waking up. We were getting serious, and the provider instinct was kicking into gear. I had never felt it before, but I was becoming preoccupied with giving all that I was to make sure she was taken care of. My heart was turning itself towards work not as a paycheck, but as a fulfillment to my duty to her and to God.

I found myself focusing more on my job, putting effort in where I had shrugged my shoulders previously. My determination to do other tasks and projects out of work was also ramping up, giving me a push to make everything of my potential. This passion to be 100% flowed in my faith walk, my relationships and even my weight-lifting. There was no time to sit on the couch and watch television. This life wasn't practice.

Reece approached his desires with the same attitude. I watched him reading books to gain insights and apply himself to his faith. He read his Bible, and did his best to workout. I was impressed that the Lord had put together two people to feed off each other like we did.

I observed Patrick in the same manner and learned many lessons from how he lived his life. He spent an hour or so a day reading and was focused on devoting time to prayer. Sometimes he would sing and worship alone in his apartment. If God wanted him to go somewhere, he may have battled against it, but he would eventually succumb. One early morning he was awakened, and the press came upon him to drive downtown and pray in front of the local strip clubs. At 2:30 in the morning, he drove his car up and down the street, praying over the strip clubs. He had no understanding of why he was doing it, but only that he should. A few days after, one of the strip clubs was shut down for a month due to excessive violence.

A similar night-time calling happened to me. It came upon me to go down to the train station. I wasn't sure why, and wasn't sure what to do. After fighting it for a few minutes, I gave in and went into the station. A man sat talking boisterously to a woman while the lone train attendant looked on. I had no clue what to do. My impatience grew and I decided to go ahead and leave. As I was walking out the door, I turned to the man and woman, asking, "Does anyone need a ride?" They both turned towards me and responded with a friendly, "No thank you". I left and drove home.

When relaying the night to Patrick, he commiserated.

"I've done the same thing," he said. "The best thing to do is wait. If you're there, and not sure why, go ahead and wait to see what happens. Pray about it. Either He will give you the next step, someone will show up, or you'll find out you heard wrong. At least you're doing your best to follow what you're hearing."

Patrick wasn't the only one who followed this form either. Many times Norm would feel the urge to go down to the coffee shop or the store and would inevitably run into someone who needed him. One day brought him to the coffee shop where I happened to be with another brother. Within a half an hour there was a table of seven or eight believers sharing the good news of God's provision and how great He was.

The amazing thing was that Patrick was teaching me it was okay to appear to fail. Norm had taught me this as well when we related different happenings in our lives. It was a moment in my life that enshrined what it meant to be a Christian. Not to be a perfect person with no screw-ups, but to eagerly seek the word of the Lord. Christ said that His flock knows His voice, and I knew the only way to discern it was to practice.

"It's kind of like a baby learning his parent's language," Patrick told me one night.

"At first, the baby can't understand the words at all, but the more the parents speak to him, and the more he listens, the more he understands what they're saying and what they mean. It's practice."

"Makes sense," I responded. Everything he was saying made me feel as though he was an archeologist, uncovering a hidden treasure. Patrick was just brushing away the clutter and confusion from the truth that was hidden deep within me.

"Now, I have to be careful with that. There's plenty of people who think they're hearing from God, and it's like 'Eh, I don't think you are on this.' It's something that requires prayer and discernment."

One story he told of stepping out in faith was the type of story very much like those in the Bible.

Patrick was told to start walking toward an unfamiliar house. Twenty-five miles away. He listened, not knowing why he was going or what he would be doing there. His feet found pavement and the walk commenced at early evening. He vividly remembers half way through the walk finding a gas station. He went in, convincing himself to find a ride for the rest of the journey.

Patrick searched for a person, but kept getting the nagging sense that he wasn't supposed to. Succumbing to the deep press, he left the gas station and continued on his way. The trip had him walking in the middle of nowhere, singing to God. He proclaimed the Lord's praises loudly, jumping and dancing while skipping down the cracked pavement.

When he arrived at the house, the man's wife answered the door.

"I can't believe it," she said. "I had a dream last night that you were going to be coming and you'd get here at this exact time."

It was then he learned that her family needed Patrick's prayer and support for a rising issue.

"I was a changed person when I got there," he said. "While I was praying, dancing and worshiping, I was being changed. It was like I just let loose."

I was inspired by the ways God led a man willing to step out on faith and perhaps even fail by his own interpretation. It was also fascinating to watch prayers that had been asked come true. I was hearing real examples of the power of God. These were events we read about in the Bible as kids, but somehow lost the child-like faith as we grew up.

The events that God lined up in my life appeared mostly in hind-sight. Through the deluge of pain and questioning of the moment, there was a struggle to keep faith in an all-knowing and loving God, but the trust was always rewarded. Each step required that I take one a little bit larger than the last. He was growing my child-like faith, but the next level was going to be even tougher.

CHAPTER 32

Reece and I spent many a Saturday afternoon pouring over our usual websites while sitting at the coffee shop. We would order our frozen mocha-lotta-crappé or some variation of drink and sit for the next several hours with eyes glued to computer screens. While we refused to get cable or internet at our apartment, we spent 20-30 dollars a month on drinks in order to keep up to date with the world at large.

I had launched a job search and application process with the hopes of landing some type of lead before I made my way to Madison. The listings poured down the screen like a waterfall, with job after job coming up in lightening quick searches. There were a few job leads that mired away into the abyss, and I wasn't passionate about anything else that was showing up. No job looked right. They all felt like shoes that were the wrong size. Some didn't interest me enough. Others interested me but were too advanced for my experience. And a few of them were downright out of my league.

"I'll give you a job when you get there," kept ringing through my head. I fought the feeling. Wasn't I supposed to be a strong steward and a go-getter? How often did Proverbs talk about the lazy man whose property wasted away? I convinced myself the press inside was just the voice in my head, a figment of my own creation trying to comfort the creeping sense that I was in over my head with moving.

It wouldn't go away.

"I feel like maybe I'm supposed to take a few months off to write the book," I said to Michelle as we discussed the job situation. She was my support structure, giving the encouragement to keep my faith, even if it looked foolish to others.

"I feel like that's what you're supposed to do," she responded.

That familiar little whisper kept resounding in my heart to start a book on my experiences in Williston, but I wondered, "Did the Lord really want me to not work in order to finish it?"

"Keep praying about it, and we'll see what happens," she said.

"Yeah, I'm going to keep looking for jobs, and if there's something that comes about, I'll test it then," I responded.

The job hunt continued, and the discontentment rose. I was hitting brick walls and the tension between what I knew I should do and my actions grew. After all the frustration, I let myself slide on filling out applications and sending out resumes.

Reece looked up from his computer screen one Saturday to gauge my job search.

"How are the applications going?" he asked.

"Not well. I've pretty much given up for now. I keep feeling that it's not going to come until I'm there, and every time I try to, I've got absolutely no motivation to find a job. It's frustrating, because I want a job, and I want to work. I hate the idea of sitting around doing nothing," I said.

"Do you still think you'd finish up that book if you did?" he asked.

"Probably." I was getting worn down by the thought of taking a few months off. It didn't jive with my logical reasoning. Hiring managers don't like to see a few months absence from work on a resume, and I was about to place a big void at the top of mine. The story of Abraham came to mind. Logic did not reason that a 90 year old couple should have a baby either.

"Well, I'm sure God will provide what you need. You just have to step out in faith and follow what He tells you," Reece responded.

It was tough nails to chew, but if a faith-filled walk was my goal, I needed to learn how to step out even when it didn't make sense.

I ceased filing applications, and the weight lifted. I was going to trust the Lord and seek Him with all my heart.

"Lord, I want to do your will. I want to follow what you have for me. I feel like I'm being told to wait until I get there, and that you have something for me, and that it'll come through someone I know. I also am really getting pressed about writing this book. I want to walk in faith, and I want to trust you. Lord, you are my guide and my shepherd, and there is no one like you. You've led me and taken care of me through thick and thin. You've provided so much in so many ways. I want to be obedient to what you have for me, because I know it's much better than what I can come up with for myself. Please show me the way. If I'm going the wrong direction, please put people in my life to stop me or redirect me. I do not want to be lazy in your eyes Father."

A story that helped calm my fears was related to me by Patrick. A close friend of his told how God had given the instruction to quit his job. This man had a family to feed, bills to pay and gas to put in the car, but he listened and quit the job. He waited, riding solely on faith in what the Lord had said.

People asked, "Don't you think you should get a job?" But he didn't back down.

Six months later a company called.

"We have an application that you turned in to us over two and a half years ago, and we were just wondering if perhaps you were still looking for a job?"

He couldn't even recall applying for the company. He snapped up the job, and was rewarded with higher pay than he had been getting before, better hours and in an industry that he was excited to work in.

I held onto that story, using it to keep my confidence in the trustworthiness of the Lord. I knew that not hearing God right could have consequences, and that thought brought on the worries and the doubts. However, confirmations came from sources I trusted deeply. They gave insight into the book, the job and the months off. It seemed no faithful voice told me I was on the wrong path.

The preparations for leaving were gaining steam. The last day of work had been set for the end of December. I would pack up everything and drive out of the little town with a big story.

A week or two before I was to leave, I reclined in my chair while Don sat across the small, dingy office. It had been my morning activity for the past two years—using the coffee pot that got me addicted to Christian Cocaine (as one brother described it) and the leather chair I sat in when I was hired. The same faded painting of three frontiersman on the North Dakota plain hung behind Don's head. There hadn't been a day when I hadn't looked at that painting and thought about the adventurous spirit of those men.

Don was moving slower than when we'd first met. The stress of buy-outs and politics was taking its toll, piling onto a platform of life lived pressing the boundaries. A man in his mid-60's looked as though he was about to pass out of his 70's. Alcohol, women, violence and war had weathered a tough face that never wanted to admit defeat. The guy was still falling off roofs and coming in to work the next day. Broken ribs or not, work needed to be done.

I noticed that in the span I had been there, he was putting Christ into more conversations. It wasn't an every day occurrence, but it happened enough to show what he was thinking.

"I'm not a perfect man, and I've screwed up in a lot of ways, but I'm trying to be better."

He gazed at me through thick glasses with vulnerable eyes.

"That's what Christ wants. If we've accepted Him as our Savior, then it's about growing the relationship," I said.

"I should go to church more. We started watching services on TV on Sunday at least," he commented.

"That's definitely a good thing."

"And I try to pray and stuff," he said. "I'm trying."

I could see tears beginning to form in his eyes. Whenever we talked about faith, there was a vulnerability that otherwise rarely showed up. His soul was bursting, warming parts of him that had been cold for a lifetime. The eagerness to drink and womanize was wasting away. I was watching a hardened military man with years of alcohol and fighting under his belt tear up. His face would soften and his demeanor shift, opening up to a young guy from Michigan who just wanted a relationship with Christ too.

The conversation continued and the hands on the clock found the 5 and the 12. I stood up, tired from a long day and longer week.

"Is there anything you'd like me to pray for?" I asked.

"Definitely me. And my family," he said. He thought about it, not wanting the question to go to waste.

"And my daughter. She could really use your prayers. She's lost right now, and really needs the guidance."

"I definitely will," I said. "Be ready to see change, because prayer is a powerful thing."

"Thank you very much," he said, eyes hopeful.

"I want to thank you Don. Thank you for everything. You were always so willing to help me out, and I want you to know how much I appreciated it. This job was an amazing experience, and I'm very thankful God put you in my life. I really feel He had you be my boss for a reason."

"Well, you helped me out. You were always willing to do whatever I asked, and never complained. I want to thank you for everything you did for us, and you're a wonderful guy," he responded.

I left that day knowing a week was not enough time to enjoy Don. I would never understand what effect I truly had, but I trusted the words I spoke were not in vain. It was obvious God was working on this North Dakota veteran's heart, and I couldn't ask for more.

"I've got a place for you to stay," Michelle said in one of our daily phone chats.

"Where's that?" I asked.

"With Ted, the place I stayed for a semester," she responded. Ted was a father of one of Michelle's best friends, and a devout Christian man. He had housed plenty of people in the past, turning his home into a half-way house for traveling Christians and workers.

"I've talked to him and he's fine with it. That way you don't have to sign a lease and you can have a place to stay. You'd be with other Christians, and he's a really great guy to get to know. I learned a lot while I was there, and he supported me during some of my roughest times," she said.

"I'm game for that," I responded. The situation sounded fine, and it would be the perfect transition. The prospect of leaving my faith community for an area steeped in liberal, progressive ideology and leaning away from christian values was a big step, and I was thankful I could immediately build faith roots. Fellowship was vital.

"I'll text you his number, and you can give him a call," she said.

I got the phone number and called. He was a kind man who sounded exhausted. I couldn't blame him though. He was always moving, always on the move to work another project for the Lord.

"I sleep maybe three or four hours a night," he commented as we got to know a little about each other.

I couldn't believe it. I wondered how a person could survive on such little sleep. He was a man stretched to his limits, but there were no questions about his faith. I prayed God could use this man to further my faith education. There was a peace that settled over me on the decision to live with him, knowing I would be guided and kept.

As for my own apartment, Reece and I discussed who was going to take over the soon-to-be vacant spot. We had a Bible-study brother named Eric who was living in a one bedroom apartment with three other men for a total of 2800 dollars a month.

"I just feel like he's the one I'm supposed to offer it to," Reece said. We had been praying the Lord would bring the right person, and Eric's name continued to come up.

"Then he's probably the one. If you think that's who it's supposed to be, then offer it to him," I said.

We had wondered if it was another guy named Josh who frequented Bible-study, but that was put to rest when Patrick felt called to offer his place to Josh. One evening they were sitting in their car discussing the matter when Josh swore he heard knocking on the window and someone telling him to make a quick move out of his current apartment.

They moved him in the next day and immediately after, he lost his job. Josh landed on his feet, when he went to Mike's church and met a man who owned a safety inspection company. They connected, and he was provided a job in a field that was his passion. We were amazed even with the man who offered him the job. He had come to Mike's church twice in about a year, and both times people who were right at the point of needing a job were provided for through him.

Reece let Eric know we would offer him my room, and he was extremely grateful. He was going from paying 700 bucks for a tiny apartment filled with other people to his own room for 350 dollars. While he had been giving us free kung-fu lessons, we were able to give back with a home and plenty of financial security.

My heart burst with happiness at what was coming to fruition around me. The Bible study that was started on a whim had become a provisional community, giving help and lending support to the brothers who came week by week. We were there for each other, giving what we could and spreading love. The Lord was working on each of us through others, and I was getting to see it first hand. It wasn't a group of perfect individuals, seeing as we occasionally gave in to our little squabbles and disagreements, but our hearts stayed in it, and even after I moved away they continued to meet.

Doug and Sarah were living a few hours away in a tiny town, down on Main street. We were fortunate enough to spend Christmas together, enjoying Sarah's amazing ham and relaxing to satellite TV. I was going to miss them, and wasn't sure when we'd be together again. They planned on coming to my wedding, and it was assured they would be most welcome. The hugs were hard to give, and I found myself slowly inching out their kitchen door, stopping again and again to keep talking for just a moment longer. Finally I found my way out of their house into a snowy North Dakota night. Despite the distance, there was no concern of losing contact. We communicated occasionally while they were living in Idaho, but we never lost a step. They were friends who loved me for who I was, and the sentiment was returned.

My last day at Life Church (what has been regarded to as Assembly) was the Sunday before I left. I had to say good-bye to many friends. As I stood at my post for Sunday School check-in, families grouped together in their familiar clusters. I could hear laughter wafting throughout the church as smiles flashed. They were living the lives they had been presented, and in that instant, a moment froze itself in time. I caught a glimpse of what it would be like after I was gone. They would attend church the next Sunday, smiles showing and laughter following. Hands would shake and backs would be patted. It would be just like it was before I arrived.

I found a firm peace in knowing that. This was a group Christ was shepherding, and despite all the people who had come and gone, they continued with open arms. There was no shrinking away from us transients. They opened the door, shook our hand and used every ounce of energy to influence each person with love.

The pastor's wife gave me a strong, powerful hug before I left. The pastor shook my hand vigorously. There was an emotional attachment on both sides that was showing itself in it's rawest form.

The youth pastor and I spoke our farewells. He had been an inspiration in my life and challenged me to bring my talents to the surface. They were no longer hiding in the basement as Brian had once told me. The people in this church had brought those gifts to the forefront, giving me the honor of using them in invigorating ways.

The day before I left, my schedule was full of errands, and I knew time was short.

Norm and I grabbed lunch together at our familiar spot. We both were on a time crunch, but couldn't pass up one last chance to say good-bye. He handed me a small book in which to write my thoughts. Inscribed on the inside cover was, "To Christian, From Norm: Very thankful for our friendship! You are a blessing! With love in Chris Jesus, Norm"

I pointed to the book, "Whose Chris?" He laughed, quickly grabbing a blue pen to fill in a 'T'.

Norm gave me blessings, praying before we left. It was hard to leave a man who'd been a great elder. I was sad to leave 'The Refuge', but assured myself it was in great hands. He would stop at nothing to do it the Lord's way, and I wanted to mirror that approach in my life. Norm was a man who impacted me with his fearless faith and shining light, always making sure to say, "It's not me they see, but Christ." We parted that day with an awareness that God brought people together for a season before separating them. We also knew it wouldn't be the last time we saw each other this side of eternity.

After meeting with Norm, running to the bank and getting my truck loaded, I was able to get in touch with Jason. We hadn't spoken much since I moved off the farm property. He had offered furniture to hold Stephen and I over when we moved into the apartment. I wanted to be able to get his things back to him. I knew if it didn't happen then, it wasn't going to.

When he showed up, our conversation was friendly and light. He looked better, and sounded healthy.

"Yeah, I'm clean now, and trying to get things back in order," he said as he stood in the doorway preparing to leave.

"You are? That's awesome man. I'm really glad to hear that," I responded. I was happy to hear he was making positive strides in life. My prayers since we met were being answered, and the change was obvious.

"I had a stroke a little while ago, and that sobered me up. I've got my kid back now and am trying to put some things together. It's kind of nice calming down," he said.

It brought a sense of relief over me. While I was living on the farm, several conversations started over what he was doing with life. I had given him words from the Lord, and tried to provide a sense of sobriety, but it had never seemed to catch on. While I was sad for the stroke, I was happy it had brought change into his life. I could see the honesty in his eyes. We gave a brisk hug and said our good-byes. We wished each other well on our new adventures, knowing we most likely would never see each other again.

"Thank you for everything you did. It meant the world to know how much you gave and provided to help me get on my feet," I said.

"No problem man, and thanks for everything too," he responded. I watched Jason walk around the corner, and I shut the door. The end was coming to the different relationships I had made, and even though there was excitement, there was also a sadness that crept next to me. These people had shaped a major shift in my life, and I never knew how I would be able to thank them or repay them.

The next relationship I had to bring to a completion was with Don. He invited me over to have dinner with his family. I didn't really have the time, but I made certain to be there. We ate and chatted, reminiscing about the past two years. When I left, I was having a hard time saying good-bye. The man had done so much for me, and I felt like there wasn't much I had done for him.

After Don's house, I rushed over to Mike's. We both were aware of the time we had missed, now that the reality was looming before us.

"We should have gone to lunch more," we both said to the other.

"I wish we could have spent more time together," we commented.

There was a pain from the loss of what could have been. I cherished him and the time we spent together on Saturday nights, or when I caught him during work. We'd sit in our trucks in a random parking lot or on site, talking about faith and life. Those were times I didn't want to let go of.

"Don't look back," he said as we hugged in the garage. The garage door was open, waiting for me to pull out of the driveway for the last time. Those words rang over and over.

"Focus on what's ahead of you. Appreciate the time you had here, but don't live half here and half there. Put yourself fully into it," he offered, giving the wisdom that helped my transition more than he'd ever understand.

"Thank you for everything you've done, and all you've given. You guys have been wonderful to me," I said.

He thanked me as well and wished me the best. I drove out of the driveway of the big white house. The lights that opened up on the tall pillars were like spot lights, drawing a person towards the home. I close my eyes and can still see the house where I drank too much coffee, sang too loud and laughed too hard. The house church had been a wonderful substitute home, and I was thankful for every moment I spent there.

My night ended with the guys from the Bible study. I sent out a text letting everyone know we were meeting if they'd like to hang out one last time. I was honored by the priority they all put on it. Eric rushed out of bed to come over. Another stopped in while he was still on the clock from work. Edward made sure to come and stay for a little while. Patrick and Reece were there before others arrived, and there after everyone left.

They had been my encouragement in a twisted town where it was easy to get lost. These brothers were men I will always remember, each finding himself in a rusty oilfield town with too many people and not enough living spaces. We were all adventuring cowboys, brought into an exciting journey by the Lord—whether we realized it or not. The opportunity of a job called, and we each had answered.

Before the numbers started dwindling, they prayed for me. It was a prayer for protection and leadership, love and guidance. Their hearts were united in asking for Christ's blessing upon me.

Saying good-bye to Patrick was easy. We knew we'd talk on the phone quite often. And I had a sense it would not be the last time I saw him.

"I love ya man," I said as I watched him leave the apartment for the last time.

"I love ya too," he responded as he turned the corner.

Reece and I stayed up for a little bit, reminiscing about the past.

"It's amazing what God brings together, isn't it?" he asked. I was leaning against the door to his room, hands shoved into my sweatpants.

"Yes it is. Thanks for being an awesome roommate. You're one of the best I ever had," I said.

Neither of us had a good idea of what to say. The words were abandoned for the unspoken understanding that this had been beneficial for both of us. We could never thank the Lord enough for the support he provided through a good roommate in a strange town.

"You too. It was a great time. I'm gonna miss ya," he said.

"I'm going to miss you too," I responded.

"Wake me up before you leave," he called as I turned to go towards my room.

"Sure thing."

The next morning I softly called to Reece from his door.

"Reece, wake up. I'm taking off."

He mumbled and fumbled his way into the living room, eyes half closed.

We gave a hug, passed along the "take care of yourself" to one another, and I shut the door to a friend who had just happened to be sitting a row behind me at church one day. He gave me support and wisdom from years of real-world experience. He was a great friend, and a cherished person.

I filled up at a local gas station that had provided me service almost every work day for the past two years. The ladies working there demanded I stop in before I left, so I complied. They lamented at seeing me go, and I returned the feelings. They were wonderful people, putting up with oilfield men who ran the gamut from hitting on them to swearing at them.

"You don't realize the affect you had on me," one said.

I perked up, not quite sure how friendly "hellos" and a smile could have had an influential impact.

"The first day I met you, I was about ready to quit. It was one of my first days and things were going wrong, people were swearing at me, and it was a mess," she said. "And then you walked in with a smile on your face, asking how I was doing and being really nice and everything. When you came in, I thought to myself, 'alright, I can do this.' I want you to know it meant a lot to me," she said.

"I'm blown away and honored. I had no idea, but thank you so much for telling me that. It lets me know it does matter, and I'm really glad I could help you in that way," I said.

She was a wonderful woman, trying to make a living with her husband in a town that ate people alive. I had seen too many workers come and go in that station, but she had been a consistent presence.

I left the gas station for the brisk new year air and got in my truck. The thought hit me: I had never even given them the gospel. I pushed it aside, figuring it was too late.

I remembered I needed ice for the meat in my truck, so I drove over to Wal-Mart, my first stop in my Williston adventure. The parking lot was quiet. There were no cars zooming every which way or tons of campers at the end of the parking lot. The lot was calm, inviting me to park one last time.

I rushed to get my ice, packed it up and drove through the lot to get to the light. I sat at the entrance, looking at the gas station.

Why not? I pulled back into the gas station and wrote the address of Life Church on the back of a couple of cards. I scratched out my work number and put my cell phone number. I opened the door and sought out my local gas station attendant. She was doing inventory in the back.

"You're back?" she said with a smile.

"I just felt the need to give you this. I want you to know that God loves you, and if you're looking for a family, go here," I pointed to the church address on the back of the card. "They're wonderful people, and they took me right in," I said. Her eyes lit up and she gave me another hug.

"That's amazing because my husband and I were just talking about how we needed a church," she said.

"The Lord works in mysterious ways," I quipped, giving a smile.

I walked to my car feeling vindicated, knowing I had made good on what the Holy Spirit had asked of me. My truck found its way onto the highway. I pointed the headlights north, heading up the same stretch that had brought me to the swath of lights tucked in the valley. Freezing rain pelted the windshield as semis and one-tons drove slowly and cautiously. I looked in the rearview mirror to catch a glimpse of my former home. A place where God had led me through some of the worst times of my life.

I had driven down the winding highway into an oil-field town as a depressed college grad with no purpose or direction, and that boomtown was spitting me out a new person on a new path.

Afterword

The temptation after reading a book such as this is to believe that everyone lived happily ever after. In reality, living a life with God does not remove a person from the troubles and pains of the world. Instead, it gives him a point of reference on which to focus. He is the foundation of truth on which you can rely when all else is failing in life.

If there was one lesson I learned through my two years in North Dakota, it is that God is faithful, even if He does not do what we expect of Him. There are moments when we believe we have Him all figured out, and things turn upside down. Other times, it takes looking back to see what He was doing. Some situations are affected by our choices, others are guided by forces outside of our control.

Many of the writers of the Bible led lives filled with danger and sufferings. Paul himself speaks of all the atrocities he faced. But he states over and over that it was for an example to other believers. "But if we are afflicted, it is for your comfort and salvation; or if we are comforted, it is for your comfort, which is effective in the patient enduring of the same sufferings which we also suffer; and our hope for you is firmly grounded, knowing that as you are sharers of our sufferings, so also you are sharers of our comfort." (Corinthians 1:6-7 NASB)

I felt called to share my story and to show the path I took in finding a relationship with Jesus Christ, so that perhaps one person might see the similarities and know that he is not alone. I pray that my story can bring comfort to anyone who is struggling or suffering, and to let him know that we aren't called to an easy, perfect life. We are called instead to show why no matter what we experience, we have a hope that surpasses all understanding. My story is the witness of how God has taken care of me and has continued to show Himself merciful despite my mistakes, my bad choices and my wrong turns. He will not abandon or forsake us. Just as a father who truly loves his children would not give up on them even when the times are extremely difficult, our heavenly Father refuses to just give up on us. He does not need us to be perfect before we may accept Him. We must only recognize that we cannot save ourselves.

I want the reader to also understand that there have continued to be situations which have stretched the faith of my friends as well as me.

Doug and Sarah eventually divorced. Doug is experiencing layers of turmoil, and I can't help but think of the book of Job. Some days, I have no words for Doug, but he is still drawing closer to God. He is recognizing that there is nothing in this world that can replace Jesus, and we are only here for a short time. No person or item can be what the Lord is to us. This does not negate his pain, and we must not be arrogant enough to say that all could be solved if only we were right with God, or if only we had a little more faith. Some situations may be worsened by sin or lack of faith, but the Lord can make clear that which we seek.

I learned how to grow with being a friend to someone who is struggling. It is easy enough for the christian to lay on the solutions and answers, when many times all we can do is pray and be a shoulder. If there is truth to be given, it must be salted with grace. And we must always humble ourselves and love our neighbor.

With regards to new life, Massey is doing wonderfully. His children are filled with of bright eyes and laughter. His home is warm and loving, growing each day with an awe in who God is.

Massey has ceased striving to make things happen, and is now trusting the Lord to manage the details of life. He works hard on each task he is given, but trusts that God will provide. And He does. Again and again and again.

My own story professes God's continuing grace and faithfulness. After leaving North Dakota, I continued to feel called to finish this book. While struggling with confidence issues and desiring to work, I refrained from finding a job and worked on the book. There were times when I would job search, and each time I felt convicted that it was not what my heavenly Father was calling me to do. I knew He had something in mind, and so I trusted. Three days after finishing the book, I was connected with a job through a person I had met once at church. I started with a company owned by a faithful man, and we continue to grow deeper together in our own friendship as well as our relationship with God.

This job has struck my pride and laid me low, but I thank the Lord for those rough months of learning a new lesson. He is building a new outlook within, and this job has been a giant blessing. I have been able to grow close to my co-workers, and share Christ in a way I never thought I could.

I wrote this book with the desire to show you the ways in which I learned to hear the Holy Spirit, the mistakes I made, and the possibilities of what He can do with those who are willing to let Him guide. God is never done shaping and honing us to bear His image, so seek Him with all that you are, and know that He loves you more than you could possibly understand.

About the Author

Christian Dell has lived a life on all sides of faith and has seen the Lord's work first hand. He was called to share his experiences with the world in order to strengthen, encourage, and teach; he is excited to bring the testimony of God to those who are struggling and in pain.

Christian lives in Madison, Wisconsin, is recently married, and is eager to see where the Lord wants to place him next.